MW00723374

Reconstructing Trauma and Meaning

Reconstructing Trauma and Meaning:

Life Narratives of Survivors of Political Violence during Apartheid in South Africa

By

Ileana Carmen Rogobete

Cambridge
Scholars
Publishing

Reconstructing Trauma and Meaning: Life Narratives of Survivors of Political Violence during Apartheid in South Africa

By Ileana Carmen Rogobete

This book first published 2015

Cambridge Scholars Publishing

Lady Stephenson Library, Newcastle upon Tyne, NE6 2PA, UK

British Library Cataloguing in Publication Data
A catalogue record for this book is available from the British Library

ISBN (10): 1-4438-8009-4
ISBN (13): 978-1-4438-8009-1

TABLE OF CONTENTS

PREFACE

The new power relationships and social structures emerging during socio-economic transition to democracy often endanger those who still carry with them the sequels to trauma of the past, gradually silencing their voices. Living myself for more than 20 years under totalitarian communist repression in Romania and witnessing directly its collapse in 1989, I have often wondered why post-conflict societies do not create more space for former victims on their journeys of healing by trying to clarify ambiguities, to facilitate the revelation of truth and to deal with injustices. Within the post-communist Romanian context of transition to democracy, I have felt the pervasive opposition of the new political power to uncovering past injustices and gross human rights violations. The conspiracy of silence at the political macro-level has increased the marginalisation of those who survived the communist repression, their voices remaining largely unheard at the societal level. The South African experience through its Truth and Reconciliation Commission has been enlightening for me in this respect. Reflecting on this process, I can see how much this journey has become my own story of making sense of past experiences lived during repressive times.

As a psychologist and family therapist at the Family Association of South Africa (FAMSA), I interacted with families and individuals from various backgrounds. In most cases, their current challenges were closely related to their traumatic experiences during apartheid. This was one of the reasons that prompted me to embark on a research study to explore survivors' current reconstructions of their trauma during apartheid and their pathways towards healing and making sense of life again. This book, therefore, is based on my PhD research for the Department of Psychology at the University of Cape Town in South Africa, during 2008-2011 (Rogobete, 2011).

The central aim of this work is to examine the narratives of survivors of political violence during apartheid and their complex ways of reconstructing trauma and recovery, almost twenty years after the collapse of apartheid in South Africa. The traumatic events experienced by victims occurred during 1960 - 1993. I interviewed twenty survivors who suffered gross human rights violations, such as detention, torture, police harassment, displacement, shootings, or the loss of a significant other.

Participants were coming from both sides of the conflict and belonged to various racial groups, ages, gender and socio-economic status. The study used qualitative research methods and thematic narrative analysis. The conceptual framework of the study was informed by contextual and narrative approaches to understanding trauma and recovery, shaped by social constructionist theories regarding reconstructions of meaning and the *self* after trauma. Central to the theoretical framework of the study was an understanding of trauma as loss of meaning and shattering of the self. Recovery was thus defined as a process of making meaning of the self, others and the world in which one lives.

The meaning-making process is multidimensional and is pursued through reflexivity, interpretation, language, human activity, interactions with others and social engagement with contextual realities. The self was understood as being constructed through narratives within a relational, moral and ethical universe shaped by social, political and cultural realities. Moving beyond a mere medical approach, the analysis highlighted complex articulations of trauma reconstructions and multiple pathways to recovery. There was no straightforward pattern or single profile that could describe experiences of trauma, but rather manifold ways of dealing with suffering and healing. In the highly unequal South African society, trauma and recovery were experienced differently across race and form of political violence. Victims of repressive political violence from black communities reconstructed trauma as an engulfing continuous process, affecting all areas of life, including the present context. Racial segregation and the ongoing oppression had a shattering effect not only on individuals but on families and communities as well. Trauma was constructed in terms of helplessness, despair and anger due to injustice, humiliation and marginalisation.

In contrast, survivors of reactive political violence inflicted by liberation movements (targeting the White population, considered as "beneficiaries" of the repressive system) reconstructed trauma as a result of the particular traumatic event in which they were involved, and not as a continuous type of violence such as Black participants had experienced. Their narratives, however, did not focus only on individual symptoms but rather on communal experiences further mediated by political, cultural and social realities. The unfolding of narratives revealed a variety of life trajectories and pathways to recovery. Findings clustered around three main categories of recovery: (1) survivors who made substantial progress by finding new meanings for their lives; (2) survivors who are still struggling in the process of meaning-making but remain committed to this journey and (3) survivors who were not able to progress and have given up searching for new alternatives in their journey to recovery. Within the whole sample it has been found that recovery is closely related to survivors' ability to *repair* or to meaningfully *transform* what trauma had destroyed in their lives. While acknowledging the limits of the research and the need for continuous development of conceptual frameworks, this work has finally argued for a contextual understanding of trauma and recovery, highlighting the complexity and diversity of survivors' experiences within the current South African context.

Knowledge does not reside in one person's mind. Thus, this book as well is the result of an interchange of ideas and co-creation of meaning developed between myself and many wonderful people I met (either in the world of ideas or in person) during this process of research and writing. I would like to acknowledge the contribution and support of my supervisor, Professor Donald Foster. I am deeply grateful for his professional guidance, encouragement, intellectually stimulating discussions and constructive feedback. Special thanks to Dereck Summerfield, Brandon Hamber and Gillian Eagle for their valuable comments and suggestions for improvement. I would also like to thank the survivors who participated in this study, for sharing with me their experiences of suffering and healing. Their stories have changed the way I perceive life and have become a source of inspiration and personal growth. I am who I am now because of my encounter with you. Several institutions graciously offered me support and assistance throughout my research. I am deeply thankful to The Khulumani Support Group, The Institute for Justice and Reconciliation, The St. James Church, The Family Association of South Africa, The Ubuntu and The Amy Biel Foundation. Their dedication and engagement with people and current challenges helped me understand the ethical and moral dimension of "being-in-the-world".

My thanks and appreciations go to Charles Villa Vicencio, Fanie du Toit, Ruben Richards and Hugo van der Merwe for their valuable time and insightful discussions. Your passion, wisdom and love for justice are highly inspiring. To my dear friends, Juliet du Mont and Pamela LaBreche, go many thanks for their careful proofreading, dedication and astute comments. Florin Vidu deserves special thanks for his technical editing. I am also grateful to my two sons, Andrei and Ralph, for putting up with a busy mother. It is my hope that their generation will stand firm against any form of oppression. Finally, I would like to thank my husband, Silviu, for his love, support and insightful philosophical discussions. From him I learnt to wrestle with injustice and to search for a voice when others want to silence it.

CHAPTER ONE

INTRODUCTION

The dehumanising effect of apartheid in South Africa has been widely documented and confirmed by various organisations both nationally and internationally. The multiple forms of political violence under apartheid shattered the lives of individuals, families and communities. In an attempt to acknowledge the complexities of people's suffering on both sides of the interracial conflict, five years after the collapse of apartheid, Desmond Tutu affirmed:

> There is consensus that atrocious things were done on all sides. We know that the State used its considerable resources to wage a war against some of its citizens. We know that torture and deception and murder and death squads came to be the order of the day. We know that the liberation movements were not paragons of virtue and were often responsible for egging people on to behave in ways that were uncontrollable. We know that we may, in the present crime rate, be reaping the harvest of the campaigns to make the country ungovernable. We know that the immorality of apartheid has helped to create the climate where moral standards have fallen disastrously. (Truth and Reconciliation Commission, Vol. 1, 1998)

Apartheid did not only cause suffering to individual victims but also destroyed the fabric of human connections, which have their basis in moral and ethical standards. It destabilised people's practical ways of life and how they perceive themselves, others and the world in which they live. Although apartheid officially ended with the release of Nelson Mandela in 1990, the process of transition from a divided nation shattered by interracial conflict to a democratic society and national reconciliation has been marked by victories and challenges, as well as excitement and scepticism. Undeniably, one of the most significant accomplishments was the role played by the Truth and Reconciliation Commission of South Africa (TRC) in achieving a peaceful transition. The new discourse based on forgiveness and reconciliation gave birth to a metaphor - the new South Africa as the *rainbow nation*. However, a question was still lingering in people's minds: Would the rainbow nation be able to repair the wreckage caused by the storms of apartheid?

The process of transition, besides successes, has also revealed many challenges in the process of rebuilding the nation. Confronted with economic poverty and marginalisation, many victims of apartheid who live in black communities continue to be victimised even in the present. Although some prominent former political activists and members of the liberation movements have become part of the new political elite, enjoying the benefits of social and economic power, there is an estimated number of 85,000 former victims of apartheid who are still fighting for their rights to reparations, established through the TRC Act (Khulumani Support Group, 2015). They feel the social contract has been breached as they consider that "the process of providing measures for amnesty and other benefits for perpetrators has not been balanced by an equal focus on the provision of redress for victims. Victims have not experienced the equal protection of the law in post-apartheid South Africa" (Khulumani Support Group, 2011). The Khulumani Support Group appears to be the only national organisation still advocating the rights of victims of gross human rights violations under apartheid. Although society may prefer to close the chapter on apartheid and its victims, it is still an ethical and moral responsibility to listen to their present stories and honour them, in order to create space for healing. Meaningful interventions for the victims of apartheid can be developed only by listening to their stories of suffering and allowing them to find their voices. This book is thus an attempt to tell the story of victims' successes and failures on their journey towards making sense of their suffering, and their lives after trauma.

With regard to the conceptual framework of this analysis, the discourse on trauma and recovery is part of a wider theoretical debate and its trajectory has been dynamic, contradictory and often elusive. With a history over a century old, discussions on the psychological effects of traumatic events have been generally prompted by significant shifts in the historical, political and cultural context in which they were developed. Significant reviews on trauma (Bracken, 2002; Herman, 2001; Joseph, Williams & Yule, 1998) have traced the first debates as early as the 1880s, within the context of train collisions and resulting spine injuries. Since then, the concept of trauma has been continuously shifting according to the socio-political realities of the last century. From the concept of nervous shock to hysteria, anxiety neurosis (Freud, 1894, 1919) and shell shock (Mott, 1919), trauma discourses have been constantly associated with political movements throughout history. Such movements include the antiwar movement after the Vietnam War and, later, the feminist movement in Western Europe and North America (Herman, 2001).

However, even in terms of formal conceptualisations, the trajectory of trauma debate has not been free of interruptions. Although the concept of *gross stress reactions* was mentioned in the *Diagnostic and Statistical Manual of Mental Disorders* (*DSM I*, APA, 1952), it was afterwards withdrawn from the *DSM II* (APA, 1968) and re-included much later in the *DSM III* (APA, 1980) as the *Posttraumatic Stress Disorder* (PTSD). In addition, as trauma concepts have been mostly developed in Western cultures, the discourse on trauma and recovery tends to be dominated by a positivist individualist framework. Such an approach views trauma as a straightforward medical condition by assuming that symptoms of trauma are directly caused by the traumatic event. It also believes that psychological negative impact and recovery from trauma takes place solely in the individual's mind and is independent of the contextual factors and socio-cultural realities in which traumatic events take place.

Nevertheless, at the end of the nineties, researchers and clinicians working with traumatised populations in non-Western contexts started to address concerns regarding the universality of PTSD and its applicability in cultural contexts which operate on different assumptions about self, relationships, community and meanings of suffering and healing (Bracken et al., 1995; Herman, 2001; Straker, 1992; Summerfield, 1991, 1997, 1998; Young, 1995). Qualitative research and clinical interventions with trauma survivors in non-Western cultures have strongly emphasised that victims' experiences of trauma and recovery have been profoundly shaped by their social, political and cultural context as well as their idiosyncratic ways of making meaning of life after suffering (Bracken, 2002; Hamber, 2009; Sideris, 2003; Summerfield, 2002; Weine, 2006).

Within the South African context, some of the earliest empirical studies with survivors of political violence have emphasised the devastating impact of detention, torture, police harassments and intracommunity violence on youth, adults, families and communities (Dawes & Tredoux, 1989; Foster, Davis and Sandler, 1987; Hirschowitz & Orkin, 1997; Skinner, 1998; Straker, 1992; Straker, Mendelsohn, Moosa & Tudin, 1996). Although after the collapse of apartheid significant conceptual discussions and studies on victims and trauma started to emerge (Kaminer, Stein, Mbanga & Zungu-Dirwayi, 2001; Pillay, 2000; Stein, Walker, Hazen & Forde, 1997), empirical research on the effects of political violence during apartheid gradually faded away after the Truth and Reconciliation Commission in 2000. It is surprising that studies on the subject of recovery after traumatic experiences of political violence are quite scarce. The trauma discourse has progressively shifted towards newer and more pressing issues such as community crime, sexual assault, domestic violence and HIV/HIDS (Kaminer & Eagle, 2010).

Nevertheless, it is worth mentioning the efforts of researchers and clinicians who worked with seriously traumatised populations during apartheid in South Africa. Gill Straker and the Sanctuaries Counselling Team (1987) brought into discussion the concept of Continuous Traumatic Stress Syndrome as a contextually specific condition developed by individuals living under continuous and intense levels of violence in townships. The debate has continued with conceptual contributions developed during the *National Symposium on Traumatic Stress in South Africa* in 2010 and 2011. The symposium aimed to develop clearer descriptions of continuous traumatic stress and its social and collective impact in South Africa, to negotiate complex relationships between various approaches and interventions, and finally, to carve space for a conceptual framework that will coherently conceptualise the theory and practice on the topic of continuous traumatic stress in South Africa (Kaminer, 2011; Eagle, 2011). Significant discussions revolved around the concept's validation and the need for further qualitative and quantitative research on trauma and recovery within the South African context, so often dominated by continuously threatening conditions, especially in economically poor communities.

The current study, therefore, is in many ways framed by these contextual realities, and aims to "remain constantly aware of, and sensitive to, issues of cultural, racial, linguistic and class differences" (Kaminer & Eagle, 2010, p. 153) when approaching the subject of trauma and recovery within the South African context. Thus, the conceptual framework of this work goes beyond the PTSD concept defined through the list of symptoms included in the *DSM IV* (APA, 1980), with the intention of exploring contextual and subjective interpretations of trauma due to political violence, its complex impact, and trajectories of recovery in post-apartheid South Africa.

The central aim is to examine the life trajectories of survivors of political violence under apartheid in South Africa. By using a qualitative approach and narrative analysis, the study seeks to unravel participants' subjective experiences of past trauma and their life journeys up to the present time. The purpose is to highlight survivors' reconstructions of traumatic experiences, their complex ways of dealing with suffering and their attempts to rebuild their lives after trauma. In addition, since political violence under apartheid was multidimensional in its form and nature, this study aims to emphasise the psychosocial impact such various forms of violence had on individuals, families and communities.

Furthermore, another important aim is to highlight how historical, socio-economic, political and cultural realities have shaped survivors' journeys to recovery after the collapse of apartheid until the present. By capturing survivors' experiences and the meaning they attach to their suffering and healing, this study attempts to facilitate the emergence of a contextually specific understanding of trauma and recovery in the context of transition in South Africa characterised as it is by socio-economic inequalities, ongoing structural violence and disempowerment among the Black population. Finally, the study aims to discern the multiple factors and interactions related to survivors' recovery processes as well as significant elements that facilitated or impeded their complex ways of making meaning of life again in the aftermath of serious traumatic experiences.

With regard to the structure of this book, the discussion begins by locating the present work within the context of previous studies and contributions in the field of trauma and recovery (Chapter Two). By highlighting some of the limitations of the PTSD concept elaborated in Western cultures, this chapter stresses the importance of the social, political and cultural context for the understanding of suffering and the reconstruction of meaning after trauma. In so doing, the discussion is carving a niche for this study as a qualitative piece of research aiming to examine the life trajectories of survivors of political violence, seventeen years after the collapse of apartheid.

Chapter Three highlights the main theoretical assumptions that constitute the epistemological framework of the study. It defines the hermeneutic key of the analysis as being sensitive to contextual and relational dimensions of human suffering, multidimensional meaning-making processes as well as to identity being shaped by culture, language and social reality. Chapter Four outlines the main elements of the methodological framework defined by a qualitative approach that adopts narrative methods for research. This chapter also includes descriptions of the study, the interviewing process, the participants and role of the researcher.

The following three chapters (Chapter Five, Six and Seven) focus exclusively on the analysis of survivors' narratives of suffering during apartheid and their search for significant ways of reconstructing meaning after trauma. The analysis takes into consideration the complex ways in which participants interpret their past experiences, their current locations in the recovery process and future perspectives about the world in which they continuously (re)create meaning for their lives. Chapter Eight concludes with an overview of central findings of the study, its contributions, limitations and a critical reflection on my journey during this research.

Since terms and concepts may have multiple connotations, it is therefore important to clarify from the onset some aspects related to the use of race terminology and concepts such as victim/survivor, political violence, trauma and recovery (De la Rey, 1999; Luthar, Cichetti & Becker, 2000). The ideology of race in South Africa has been an integral part of the apartheid repressive system in the past and terms such as Black[1], White and Coloured may carry with them painful memories of the "old times". Although there have been debates over such issues, these categories do not bear value demarcation anymore. They are used purely as technical terms to distinguish demographically between various race groups who are part of the current South African society (TRC Report, Vol. 1, 1998). Similarly, in this book, *White* and *Black* are the terms used most frequently. White refers to members of the groups who were full citizens of the apartheid state, thus enjoying the rights and benefits of such identity. The term Black refers to all members of the group who were disenfranchised under apartheid. *Coloured* is a sub-grouping within the category Black and is used in this work to signify mixed race and people of Indian origin. When not otherwise specified in this study, the term Black includes the Coloured and Indian participants in the sample.

The terms *victims* and *survivors* are used interchangeably in the study without conferring a higher value to one or the other. Therefore, when using the word *victim*, there is no intention to convey weakness to the individual, since both victim and survivor are used to signify the experience of gross violations of human rights as described in the Promotion of National Unity and Reconciliation Act, Section 1 (TRC Act). The word *victim* is also the accepted term within the framework of the Truth and Reconciliation Commission of South Africa. Differences between these terms are, however, highlighted in the study when participants themselves make a distinction between their meaning attributions.

The oppressive apartheid system used various forms of political violence, which will be presented in Chapter Two. Although *repressive* violence refers to the violence inflicted by oppressive structures of the apartheid state on the Black population (as the oppressed), in this work,

---

[1] When referring to persons, these terms are capitalised as recommended in the *Publication Manual of the American Psychological Association*, 6th edition, 2010, p. 75.

the expression 'victims of *repressive* political violence' includes also some victims who are White. Even if the victims of repressive violence were predominantly Black, there were also White people (even from outside the borders of South Africa) who actively opposed the system of apartheid and thus suffered the consequences of repressive violence as well. In a similar vein, it has to be mentioned that political violence inflicted by anti-apartheid movements, while targeting the White population, made victims among Black and Coloured people as well (for example the massacres in 1993).

Finally, the term *trauma* has been used in this study to refer both to clinical trauma as described by symptoms of *Posttraumatic Stress Disorder* as well as to a *crisis of meaning* created in an ongoing multidimensional traumatic context during apartheid and in some ways also perpetuated during the period of transition. Therefore the term trauma includes not only the psychological trauma of the individual but also historical, structural and communal trauma within the context of ongoing threat and adversity (Kaminer & Eagle, 2010). Such a situation makes it difficult to distinguish between the effect of a single traumatic event and its subsequent impact; therefore the term *trauma*, depending on the context, refers both to the nature of an event (as being traumatic) as well as to the suffering produced by such an event (as the traumatic aftermath). In a similar vein, the term *recovery* has been used to signify both psychological recovery as well as relational and contextual recovery. Recovery has been defined as a continuous and multidimensional process of making meaning of life after trauma.

Having briefly presented the general map of this work, I will turn now to a more detailed description of the contextual location of this analysis within existent conceptual and empirical studies in the field of trauma and recovery.

CHAPTER TWO

TRAUMA AND RECOVERY: HISTORICAL ROOTS AND PARADIGM SHIFTS

At various times in human history, violence, wars and natural disasters have shattered the lives of people and communities in many parts of the world. The pain and suffering experienced by people has been interpreted in multiple and, often, contradictory ways, which in fact has mirrored victims' confusion and devastation in the aftermath of trauma. It has been widely acknowledged that people who experience political violence have suffered various forms of trauma. Depending on the historical context and type of traumatic event, the psychological suffering is conceptualised as war neurosis, shell shock or most often as Posttraumatic Stress Disorder (PTSD). The continuous transformation of such concepts throughout history clearly show that trauma has a dynamic and elusive nature, being in constant need of re-thinking and re-shaping according to context, history and culture. This chapter, therefore, seeks to answer several questions: What are the main ways of understanding trauma and recovery within the literature? What is the meaning of these concepts within the context of apartheid? Is there sufficient empirical evidence showing that people suffered trauma under apartheid? If there is, what types of trauma and what was the extent of traumatisation? Considering the racial differences, how was trauma and recovery experienced differently by Black and White people in South Africa? What is the meaning of recovery and what was people's experience of recovery in the aftermath of the collapse of apartheid until present?

In addressing these questions, the aim is to provide an overview of relevant studies and contributions in the field of trauma and recovery in general and the application of these concepts within the context of apartheid in particular. While there is abundant literature on the conceptualisation of trauma and recovery in general, it is surprising to notice the scarcity of empirical studies exploring such concepts within the South African context. The focus of discourses on apartheid trauma and political violence has gradually faded away and has been replaced by concerns with other types of violence such as sexual abuse and crime (Kaminer & Eagle, 2010). Consequently, some of the questions regarding recent empirical evidence on trauma and recovery within the context of apartheid would largely remain unanswered in this chapter. This fact highlights the importance and relevance of the present work that takes place more than fifteen years after the collapse of apartheid in South Africa. The aim is to find out what happened with former victims of apartheid, how they recovered (if they did), how they remember their trauma and how they have been trying to make sense of their lives after trauma.

In so doing, the discussion will map relevant material in the field of trauma in general and the traumatic effects of apartheid in particular, focusing especially on the contested nature of PTSD. The structure of the argument will initially deal with the main ways in which trauma is understood, showing how various changes in conceptualisation have been prompted by significant transformations in the socio-political context (Herman, 2001[1]; Joseph et al., 1998; Moon, 2009). Secondly, the chapter will explore psychosocial and broader approaches to trauma and recovery, highlighting some of the limitations of PTSD concepts and thus emphasising the importance of historical, ideological and cultural aspects for the understanding of suffering and the reconstruction of meaning after trauma (Bracken, 2002, 2007; Brison, 2002; Etherington, 2003; Herman, 2001). Third, the argument will turn towards the actual context of apartheid and the way trauma and recovery has been conceptualised through empirical studies and conceptual analyses in South Africa (Foster et al., 1987; Gobodo-Madikizela, 2009; Hamber, 1995, 1998, 2004, 2009; Kaminer, Grimsrud, Myer, Stein & Williams, 2008; Kaminer et al., 2001; Manganyi & du Toit, 1990; Straker, 1992). In conclusion, the chapter will emphasise the place of the current study among previous research and its contribution to the furthering of knowledge on apartheid trauma and survivors' ways of rebuilding their lives after massive suffering.

2.1. Understanding trauma and recovery

It should be stated from the onset that the literature on psychological trauma is vast and it is beyond the scope of this chapter to provide an exhaustive account of the historical development of trauma. Moreover,

---

[1] This is the 4th edition of Herman's book *Trauma and Recovery*, published in 2001 with a new afterword. However, it should be mentioned that the book was first published in 1992.

comprehensive reviews on understanding trauma have been already presented in various clinical books and empirical studies (Andreasen, 1985; Bracken, 2002; Herman, 2001; Joseph et al., 1998; Wilson, 1994). Thus the key purpose in this chapter is to discern from among various approaches, which type of trauma concepts provide the current discussion with a suitable framework for the exploration of traumatic experiences of survivors of political violence during apartheid.

This section will start by briefly presenting some historical roots of the main concepts of psychological trauma and will continue with an analysis of PTSD and complex PTSD. The last part of this section will highlight some important limitations of the PTSD framework, thereby claiming that the understanding of trauma and recovery could be enhanced if contextual factors are taken into consideration. This argument will draw on evidence from significant studies emphasising the impact of trauma on wider social systems and the importance of relationships, family support, cultural beliefs and spiritual values in the process of rebuilding one's life after trauma. The concept of resilience and post-traumatic growth will also be explored, as relatively recent views on recovery that highlight the ability of survivors to access their strengths, transform themselves and even grow as a result of their trauma. However, not all survivors experience visible growth as some may admit that their situation is even worse than before the traumatic event. The section, therefore, will end with a brief description of the concept of posttraumatic embitterment as a challenging way of coping with trauma.

The earliest ideas about trauma begun to surface more than a hundred years ago and expanded in the context of discussions regarding the impact of various traumatic events on individuals. Throughout various periods of time, the development of trauma concepts has never been linear but always surrounded by heated debates concerning definitions of traumatic events and trauma, the presence (or absence) of certain symptoms and types of interventions employed for recovery. Approaches to trauma have been heavily influenced by philosophical ideas regarding the understanding of human beings and the meaning of the world in which they live, aspects that contributed to the continuous reshaping of trauma concepts.

Chronological reviews in the field of trauma emphasize that changes in conceptualisation are prompted by major shifts in the historical, cultural and political context, this fact highlighting once again the dynamic nature of trauma (Bracken, 2002; Herman, 2001; Joseph et al., 1998; Moon, 2009). Herman (2001) argues that significant developments of trauma concept are closely related to political movements throughout history, for example, *hysteria* that emerged out of the anticlerical political movement at the end of the nineteenth century in France, the PTSD developed within the context of the Vietnam War and the anti-war movement, and trauma caused by sexual and domestic violence which coincided with the feminist movement in Western Europe and North America (p. 7-9).

Some of the first discussions on trauma in general, or more precisely on the psychological effects of traumatic events, trace their roots back to the nineteenth century and are linked to the context of train collisions, described in Ericksen's book from 1866 through the concept of *spinal concussion* and *railway spine* (Joseph et al., 1998). Further concepts have followed along the chronological line: nervous shock, traumatic neurosis, anxiety neurosis (Freud, 1894, 1919), fright neurosis (Kraeplin, 1886) and shell shock (Mott, 1919; Southward, 1919).

The first concept used to describe war trauma was *the shell shock* (Mott, 1919) developed in the context of the First World War. This diagnosis was attributed to soldiers who suffered brain injuries during explosions and, as a result, displayed symptoms such as trembling, paralysis of the limbs, loss of speech, convulsions, amnesia, insomnia, nightmares and depression. However, similar symptoms were discovered among soldiers who did not experience explosions, a fact that led to the execution of many soldiers accused of cowardice. After the Second World War, Kardiner (1941) brought further contributions through his post-trauma-syndrome (Joseph et al, 1998), although the descriptions of its symptoms did not differ from the previous ones. In terms of interventions, the role of the treatment consisted in "integrating the repressed events so that the patient may once again become master of what (it was assumed) had become a dissociated self" (Moon, 2009, p.74).

Posttraumatic stress disorder

The most acknowledged term used in connection with war trauma is the concept of Posttraumatic Stress Disorder (PTSD), elaborated in the aftermath of the Vietnam War and formally adopted by the American Psychiatric Association as a psychiatric disorder in 1980 (APA, 1980). However, stress reactions to trauma were mentioned earlier in DSM I (APA, 1952) as *gross stress reactions* but withdrawn from DSM II (APA, 1968) and much later reintroduced in DSM III (APA, 1980) as PTSD. From this perspective, trauma was defined in terms of exposure to a traumatic event and the symptoms experienced in the aftermath of the traumatic event (Joseph et al., 1998).

PTSD has its conceptual roots in Horowitz's (1975) two-factor model based on the information-processing theory. According to his model, in the aftermath of a traumatic event, the person would experience intrusive disturbing memories of the traumatic event and also avoidant attitudes to escape the distressing feelings and images. These alternating phases of intrusion and avoidance became the framework for the new concept of PTSD that was included in the DSM III. PTSD was used as a diagnosis if the patient exhibited a set of symptoms that could be organised into three main categories: symptoms of intrusion (flashbacks, recurring nightmares and recurrent thoughts about the trauma), symptoms of constriction (numbing, feelings of detachment, avoidance of thoughts, places or activities reminiscent of trauma) and hyperarousal symptoms (irritability, insomnia, poor concentration, hypervigilance and guilt about surviving) (Blake, Albano & Keane, 1992).

Depending on the onset and duration of symptoms, DSM III distinguished three forms of PTSD: acute (the onset within six months from the event and a less than six months duration), chronic (duration of symptoms for six months or more) and delayed (the onset of symptoms at least six months after the trauma) (APA, 1980). The time constraints were better defined in the revised edition of DSM III – R (APA, 1987). In order to meet the diagnostic criteria of PTSD, the symptoms had to begin in the immediate aftermath of the traumatic event and last for no less than one month, although re-experience and avoidance symptoms were considered to appear even several years after the event.

Regarding PTSD conceptualisation, a major theoretical shift was introduced in DSM IV (APA, 1994) both in terms of time limits and the definition of a traumatic event. In contrast with DSM III-R, the new edition reintroduced *the acute stress disorder* characterised by symptoms that lasted for "minimum of two days and a maximum of four weeks" (Joseph et al, 1998, p. 12). Regarding the definition of a traumatic event, DSM III-R vaguely defined it as "an event outside the range of usual human experience" (APA, 1987). Therefore, DSM IV excluded the previous definition and considered that a traumatic event should consist of both: (1) experiencing or witnessing an event or events that "involved actual or threatened death or serious injury, or a threat to the physical integrity of self or others" and (2) the person's subjective reactions of "fear, helplessness or horror" (ibidem, p. 13).

Individual responses to traumatic events and modes of recovery were explained through emotional cognitive approaches based on a series of theories such as emotional processing, conditioning theory, learned helplessness and information processing.[2] Recovery was thus conceived in terms of therapeutic processes based on cathartic techniques of re-experiencing the memories of the traumatic event, followed by their integration into consciousness (Moon, 2009). Continuing the cognitivist tradition, Janoff-Bulman (1989, 1992) described trauma as the shattering of mental *schemas* and fundamental assumptions about the world as meaningful and benevolent. While these models and theories are helpful in explaining trauma and post-trauma responses, they fail to provide clear explanations of individual differences in reactions (including the fact that not all people exposed to traumatic events develop PTSD) as well as differences between PTSD and other psychiatric disorders such as depression and anxiety (Bracken, 2002; Summerfield, 1991; Yehuda, 1998). It has become apparent that, in order to understand the complexity of trauma and recovery, there was a need to go outside the intra-psychic world of the individual by trying to explore contextual factors that may mediate the outcome of traumatic experiences.

Complex posttraumatic stress disorder

Although initially a traumatic event was defined as an event "outside the range of the human experience", in Herman's view (2001), this definition has proved to be incorrect, since, for example domestic violence, rape and atrocities are a common aspect of human experience. She argues that "traumatic events are extraordinary, not because they occur rarely, but rather because they overwhelm the ordinary human adaptations to life" (p. 33). Within this context, Herman brings a dynamic perspective to the initial static understanding of PTSD by introducing the "dialectic of trauma" (p. 237-247). This concept is defined as a prolonged tension between intrusion and constriction symptoms, between remembering and forgetting, a process that emphasises the ambivalence, confusion and the helplessness of victims as well as the "self-perpetuating" character of trauma (Herman, 2001, p. 47). As a result of chronic repetitive trauma (such as the situation of child abuse and repression), Herman argues that survivors develop "characteristic personality changes, including deformation of relatedness and identity", that are often misdiagnosed with borderline personality disorder and multiple personality disorder (p. 119).

---

[2] Space does not permit a description of these theories. For thorough descriptions see Rachman (1980) on emotional processing, Seligman and Maier (1967) on learned helplessness and Horowitz (1975) on information processing.

These were some of the premises leading to Herman's (2001) new concept of *Complex Posttraumatic Stress Disorder*, developed in order to account for situations in which victims experienced repression and were subjected to "totalitarian control over a prolonged period (months to years)", examples including hostages, prisoners of war, concentration-camp survivors, survivors of some religious cults, survivors of sexual abuse and domestic battering as well as childhood physical or sexual abuse and organised sexual exploitation (p. 121). In her view, complex PTSD is based on seven diagnostic criteria, the first being a prolonged exposure to trauma instead of a traumatic event as was mentioned in the PTSD diagnostic criteria. The next six types of symptoms were defined as: (1) alterations in affect regulation (persistent sadness, suicidal ideation, self-injury) (2) alterations in consciousness (amnesia, dissociation, relieving experiences) (3) alterations in self-perception (helplessness, shame, guilt, sense of stigma, self-blame) (4) alterations in perception of perpetrator (preoccupation with relationship with perpetrator, revenge or idealisation of perpetrator), (5) alterations in relations with others (isolation, withdrawal, broken relationships, persistent distrust, search for a rescuer) and (6) alterations in systems of meaning (loss of faith, hopelessness and despair (ibidem).

In addition to the traditional understanding of PTSD, complex PTSD defines trauma as a loss of coherent self, psychological fragmentation, loss of control, trust and self-worth, insecure attachment bonds and significant risk of re-victimisation (Ide & Paez, 2000; Van der Kolk, Roth, Pelcovitz, Sunday & Spinazzola, 2005). Recovery, in Herman's view, follows three well-defined stages: the establishment of safety, remembrance and mourning loss and reconnection with ordinary life, community and society (p. 155). Vital for the process of recovery is the context of a healing relationship that has also an empowering effect on the victim.

Although complex PTSD brought significant improvements to the understanding of trauma and recovery by drawing attention to the impact of continuous repetitive traumatic events and the importance of relationships and contextual factors in recovery, the category has not been formally included in diagnostic systems such as DSM or International Classification of Diseases (ICD). The fragility of complex PTSD comes from a lack of empirical evidence able to clearly differentiate between complex PTSD, PTSD and borderline personality disorder (BPD). The next section will explore some critiques on the positivist approach of PTSD by highlighting contributions coming from contextual perspectives on trauma and recovery which take into consideration the social and cultural aspects in which people's traumatic experiences take place.

2.2. Trauma, recovery and transformation:
From loss of meaning to posttraumatic growth

Looking retrospectively at the context in which trauma concepts have been shaped, it can easily be noticed that most conceptualisations have a Western cultural background, which bears the individualist positivist imprints and ways of thinking, an aspect that has been emphasised by Young (1995), Bracken (2002), Bracken and Petty (1998) and Summerfield (1998, 1999) on numerous occasions. The immediate question to be addressed concerns the applicability of such concepts in non-Western contexts, which operate on different assumptions about meaning, self, community and society. It is, therefore, important within the context of the present study to establish to what extent the PTSD framework is suitable and sufficient for the understanding of trauma and recovery in post-apartheid South Africa. In order to make an informed decision, this section will discuss first several contested aspects of PTSD and then will examine conceptual analysis and empirical studies using broader psychosocial and contextual frameworks for the understanding of trauma.

Major criticism of the PTSD conceptualisation concerned its universality and linear causality, aspects that are closely interrelated. Within the positivist Cartesian framework based on linear causality, the first contested aspect addressed the view of trauma as a straightforward medical condition that has a clear "aetiology, diagnosis, psychopathology, treatment and prognosis" (Bracken, 2002, p. 47; Summerfield, 1991). Hence, it was assumed that symptoms of trauma represent a direct reaction to the traumatic event, happening in the individual's mind, independent of the characteristics of the outside world and the socio-cultural context in which traumatic events take place. However, in contrast with this view, empirical evidence has shown that not all people who experienced a traumatic event develop PTSD (Breslau, 1998; Herman, 2001; Shalev & Yehuda, 1998) and that other factors such as "individual characteristics, environmental aspects, objective components and subjective interpretations" mediate the development of PTSD symptoms (Foa & Meadows, 1998, p. 179).

Secondly, it has been also implied that the PTSD is a universal model that can be applied in any cultural context regardless of its historical, social and ideological characteristics. As in the case of other Western theories, the PTSD concept has been applied in various non-Western contexts (including South Africa, as will be expanded on in the second part of this chapter) in which empirical studies have confirmed a high prevalence of PTSD in the aftermath of traumatic events. Yet, some studies conducted with traumatised people in non-Western cultures have shown that trauma did not fit the PTSD understanding. Direct clinical interventions and research with trauma survivors in various cultural contexts highlighted the importance of psychosocial factors (Joseph et al., 1998) and the role of people's cultural and idiosyncratic beliefs for the understanding of trauma (Bracken, 2002; Bracken et al., 1995; Johnson, Thomson & Downs, 2009).

In a similar vein, anthropological and philosophical analyses see trauma as the 'shattering of the self' and 'loss of meaning' that challenge the very notion of personal identity (Bar-On, 1999; Brison, 2002; Crossley, 2000; Etherington, 2003; Kaplan, 2005). Since trauma is perceived as the "disintegration of the self", recovery is understood in terms of the "re-making of the self" through a narrative reconstruction of meaning (Brison, 2002, p. 4) based on interpretive processes governed by social contexts and cultural models for memories, narratives and life stories (Antze & Lambeck, 1996, p. 191; Frank, 1995). These aspects point once again to the limitations of the PTSD concept. However, reflecting on what has been said so far, the problem does not seem to reside within the PTSD concept itself but rather in the framework of understanding trauma and its research tools. In other words, researchers studying trauma (especially trauma of political violence and oppression) should not stop at the border of PTSD but should dare to explore further the characteristics of trauma and ways of recovery by using more descriptive instruments rather than just lists of symptoms. In exploring the experience of trauma, it is more important to analyse the multiple meanings victims ascribe to their experiences rather than describing to victims the meaning of a pre-established list of symptoms.

In this context, Patrick Bracken's (2002) approach should be seen as a major contribution to the field of trauma. Arguing primarily from a phenomenological position informed by Heidegger's view of the *self*, he challenges the reductionist perspective of psychiatry and psychology of trauma. In so doing, he advocates an ontological and contextual dimension of trauma, thus taking into consideration survivors' ways of interpreting suffering and healing within their specific cultural context. Consequently, instead of symptoms and diagnostic criteria, Bracken views trauma as "loss of meaning" and recovery as a meaning-making process taking place in three main contexts: social (defined by survivors' relationships with family and friends, their economic status, employment), political (referring to survivors' beliefs on gender, class, ethnicity, political views) and cultural (spiritual and religious beliefs, values, concepts of self, community and views on illness) (Bracken et al., 1995, p. 7). For example, especially in the context in which trauma is related to displacement, loss of house and oppression, recovery after trauma may mean the rebuilding of the ordinary "ways of life" described by a safe shelter and a decent job.

In addition, Bracken and Thomas (2005) propose a new epistemological paradigm, namely the concept of postpsychiatry[3]. As a conceptual theoretical position, postpsychiatry is not antipsychiatry and "does not negate the importance of a biological perspective, but it refuses to privilege this approach" (Bracken & Thomas, 2001, p. 726). Postpsychiatry is concerned with meaning and interpretation, arguing for openness towards people's experiences of trauma without imposing models and interventions that are not suitable in their context. One of the most important theses of postpsychiatry is that psychiatric symptoms could be seen as meaningful rather than pathological (Thomas & Bracken, 2008). *The Hearing Voices Network* established in Britain in 1990 is an example of how patients with psychiatric symptoms such as 'hearing voices' can develop meaningful explanations of their experiences, a fact that has a normalising effect thus helping them to cope better with their illness.

Furthermore, Johnson et al.'s (2009) recent qualitative study with nine non-Western interpreters, who experienced trauma of oppression in their countries of origin, highlighted new factors, which are not included in the PTSD concept. Such factors represent specific beliefs of survivors related to ethnicity, experiences of oppression, causal attributions, religious beliefs and social support. The results showed that the anticipation of violence and the understanding of ethnic oppression had a normalizing effect for victims. This created a sense of predictability and control that had an empowering effect on survivors by helping them to cope better, resist and even respond to repression. Religious beliefs helped participants to manage painful emotions and try to find a purpose for their suffering, a fact that facilitated the process of finding meaning in trauma and even experiencing a sense of growth. As a result of their traumatic experiences, survivors considered that "they had learned to be patient and that they had the ability to be courageous and strong" (p. 415). The study is helpful in importing new beliefs about trauma within non-Western contexts. However, it is not clear what is actually the understanding of trauma within that particular context, and although the authors view recovery as a process of adaptation, yet a description and the mechanisms of this process are not provided.

---

[3] The concept of postpsychiatry was first used by Peter Campbell in Read and Reynolds' anthology published in 1993.

A preliminary concluding point that needs to be made here is that trauma is an ever-changing construct (Lutz, 2003; Morris, 2003). Although various attempts have been made to conceptualise trauma and recovery as being more than a traumatic event or PTSD, a new and clear conceptualisation has not been produced yet (Bracken, 2002). The difficulties reside probably in the attempt to make universal and general something that cannot be generalised. However, new avenues for understanding trauma and recovery have emerged as a result of contextual and systemic interventions with traumatised groups and communities. Such approaches have proved to be successful in being able to work with individuals within the context of their multiple relationships in their families, work place, community and society at large.

Multisystemic integrative perspectives on trauma and recovery

Empirical evidence resulting from research and systemic interventions with survivors of political trauma strongly emphasise the importance of relationships both in the way trauma is experienced and the way in which recovery takes place (Danieli, 1998; Johnson, 2002; Landau & Saul, 2004; Weingarten, 2000). It has been suggested that trauma affects not only the individuals, but their families, friends and community as well. Family therapy with trauma survivors showed that the effects of traumatic events are more bearable if they are shared or if survivors allow those around them (family and friends) to bear witnesses to their suffering (Weingarten, 2004). Also, multigenerational studies with families of Holocaust survivors have shown that trauma can be passed on to the subsequent generations through a complex process of intergenerational transmission taking place at the level of the family and society (Auerhahn & Laub, 1998; Felsen, 1998; Hardtman, 1998; Rosental & Volter, 1998; Simpson, 1998; Solomon, 1998).

Working with Bosnian refugee families in Chicago, Weine et al. (2004) studied the effects of displacement and constructed a model that describes "displaced families of war" (p. 147). Results of the study point to the fact that political violence and particularly refugee trauma lead to multiple changes in the life of families displaced by war. The impact is "not limited to symptomatic consequences of discrete traumatic events, but represents multiple changes that war brings to the lives of families and their members" (p. 158). A significant change in family roles concerns the fact that parents found "little purpose or meaning in their own lives compared to their hopes for their children" (p. 152). In response to this type of change, some families are able to show flexibility, tolerance and trust, thus finding ways to manage these changes, as the children's success is restorative for the parents in the healing process. However, as the study points out "there is a built-in fragility because if parents see that their children are having difficulties, their letdown can be equally tremendous" (p. 152).

Additionally, systemic interventions are solution-oriented, emphasising personal strengths, resilience and the importance of secure emotional attachments in recovery after trauma (Harvey, Mondesir & Aldrich, 2007; Johnson, 2002). Major improvements have been registered when spouses were included in the treatment of trauma, alongside their traumatised partner, accounting for an increase of the success rate from 46% to 82% (Cerny, Barlow, Craske & Himadi, 1987). Also there is empirical evidence showing that social and family support is related to lower PTSD levels (Solomon, 1990; Van der Kolk, 1996) and both factors are strong predictors of adjustment and PTSD symptomatology (Brewin, Andrews & Valentine, 2000). In Johnson's (2002) view, the growing tendency to include couple and family interventions in psychotherapy with veterans of the Second World War comes to validate the importance of the closest relationships in people's lives, which can either exacerbate the negative effects of traumatic experiences or become a source of healing. The ability of the other partner to express compassion and support helps the victim to 'face the dragon' from a more secure base. As Johnson (2002) argues, if survivors experience secure attachments in their relationships with significant others, they become more resilient and cope better with the effects of the traumatic events.

Furthermore, the importance of resilience in the process of recovery from trauma has been emphasised by several clinical studies and interventions with survivors of trauma from various ethnic backgrounds (Falicov, 2007; Harvey et al., 2007; Landau, 2007; Sideris, 2003). A considerable contribution to the understanding of recovery after trauma was made through the Linking Human Systems (LHS) Approach, designed and defined by Judith Landau as culturally informed multisystemic interventions based on "the theory of resilience in individuals, families and communities facing crisis, trauma and disaster" (Landau, Mittal & Wieling, 2008, p. 194). The model highlights that recovery is closely related to human connections, extended social support systems, a sense of continuity with past and future and resilience. The LINK model is based on interventions with individuals, family and groups, a core element being the recruitment of a family member or a community member "who can act as natural agents for change" (p. 197). The first stage of intervention is based on the assessment of family and community resources, the overall level of stress within the system, the balance between stressors and resources and continuity/disruption of transitional pathways (stories about past adversities and how they were overcome). The intervention stage consists of interactive group meetings that foster resilience, develop strengths and empower survivors. Methods are based on storytelling, exploring the family of origin, stories of resilience and themes of positive continuity and connectedness in the future.

Although space does not permit a full description of the Link model[4] here, a few points will be made regarding the systemic approach to understanding trauma and recovery, which will be further detailed in the next chapter. First, this model adopts a relational approach by assessing the impact of trauma on the family and larger system while not losing focus on the individual. Second, it is stressed that family support and social support from extended systems "can moderate the effect of trauma on family members" (Landau et al., 2008, p. 195). Third, unlike the PTSD concept, this model focuses on strengths, resources and the ability to build resilience. The interplay between psychological resilience and recovery after trauma will be explored in the next section.

Resilience and recovery after trauma

Throughout more than three decades of resilience research, the concept of resilience has been defined and operationalised in various ways, without reaching a certain form of consensus. Several concerns have been raised regarding ambiguities in definitions, terminology and the rigour of theory and research (Cichetti & Garmezy, 1993; Luthar, Cichetti & Becker, 2000; Rutter, 1985). In relation to psychological trauma, the concept of human resilience has been often used to describe positive functioning indicating recovery after trauma. Garmezy (1991), one of the pioneers in resilience research has defined psychological resilience as a dynamic process involving the maintenance of positive adjustment within the context of significant adversity. Since there are multiple understandings of both positive adjustment and adversity, the next paragraphs will describe several theoretical models of resilience that include definitions, main

---

[4] The Link Approach is a complex model containing three-level intervention methods and five transitional assessment tools. The model has been successful in various cultural contexts and with multiple types of problems such as addiction, HIV, mass trauma and disaster. Empirical results are currently in press. For more details see Landau & Garrett (2006) and Landau & Saul (2004).

constructs of the model and the underlying mechanisms explaining the functioning and interaction between the elements of the model. Although most resilience research has focused on children, it has been argued that resilience can develop at any point in the life cycle and is distinct from the process of recovery (Bonanno, 2004, 2005; Luthar et al., 2000). Yet, there is empirical evidence showing that psychological resilience influences recovery by facilitating adaptive and restorative processes (Ong, Bergeman, Bisconti & Wallace, 2006). The most common understanding of resilience concerns three main aspects: (1) better than expected developmental outcomes, (2) competence under stress and (3) positive functioning indicating recovery after trauma (Ungar, 2008). Although these elements overlap in many ways, the major aspects they have in common are the presence of adversity and positive adaptation under challenging life situations. Regarding the definition of resilience as a personality trait versus a dynamic process, it has been decided that *ego-resiliency* would be used to describe a characteristic of the individual's personality and *resilience* would be exclusively used for the process describing positive adjustment within the context of adversity (Luthar et al., 2000).

Luthar et al. (2000) have emphasised the multidimensional nature of resilience arguing that people manifest competence in some areas but show problems in other areas of life. Moreover, they do not maintain the same level of competence throughout life and there are high fluctuations over time even within specific adjustment domains. This fact highlights the importance of vulnerability and protective factors that influence positive adjustment at various life stages. As highlighted by Luthar et al.'s (2000) critical evaluation of resilience research, multiple studies have emphasised as protective factors the importance of close relationships, effective education and connections with wider community. There is also high variation in the way risk and adaptation is operationalised, as well as differences in subjective perceptions of risk and resilience.

In terms of theoretical models of resilience, Garmezy (1985) and Werner and Smith (1992) have proposed a model which considers that vulnerability and protective processes operate at three levels of influence on children's adjustment: (1) community (social support, neighbourhood), (2) family (parental care, nurturing, maltreatment) and (3) the child (intelligence, social skilfulness) (in Luthar et al., 2000, p. 552). Other similar models include the ecological-transactional integrative approach (Baldwin, Baldwin, Kasser, Zax, Sameroff & Seifer, 1993) and the structural-organisational theory (Cichetti & Schneider-Rosen, 1986) that emphasises continuity and coherence in the development of resilience over time. An integrative model used in a study with minority youth was described by Luthar et al. (2000), highlighting eight major constructs for the understanding of resilience: (1) social position variables (race, gender), (2) racism and discrimination, (3) segregation, (4) promoting/inhibiting environment, (5) adaptive culture (traditions, legacies), (6) personal characteristics (age, temperament), (7) family values and beliefs and (8) child developmental competencies (p. 550).

Although research on resilience has flourished in the last decade, according to Ungar (2008), "there has been little investigation into the applicability of the construct of resilience to non-western majority world", as main elements of resilience have been primarily defined in Western terms (p. 221). Based on the findings of a mixed method study (The International Research Project) with 1500 youth from five continents, Ungar (2008) has advanced a "more culturally and contextually embedded understanding of resilience" (p. 218). His contextualised definition of resilience takes into consideration both the individuals and their social environment. As he defines it, "in the context of exposure to significant adversity, whether psychological, environmental or both, resilience is both the capacity of individuals to navigate their way to health-sustaining resources, including opportunities to experience feelings of well-being, and a condition of the individual's family, community and culture to provide these health resources and experiences in culturally meaningful ways" (p. 225). Resilience is therefore considered not only a characteristic of the individual but also a quality of the environment in which people live.

As a major contribution to the understanding of resilience across different cultures, Ungar's model considers that resilience is defined thorough the ways in which individuals resolve seven tensions between themselves and their cultures and contexts. These are: (1) access to material resources, (2) relationships, (3) identity, (4) power and control, (5) cultural adherence, (6) social justice and (7) cohesion. The resolution of these tensions is governed by four main principle: the navigation of the individual towards health resources (personal agency, self-esteem), the negotiation and provision of resources in ways that are meaningful to individuals in their culture, the principle of homogeneity (convergence in how people behave across cultures) and the principle of heterogeneity (diversity within and between populations) (Ungar, 2008, p. 230-232). Within this conceptual framework, outcomes and protective processes are defined in ways that are meaningful to people in a particular culture and social context, thus avoiding "colonizing people's experiences" and promoting appreciation for cultural diversity and local truths (Ungar, 2008, p. 233; see also Arrington & Wilson, 2000).

Summing up main ideas and also trying to define the concept of resilience adopted in the present study, it can be concluded that resilience is a dynamic multidimensional process, which is shaped by global as well as culturally and contextually specific constructs (Lifton, 1993). In the context of significant adversity, it emphasises both the capacity of individuals to access resources and the ability of their context to provide these resources in culturally meaningful ways. Within this context, the concept of resilience becomes a useful tool in exploring survivors' experiences of coping with challenges in the aftermath of trauma. It is also a window into people's realities and a lens for distinguishing resilient life trajectories among various life trajectories of other participants in the sample who had different experiences and perceptions of social reality. Moving beyond resilience, next section will explore another construct that focuses on positive aspects resulting in the aftermath of traumatic experiences – the concept of posttraumatic growth.

Posttraumatic growth and the transformed self

Besides developing resilience, it has been argued that survivors can experience a positive transformation and even growth in the aftermath of trauma. This idea has been conceptualised by Tedeschi and Calhoun (1995, 1996) under the notion of posttraumatic growth (PTG). Tedeschi (1999) argues that trauma due to violence "can be a catalyst for personal and social transformation" and that survivors can live life "more fruitfully than it was prior to the trauma" (p. 320). Through an overview of empirical work, he further develops the concept of posttraumatic growth[5] experienced by trauma survivors as a result of their copying strategies in the aftermath of trauma. Posttraumatic growth is described by three main dimensions: positive perception of self (discovering personal strengths as a result of going thorough trauma), healthy interpersonal relationships (based on more self-disclosure and emotional expressiveness) and spiritual development and wisdom as the ability of survivors to create "an affirmative identity that incorporates the painful, allowing serenity despite difficult history" (Tedeschi, 1999, p. 325). Since this model was based on a self-report questionnaire, it has been suggested that the concept of PTG needed further explorations using qualitative methods.

---

[5] For more details on previous conceptualisations of posttraumatic growth see Tedeschi & Calhoun (1996).

Pals and McAdams (2004) developed the previous model by using a narrative methodological approach to understanding PTG. They argued that the "analysis of narrative accounts may constitute the most valid way of assessing PTG" as the life story should not be seen as "just one piece of the complex puzzle of posttraumatic growth (…) but rather as the fundamental frame that holds the entire puzzle together" (p. 65). Growth outcomes can be assessed by examining the extent, the types and the meanings of growth as they naturally emerge in people's narrative reconstruction of the traumatic event and the self. PTG is influenced by other factors such as personal ones (openness to feelings, activity and positive emotions), contextual factors (talking to others, praying, writing about trauma) and cultural narratives that "shape people's understandings and expectations of PTG" (cultural stories and values regarding the understanding of suffering, development, optimism/pessimism, etc.) (Pals & McAdams, 2004, p. 67; see also Tedeschi, Park & Calhoun, 1998 and Weiss & Berger, 2010).

More specifically, it has been suggested that there is a two-step narrative process in which a person gets to perceive the positive transformation of the self as a result of the traumatic event. The first step consists of open acknowledgement of "the disequilibrating impact of the traumatic event on the self" and the second step concerns the ability to "construct a positive ending to the story" that highlights and explains "how the self has been positively transformed" (p. 66). It has been argued that an emphasis on the negative impact of the traumatic event in people's narratives is related to the ability to integrate the negative emotional responses and develop positive ones, aspects that can lead to the experience of posttraumatic growth. Although Pals and McAdams (2004) bring an important contribution to Tedeschi and Calhoun's model by providing a narrative methodological framework to the understanding of PTG, the study fails to provide empirical evidence and clear examples of how PTG can be interpreted in people's narratives. Their entire description of PTG relies on a single quotation taken from a "middle-aged woman's narrative account of her most traumatic experience in adulthood" (p. 65) without even providing the core narrative of the story. In this context, the current work based on a series of full trauma narratives and stories of recovery could provide additional evidence for the efficacy of such a model. It may also bring new perspectives on how survivors interpret growth and transformation after trauma.

Posttraumatic embitterment disorder

Although for some survivors, posttraumatic growth is a reality, there are still situations in which people do not recover. If trauma has been intentionally inflicted by human beings causing continuous feelings of pain, unfairness and disappointment, especially due to injustice in repressive political systems, victims may develop intense anger and become embittered. As Edwards (2009) argues, such persons "instead of focusing on building a future, they spend considerable time ruminating about what was done to them, how no one cares about what happened to them, or how they should be compensated or the perpetrators punished" (p. 55). This situation can become chronic and develop into a syndrome that was conceptualised by Linden, Rotter, Baumann and Lieberei (2007) as the 'posttraumatic embitterment disorder' (PTED). By summarising Linden et al.'s description, Edwards emphasised the following symptoms of PTED: "intrusive thoughts or memories of particular events when they felt they had been unjustly treated", "upset when reminded about the event", depressed, agitated, activated when thinking of revenge (p. 56). PTED was developed in the context of clinical work with individuals from the former German Democratic Republic who, ten years after the reunification of Germany, were seeking psychological help due to symptoms of depression and PTSD related to "negative changes in their lives that followed reunification" (Edwards, 2009, p. 55). Within this context, taking into consideration the current disappointments of former victims of apartheid, exploring posttraumatic embitterment may prove to be particularly relevant.

2.3. Summary and preliminary conclusion

As a preliminary conclusion and as a result of multiple shifts and difficulties in defining the meaning of a traumatic event, trauma and recovery, it can be stated that the concept of trauma has an elusive and multidimensional nature. Conceptualisation differs according to theoretical assumptions, philosophical paradigms and socio-cultural contexts. Within the context of the present work, trauma is defined as a profound form of bio-psycho-social distress, experienced by survivors as 'shattering of the self' and 'loss of meaning' in life. Such psychological disorientation can emerge in the aftermath of a traumatic event or can gain continuity due to the reoccurrence of further traumatic events (as experienced by former victims of political oppression). PTSD is part of this definition, perceived as one way of understanding trauma at a certain moment in time and characterised by specific symptoms such as those described by DSM IV and Herman's complex PTSD. However, trauma is "far broader than PTSD alone" (Kaminer et al., 2008, p. 1594) and is continuously shaped by survivors' idiosyncratic ways of interpreting their traumatic experiences, which are imbedded in history, traditions and culture (Bracken, 2002). Therefore, it is suggested that trauma and recovery are not completely separate processes, but are closely interrelated and can coexist. For example, a person may experience recovery and growth in his/her spiritual domain of life by feeling wiser and trusting more in God, but still experience major suffering seeing the permanent physical damage of a family member.

Thus, in this book, recovery is not seen as the absence of symptoms but rather as the survivor's openness and commitment to continue the process of reconstructing meaning by showing hope, action/agency and a purpose to rebuild the self, relationships with others and ordinary ways of life which may mean (depending on the situation) getting a job or being able to take care of one's family. Recovery may also involve resilience and posttraumatic growth but their meaning will be explored through people's personal interpretations of what these concepts may mean for their lives and in which particular areas (personal strengths, aspirations, relationships, spiritual values, etc) it may exist. For example, it may be possible that some survivors experience growth in some areas but devastation in other areas. Therefore, it is desirable to adopt a view of recovery, resilience and transformation of the self as based on a spectrum of situations, hypothetically ranging from embitterment as described by Linden et al. (2007) to growth, including a variety of categories in between the two ends of the scale, as survivors incorporate both victories and struggles in their narrative identity reconstruction. Since it has been repeatedly suggested that trauma and recovery are shaped by history and culture, the next section will explore these concepts within the South African context, by trying to highlight the particular contextual understanding of people's traumatic experiences during apartheid.

2.4. Perspectives on trauma and recovery in South Africa

In the last two decades, increasing concerns have been expressed over the high incidence of violent crime, domestic violence, rape, alcohol abuse and the psychological effects of such events on people living in South Africa (Carey, Stein, Zungu-Dirwayi & Seedat, 2003; Kaminer & Eagle, 2010; Kaminer et al., 2008; Stein, Seedat, Herman, Moomal, Heeringa & Kessler, 2008; Stein et al., 1997). Most analyses, trying to provide explanations for this situation, have pointed towards legacies of oppression and political violence during apartheid and economic inequalities that continue to characterise the post-apartheid South African landscape (Mengel, Bnorzaga & Orantes, 2010; Vogelman & Simpson, 1990). While there have been many discussions and debates over these issues, yet only a small number of empirical studies have focused specifically on the psychological impact of apartheid political violence on the lives of people in South Africa. Surprisingly, there seems to be no review of empirical research on apartheid trauma and recovery in South Africa and only a few survey reports and qualitative studies have been found so far.

Quantitative surveys have emphasised the high prevalence of mental disorders (including PTSD) among former victims of political violence (Hirshowitz & Orkin, 1997; Kaminer et al., 2001; Kaminer et al., 2008; Pillay, 2000) and mixed or qualitative studies have described the traumatic context of apartheid, types of traumatic events and ways of coping in the aftermath of trauma (Foster et al., 1987; Skinner, 1998; Straker, 1992). Some conceptual analyses have commented on victims' narratives given during the TRC hearings. Such materials have been more concerned with victims' perceptions on transitional justice, the TRC, forgiveness and reconciliation (Backer, 2010; Colvin, 2006; Van der Merwe & Gobodo-Madikizela, 2007) rather than with victims' trauma and recovery after the collapse of apartheid.

This section will critically examine the existing works in the apartheid context, trying to find empirical evidence confirming traumatic experiences, the nature of traumatic events, PTSD prevalence and specific characteristics of trauma and recovery within the South African context.

Political violence and the repressive context of apartheid

A quantitative survey conducted by Hirshowitz and Orkin (1997) highlighted the effects of political violence on mental health in South Africa, focusing particularly on PTSD and its symptoms. The study was part of a nation-wide survey on health inequalities in South Africa that took place in 1995 and covered 4000 households, out of which 3 870 individuals aged between 16 to 64 years were asked questions related specifically to their mental health status. Weighted results indicated that more than five million people (23% of the population aged 16 to 64 years) had experienced one or more traumatic events such as "being attacked, participating in violence and witnessing one's home being burnt" (p. 169). 78% of the adults who had experienced at least one traumatic event reported one or more symptoms of PTSD and 87% of Black adults experienced at least one symptom of PTSD. Also 17% of those who had experienced a traumatic event described their emotional state as poor compared to only 2% of those who did not experience political violence. In addition, the study emphasised feelings of anxiety and depression present in 60% of those who had experienced a traumatic event compared to those who did not (only 26%). Results of the survey led to the conclusion that PTSD was not an "illness affecting only a few individuals" since a "large proportion of the population" in South Africa suffered one or more symptoms of PTSD. Such symptoms correlated highly with exposure to a traumatic event and symptoms of anxiety and depression (p. 180).

High prevalence of PTSD was also reported by Pillay's (2000) study with 147 victims of political violence in Kwa Zulu-Natal and Free State Provinces, who gave testimonies at the TRC. The highest PTSD incidence was 56 % in Port Shepstone, 48% in Durban, 34% in Free State and 25% in Newcastle. In addition Kaminer et al. (2001) found that in a sample of 134 survivors of human rights abuses, 55% were clinically depressed, 42% had PTSD, 27% had an anxiety disorder and 54% of the sample had multiple diagnoses (p. 374). Also, a more recent study based on nationally representative data, dealing with the risk of PTSD as related to various forms of violence, showed that "among men, political detention and torture were the forms of violence most strongly associated with lifetime diagnosis of PTSD" (Kaminer et al., 2008, p. 1594).

The quantitative studies mentioned above provide clear evidence of the widespread nature of physical and psychological distress and PTSD symptoms experienced by victims of political violence, in the aftermath of the collapse of apartheid. In addition, these findings could be enhanced with empirical results coming from more qualitative research. One of the first predominantly qualitative studies providing clear empirical evidence of the reality of political violence and its damaging effects on victims in South Africa is Foster et al.' s (1987) study on torture and detention. A preliminary report of the main empirical results was released at an earlier date on 11 September 1985 (Foster & Sandler, 1985). The aim of the study was to investigate claims from former detainees regarding conditions, events and actions prior to and during detention and to explore reactions and symptoms during and following detention. The study investigated 176 cases of detention. Although the unit of analysis was the case of detention, since several persons reported multiple detentions, the total number of people interviewed was 158 (82 % males and 18 % females, 72% African, 10 % Coloured, 10% Indian and 8% White). Individual interviews using semi-structured questionnaires took place in major cities in South Africa during 1983 – 1984.

The results of the study showed clear empirical evidence of police harassment experienced by victims before detention (60% of the sample, Blacks being more harassed than Whites and youngsters below the age of 20 years being the most harassed). The extreme severity of the treatment during detention highlighted in the study was characterised by severe forms of physical torture such as beatings, strangulation, electric shocks, food/water deprivation, wet bag over head, application of cigarettes and chemicals, genital abuse, excess heat/cold, pulling hair/beard and others. Psychological torture was also reported under the form of solitary confinement, witnessing or knowledge of another's torture, being threatened with the execution of self and family, being forced to undress, excrement abuse, sham executions and the administration of drugs.

Among physical and psychological problems experienced during detention, detainees mentioned: sleeping difficulties (60%), headaches (53%), fantasising (45 %), weight loss (45%), appetite loss (44%), concentration difficulties (44%), nightmares (41%), fatigue (36 %) and memory problems (34%). After detention, participants reported feelings of depression (25%) and social problems such as: difficulties relating to friends (39%), to family (35 %) and to others (18%). A significant relation was emphasised between the increase of physical and psychological symptoms and a longer period of detention, experience of solitary confinement, a higher number of interrogations and severity of treatment during detention.

Although a definite conclusion confirming posttraumatic stress disorder was difficult to reach, still numerous symptoms reported by former detainees resemble the intrusion, avoidance and hypervigilance reactions listed in the PTSD definition (DSM III). As Foster et al. (1987) conclude, trauma experienced by detainees meant serious physical and psychological suffering and was described through multiple symptoms such as "stress anxiety, depression, cognitive dysfunctions, psychosomatic pain and emotional anaesthesia with difficulties in interpersonal relationships." (p. 162). The study provides enough empirical evidence to confirm the severity of trauma due to detention and torture and it clearly shows the negative psychological effects of political violence on former detainees.

Commentaries and conceptual analysis have drawn attention towards the widespread form of political violence in South Africa and its damaging effects on children and youth who were at the centre of protests and liberation movements (Chikane, 1986; Gibson, 1989; Marks, 2001; Swartz

& Levett, 1990; Van Zyl, 1990). In addition several authors have emphasised the damaging effects of a victimological discourse (Foster & Skinner, 1990; Marks & Andersson, 1990; Posel, 1990; Swartz, Gibson & Swartz, 1990). Although observations and proposals have been made, there are not many empirical studies analysing the impact of violence on children. A valuable perspective on this topic is offered by Gill Straker's (1992) study on a group of 60 youngsters from Leandra township. In 1986, following a six week period of various forms of violence in Leandra (such as police harassments, arrests, beatings, threats and shootings), the youngsters were forced to flee their homes and tried to find safety in a church centre. The study was based on clinical case histories, in-depth interviews with eight counsellors who assisted the youth during that time, interviews with the house-mother and field workers and three-year follow-up interviews with 25 individuals (8 girls and 17 boys) representing 40% of the actual group.

Results following the analysis of 300 hours of interviews asserted that although in the immediate aftermath of the violent events, almost all youngsters showed signs of PTSD, they were able to recover in a relatively short time. However, at three-year follow-up assessment, 20 % of the group were abusing alcohol or marijuana, 10% were involved in gangsterism and 20% showed clear signs of acute PTSD. Consequently, a pessimistic view would conclude that three years after the traumatic events 50% of the group were not coping well. In fact, Straker and the Sanctuaries Counselling Team (1987) have signalled before the devastating impact of continuous traumatic stress experienced by individuals living in black townships, emphasising that the damage is "already inestimable" and "should it continue it may well become irreparable" (p. 76).

However, the opposite was also true, especially taking into consideration the difficult living conditions in which the youngsters continued to live after the traumatic events. The fact that the rest (50%) of the total number of youth were highly functional is interpreted by Straker (1992) as a "testimony to the resilience of human spirit" (p. 35). These youngsters were able to initiate projects, "to love, to play, to think well of themselves, to evidence pro-social behaviour, and on the whole maintain a positive sense of well-being despite the harshness of their environment" (ibidem). As mediating factors in fostering resilience, the study highlighted the importance of constitutional factors (age, temperament), supportive family relationships and an external social support system. Finally, Straker emphasised that "young people are potentially resilient and that given the opportunity to heal, they do" (p. 85). This is yet another proof of the fact that the ability to recover fundamentally depends on a safe environment in the aftermath of trauma, and furthermore, social support (Herman, 2001).

Another significant study on trauma and recovery was conducted by The Trauma Centre for Victims of Violence and Torture during 1994 – 1995. The aim of the study was to explore the types of trauma, coping mechanisms and current life circumstances experienced by former victims of political violence (Skinner, 1998). The study adopted a mixed methodological approach, using surveys and individual interviews with 157 former victims of political violence (87 % were victims of apartheid political violence) from several urban and rural areas in Western Cape. Regarding ex-political prisoners and torture survivors, it was strongly emphasised that the impact of past traumatic events continues to affect survivors through symptoms of depression (25-30%), PTSD symptoms (25-30%), anxiety (20-25%), frustration and anger (50%), medical problems (pain, physical weakness, high blood pressure, ulcers), difficulties integrating into local communities, lack of trust in others, inability to develop intimate relationships as a result of past experiences. A third of the sample felt that their families have suffered as a result of their traumatic experience. However, the study does not explicitly analyse the impact of trauma on the family, this being acknowledged as an area that needs further exploration.

Regarding the process of recovery, the report emphasised significant barriers impeding healing. These include the ongoing violence in black communities, racism and sexism, poverty, discrimination and poor coping methods such as alcohol and drug abuse. Most respondents complained of difficulties in accessing housing, employment and education. As a result they often felt ignored by community and society, thinking "that their contribution was forgotten and lost and that they should now just disappear" (p. 209). Regarding the recovery of former political activists, the study also infers that "long term prisoners who were better educated or held more senior positions have derived concrete benefits and now sit in senior positions in the country, but for the majority it appears that there have been few benefits at a grassroots level" (p. 208).

Reflecting on what has been discussed in this section, the studies presented so far have explored primarily the impact of state repression, defined as unidirectional political violence coming from the repressive structures of apartheid (Foster, Haupt & De Beer, 2005). However, this was not the only form of political violence under apartheid. Liberation movements such as the African National Congress (ANC), Pan African Congress (PAC), United Democratic Front (UDF) and Azanian People's

Organisation (AZAPO) have also organised violent acts against the state repressive structures, this form of violence being defined as bi-directional violence (ibidem). The context of political violence after 1980 had become even more complicated as new forms of violence rose up among black communities and were directed towards those suspected of collaborating with the state repressive structures. This form of violence labelled as horizontal or lateral violence or, pejoratively, 'Black-on-Black' violence consisted of executions and 'necklace' killings among black communities, vigilante attacks and other conflicts between different anti-apartheid groups (Allwood, 1986; Hirshowitz, Miller & Everatt, 1992; Swartz & Levett, 1990). Duncan and Rock (1997) defined the political violence of apartheid as including one or a combination of the following elements: (1) state oppression, (2) "counter-violence resulting from Black people's attempt to challenge their oppression, as well as repressive reactions by the state and its agents in the form of torture, murder, vigilante activities and detention without trial" (p. 135) and (3) intra-community violence resulting both from political rivalry and destabilisation processes.

The quantitative and qualitative studies combined with conceptual analysis of various forms of political violence have provided significant empirical evidence confirming that the people's suffering under apartheid was real. People living in black communities experienced continuous harassment, terror, displacements and arrests from repressive structures. The violence was continuous and in the aftermath of traumatic events, victims could not find a safe place or a healing relationship to help them recover (Herman, 2001). Still, it has been suggested that although most victims experienced PTSD symptoms, some of them, especially youth, developed good coping skills and became resilient. Others, on the contrary, have become aggressive and alcohol abusers. Surprisingly enough, there seems to be no empirical study to provide evidence on how trauma and recovery might be experienced differently by White and Black victims of political violence. For example, in what ways does the experience of trauma and the process of recovery of victims of St. James Church massacre (a predominantly White Anglican Church) differ from that experienced by Black victims in townships? This is one of the issues this book is trying to address. The next section will continue to explore a particular form of dealing with trauma and recovery, namely through public trauma narratives at the Truth and Reconciliation Commission of South Africa.

Healing through storytelling and forgiveness

The South African Truth and Reconciliation Commission (TRC) is, arguably, one of the most prominent and analysed truth commissions in the world (Skaar, 2009). Since the establishment of the TRC in April 1996 until now, scholars from various fields have been tirelessly analysing the South African TRC from multiple perspectives and angles.[6] However, since the focus of this study is not on the TRC, this section will only explore the role of the TRC in dealing with evidence of trauma and its impact on victims' recovery. In so doing the discussion will draw from data provided in the TRC Final Report that deals particularly with gross violations of human rights from the victims' perspective and on empirical studies evaluating the impact of the TRC on victims' healing processes.

One of the main goals of the TRC was to "provide the space within which victims could share the story of their trauma with the nation" (Truth and Reconciliation Commission, 1998, Vol. 1) with the purpose of uncovering the truth about human rights abuses under apartheid, of having their suffering publicly acknowledged and in this way for them to be able to embark on a healing journey (Villa-Vicencio & Du Toit, 2006). Reparations for victims, amnesty for truth-revealing perpetrators as well as forgiveness were also integral aspects of this complex process. Truth recovery was considered to be an important aspect in the process of dealing with the past injustices of apartheid and for the reconciliation and healing of victims (Boraine, Levy & Scheffer, 1994; Hamber, 1995, 2009; Kgalema, 2002; Simpson & Van Zyl, 1995). Although the TRC was successful in avoiding a much-feared bloodshed in the aftermath of the apartheid's collapse, the issue regarding the degree to which victims were helped through the TRC process is still under controversy (Guthrey, 2015; Hamber, 2000; Moon, 2008, 2009).

Following the submission of the first five volumes of the TRC in 1998, researchers became more sceptical about the ability of the TRC to reveal *objective truth* and contribute to the individual healing of the victims of apartheid (Backer, 2010; Chapman & Van de Merwe, 2008; Colvin, 2000; Hamber & Wilson, 1999; Hook & Harris, 2000; Moon, 2008, 2009; Statman, 2000). As Statman (2000) argued, the expressions of 'truth' produced at the TRC hearings were in fact "shaped, coerced and

---

[6] The space and purpose of the present study does not allow a comprehensive discussion on the structure, aims, mandate and impact of the TRC. These issues are thoroughly analysed in: Asmal, Robers & Asmal (1998), Hamber (1995); Villa-Vicencio & Verwoerd, 2000; Villa-Vicencio & Du Toit (2006); Doxtader & Salazar (2007).

constructed" (p. 30) through a psychosocial process defined by a positivist research methodology and the dominant ideological discourse on reconciliation. Such discourses encouraged public forgiveness and reconciliation by creating a collective atmosphere in which individual feelings of anger and revenge felt inappropriate. He points out how the TRC's focus on victims changed gradually towards "finding perpetrators and naming names" (p. 25).

Furthermore, to strengthen his argument, Statman (2000) considers Hugo van der Merwe's (1999, 2001) analysis of two communities hosting TRC hearings, which described the victims who were not offered the opportunity to testify, as being disappointed and doubtful as to whether the Commission found their case to be "sufficiently important to warrant a public hearing" (p. 26) as well as to if they would have any chance of receiving reparations. However, taking into consideration the results of this study and the more recent discussions related to Khulumani Support Group, a leading South African organization of victims of political violence, it seems that victims viewed their healing as being more related to reparations, or at least that the truth recovery would lead to reparations eventually. This trajectory would mean for them that in telling and revealing their stories, they were heard and their suffering was acknowledged (Statman, 2000).

However, "*just* revealing is not *just* (accurate, right, correct)[7] healing" and "unstructured truth telling and truth for the truth's sake is pointless" and furthermore, "effective trauma counselling and support for victims should not be equated with dealing with the past" (Hamber, 1998, para. 9). Indeed, several authors have emphasised that complex individual and social processes need to be involved at many levels in the process of recovery, including dealing with reparation, economic inequalities and the rebuilding of the social and moral fabric of society (Hamber, 2000; Hamber & Wilson, 1999; Hook & Harris, 2000). These tasks were, however, too complex for a single organism such as the TRC, which "was imbued with a local mandate to be achieved in a very short time span" (Chapman and Van der Merwe, 2008, p. 281). Moreover, a major critique of the TRC concerned the overtly psychological discourse that had as a goal political ends rather than psychological ones (Moon, 2008, 2009; Colvin, 2006).

In her argument, Moon (2009) shows how the TRC assumed a therapeutic role in South African society, working "to construct a particular political moral order in South Africa grounded in a form of

---

[7] My adding of synonyms

legitimacy that was neither traditional (based on nature, family or God) nor 'modern' (based on security, justice or prosperity), but one that was infused with a concern with the self, emotional expression and victimization" (p. 84). As she argues, the TRC model is "grounded in a grammar of trauma and suffering underpinned by claims that repressed memory causes untold and ongoing psychological problems; that 'revealing' or truth-telling leads to healing; and that 'closure' on the past must be reached in order for the present to be lived and the future to be faced" (p. 79).

The consequence of the TRC's therapeutic ethos "transformed the moral and political crisis about South Africa's apartheid past into an emotional or psychological one with the effect of eliding the broader context within which party political violence had emerged" (Moon, 2009, p. 84). The further outcome was a "deep depoliticalization of apartheid and the struggle against it" and the reduction of apartheid to a "pathological entity amendable to therapeutic management" (ibidem; also see Mamdani, 1996). In other words, by using therapeutic means to obtain democratic ends, the TRC used the grammar of trauma emphasising the importance of victims' experience and the importance of forgiveness and reconciliation in achieving societal healing.

Trying to be even more specific, it could be said that victims' stories were used at the TRC with the primary purpose of achieving national reconciliation and only implicitly for a victim's benefit in fostering personal healing. This is not necessarily problematic, if forgiveness is authentic and if as a result, victims would feel liberated and helped by this process. Unfortunately, as was discussed before, victims did not find it helpful both at the time of the TRC and also more recently (Colvin, 2000; Statman, 2000; Van der Merwe, 1999). As Backer's longitudinal study with 153 former victims points out, there is a decline in support for the TRC process, "an increased sense of the unfairness of amnesty and dissatisfaction with the extent of truth recovery" (p. 443).

In a similar vein, Colvin (2006) argued that the traumatic storytelling used at the TRC "had the effect of reducing the meaning of 'violation' to the violent" and that it emphasised "spectacular suffering of certain individuals rather than the structural and everyday violence visited on millions of individuals and communities during apartheid" (p. 171). The stories, however, had the function of crafting new borders and social identities: borders of race between Blacks and Whites, temporal borders between past and present, social borders between healed and unhealed and political borders between the new state and the old state. New social identities "as long-suffering victims, repentant perpetrators, empathetic witnesses, or high-minded political leaders" (ibidem) were also part of the social-construction processes developed during the TRC.

Nevertheless, conflicting ideas and debates should not be seen as a threat but rather as a constructive dialogue. As Chapman and Van der Merwe (2008) argue "competing versions of history (…) are all indicators of a healthy public debate" (p. 283). It must also be stressed that the TRC was tasked with "promoting reconciliation not with achieving it" (p. 298). Its reports made important recommendations regarding victims' reparations (Truth and Reconciliation Commission, Vol. 5, 1998) and the implementation of such proposals were entirely the duty of the government. Unfortunately for victims, "the Mbeki administration has been reluctant to implement the TRC's recommendations, thereby diminishing its standing and legitimacy" (Chapman & Van der Merwe, 2008, p. 298). It is also worth mentioning that the TRC was just one organism having to deal with an enormous task over a very short time span and its efforts should be seen as "one phase of a longer process of societal recovery and reinvention" (ibidem, p. 300). However, further aspects related to healing bring into focus the issues of forgiveness and reconciliation, which were considered important not only by the TRC but also, according to various psychological approaches, to recovery as well.

Recovery, forgiveness and reconciliation

In the post-apartheid context and more specifically through the TRC's approach, the notions of forgiveness and reconciliation were considered important both for the recovery of individuals and the healing of the nation. Since the literature on the meaning of forgiveness and reconciliation is too extensive for the purpose of this study, this discussion will consider only materials dealing with the question of whether or not forgiveness and reconciliation are helpful in the process of victims' recovery from trauma. The argument will draw on results from empirical studies analysing the ability of the TRC to facilitate forgiveness and its impact on the recovery process of victims as well as on some conceptual analysis presenting various perspectives on forgiveness.

Opinions related to the potential benefits of forgiveness and reconciliation in victims' healing are often polarised and contradictory (Summerfield, 1997, 2002). The TRC's approach strongly supported the idea that publicly testifying, forgiving and reconciling with perpetrators would have a healing and restorative effect on the human dignity of former victims (Tutu, 1999; Chapman, 2008). The type of forgiveness promoted by the TRC was often unconditional as it was "unrelated to the nature of the crime, perpetrator acknowledgement of wrongdoing and expression of regret, or efforts to compensate the victims" (Chapman, 2008, p. 67). Forgiveness was rather understood as a metaphysical act (Griswold, 2007), as "abandoning your right to pay back the perpetrator in his own coin" and although this could be perceived as a loss, yet "it is a loss that liberates the victim" (Tutu, 1999, p. 272).

The positive effects of forgiveness on victims' recovery have been emphasised and described in numerous conceptual analyses (Bar-Tal, 2000; Van der Merwe & Gobodo-Madikizela, 2007). Even at the TRC public hearings, some victims admitted they felt a sense of relief and peace after publicly telling their stories (Daly & Sarkin, 2007). However, empirical studies with former victims of apartheid who testified publicly, in writing, or did not testify at all, show little evidence that testifying in a public hearing or forgiving those responsible for their suffering was beneficial for victims (Chapman & Van der Merwe, 2008; Kaminer et al., 2001; Daly & Sarkin, 2007). On the contrary, victims experienced testifying as painful and stressful, something that brought back sadness, anger and sorrow. Many victims felt that "their experience at the hearings was disempowering and made their encounters with their perpetrators more difficult" (Chapman, 2008. p.82). Furthermore, victim advocates argued in fact that forgiveness "does not necessarily confer benefits, and (…) when imposed on victims, may even be harmful" (ibidem, p. 81).

An empirical study analysing transcripts of victims' testimonies at the TRC and transcripts of focus groups with former deponents showed that only 2% out of 429 participants in the study were ready to forgive unconditionally. The majority of deponents were critical towards forgiveness and "more oriented to truth and justice than to forgiveness and reconciliation" (Chapman, 2008, p. 68). Also, a survey in Cape Town on 228 members of Khulumanyi Support Group revealed that 50% did not forgive and most of them would mention various conditions to be met before they would be able to forgive. Similarly, Kaminer et al' s (2001) study on the relationship between TRC testifying, forgiveness and psychiatric status showed that testifying at the TRC did not have a visible therapeutic effect on victims and did not influence in any way the level of forgiveness. However, the study highlighted a correlation between lack of forgiveness and poor psychiatric adjustment, although a causal relationship could not be established.

In trying to find an explanation for such a negative view by victims on forgiveness, most studies pointed towards the absence of an appropriate setting at the TRC, in which victims and perpetrators could come together, listen to perpetrators describing the situation and find out "why the abuse occurred" (Chapman, 2008, p. 75). In addition, the perceived lack of justice at the TRC, the amnesty and the inability of perpetrators to show remorse and to reveal 'the whole truth' also contributed to the negative feelings of victims regarding forgiveness. As Van der Merwe and Chapman (2008) argue, "the TRC did become increasingly aware of their limited ability to impact on individual process of reconciliation and forgiveness", a fact that prompted one of the commissioners to acknowledge that "forgiveness and the healing of wounds is an individual process that cannot be handled by a committee or structure" (p. 257).

However, truth commissions can provide institutional support to promote forgiveness "as one option" or as an alternative between extreme positions such as unconditional forgiveness and anger (Daly & Sarkin, 2007, p. 155). Consequently, the act of forgiveness could have a positive impact on victim's recovery if additional counselling and negotiation services are employed, and an appropriate setting is provided with the purpose of facilitating an authentic human encounter between victims and perpetrators (Gobodo-Madikizela, 2003; Staub, 2006). It seems, however, that the balance between caring for the individual on the one hand and the society on the other hand, between a violent past and the need to move forward, between retributive justice and restorative justice is highly complex and inherently constitutive of the makeup in which we try to understand the trauma of the apartheid.

2.5. Concluding remarks and possible ways ahead

This chapter began by posing questions regarding particular approaches to the understanding of trauma and recovery within the context of apartheid. By looking at the available literature in the wider field of trauma and recovery as well as within the South African context, it can be firmly emphasised that there is enough empirical evidence to conclude that people under apartheid were traumatised in multiple ways and to different degrees by various forms of political violence. Although hypothetically, the extent of apartheid trauma cannot be compared (in terms of number of deaths) with that of the Holocaust or with the suffering of war victims in Mozambique, victims still suffered profound trauma during apartheid, as described by PTSD symptoms and other mental disorders. There is clear empirical evidence showing that victims suffered gross human rights violations such as torture, detention, bomb attacks, shootings and killings. For instance, taking the example of the St. James massacre, the experience of sitting in church and having one's mother killed (next to you) by four men opening fire in the congregation, is horrendously traumatizing regardless of context or culture.

Reflecting on the section on apartheid trauma, there is one neglected area that needs to be emphasised at this point. This area concerns the lack of empirical research on how trauma was experienced differently across race. Since apartheid meant racial segregation and oppression, there might be major differences related to victims' traumatic experiences across race, culture and identity. The large majority of the Black population (representing the oppressed) experienced continuous, repetitive traumatic events without the possibility of a safe haven in which, as Herman (2001) suggested, recovery could begin. In contrast, most White people (excepting those who adopted various forms of protest against apartheid) being the beneficiaries of the repressive system experienced trauma as a result of individual traumatic events (such as attacks and massacres). By virtue of their position, they would most likely have the possibility of finding safety and support in the aftermath of trauma. Would these differences have any impact on the way trauma is experienced and the way victims recover? This is yet another concern of this book.

Regarding recovery after trauma suffered under apartheid, it has been widely acknowledged that although, at a practical level, the TRC created some premises for healing, the emphasis was more on the collective aspect of reconciliation than the recovery of individual victims (Guthrey, 2015). Sufficient empirical evidence showed that traumatic story telling in public hearings at the TRC was not particularly helpful and that additional means had to be considered for the healing of victims.

This represents one of the major gaps this work is trying to bridge. Moreover, although there are various objections raised related to the individualist positivist framework of PTSD, there are only a few conceptual alternatives in general that clearly articulate a different way of understanding trauma and recovery. Most of these approaches consist of psychosocial, contextual and systemic interventions delivered within a therapeutic context. Empirical studies adopting a contextual/systemic framework seem particularly relevant here since contextual characteristics of race, culture and identity play a major role in the understanding of trauma and recovery in post-apartheid.

This book adopts a contextual/systemic framework for the understanding of trauma and recovery using life narratives of trauma survivors, an approach that will be further described in the next chapter. This approach resembles Bracken's (2002) contextual approach, Herman (2001) and Landau et al.'s (2008) Link model as it aims to be holistic, process oriented, focused on resources, culturally sensitive and based on relationships. By interviewing former victims (Black, Coloured and White) who suffered serious trauma due to political violence (torture, detention, displacement, police harassment, the loss of a significant person, shootings, etc), the major goal was to explore victims' narratives and their particular ways of reconstructing trauma and recovery after the collapse of apartheid. Since their stories concern past experiences, their narratives are inevitably shaped by interpretations and identity processes (the reconstruction of the self) rooted in subjectivity, social relationships and cultural values.

Summing up, the analysis of survivors' narratives will have two major foci: (1) questions regarding the reconstruction of trauma and its impact and (2) the process of recovery from the aftermath until present. These processes are not separate but interact in various ways in people's narratives. On the one hand, their reconstruction of trauma is influenced by idiosyncratic understandings of the self and the world. On the other hand, the process of recovery, since it involves the reconstruction of the self, relationships with others and the world, is also shaped by past experiences including trauma. Consequently, the impact of trauma will be assessed in the context of individuals' interactions with other significant subsystems such as family, community, place of work, political institutions and organisations. Within this frame, PTSD symptoms could be understood as a characteristic of the individual's trauma at certain points during their life trajectories, experienced either in the immediate aftermath of traumatic events or even at later stages in life. Recovery will be explored systemically by looking at how survivors try to rebuild their lives in relation to their social context.

At this point, it suffices to say that from a systemic point of view, the process of recovery is viewed in terms of individuals' openness to change, desire to explore new options in life, hope and commitment to continue searching for meaning and new alternatives. Difficulties or conflicts are not necessarily viewed as dysfunctional but (depending on participants' views) they could be seen rather as opportunities for change and transformation (Watzlawick, Weakland & Fish, 1974). Such a perspective has the potential to broaden research opportunities and to open up new avenues for a deeper understanding of human suffering and healing. The next chapter will try to create the conceptual framework, including the theoretical assumptions and the hermeneutics that set the ground for the analysis and interpretation of survivors' life narratives.

CHAPTER THREE

CONCEPTUAL FRAMEWORK

This chapter aims to highlight the main theoretical assumptions that constitute the epistemological framework used in this work with the purpose of exploring narratives of victims of political violence during apartheid and their life trajectories to the present. Since the survivors interviewed in this study experienced trauma more than twenty years ago, their stories (about stories) are interpretations about events, people, actions and feelings that happened in the past and are brought into the present through a process of social reconstruction. Trauma experienced in the past was considered to have a shattering effect on the self and the meaning of the world and, from this perspective, the reconstruction of victims' life narratives represents also the reconstruction of their selves.

However, I realised that, as a listener of these stories, I had to be aware of the hermeneutical lenses I am wearing while interpreting people's texts. Theories of trauma are profoundly embedded in the Western individualistic culture dominated by Cartesian dualism, behaviourism and cognitive approaches to understanding the subject and his/her world (Bracken, 2002; Crossley, 2000). A major question comes up regarding the suitability of this type of approach for the South African context in which people of various cultures, races and experiences of repression try to coexist by sharing the same geographical space and time. White people with a predominantly Western cultural background experience anxiety and meaninglessness in an utterly different way from Black people living in townships or even Black people representing the new political elite of the nation. All these differences point to a careful consideration of peoples' beliefs, values and ways of life in the process of interpreting their narratives. In addition, an understanding of trauma is closely related to how anxiety is experienced in the cultural matrix (Kaplan, 2005). Nevertheless, since such a discussion is taking place in these so-called postmodern times, an exploration of current philosophical assumptions about knowledge, self and the world is vitally important at this stage.

There are three main presuppositions that informed and shaped the conceptual framework of this work. First, no single paradigm or approach can sufficiently explore on its own the trauma of political violence and the construction of the self after trauma. As Paolo Bertando (2000) argues, all theories have limitations and internal inconsistencies. In trying to strictly consign the research to one of the main theoretical approaches, I often found myself trapped in the dialectic of positivism versus constructionism, objectivity versus subjectivity, one truth versus multiple truths, individual versus collective, losing the subject versus losing the discourse and the list can endlessly continue. In this context, Kenneth Gergen and Mary Gergen's (2003) perspective on knowledge, meaning and the self felt liberating through the celebration of the multiple opportunities offered by postmodernity and the emphasis on language, culture and history claimed by social constructionism. In saying this, however, I do not suggest that postmodern theories are flawless or free of inconsistencies. I just argue that postmodernism confers a better framework than positivism and individualism for the exploration of trauma and its impact in post-conflict non-Western societies.

Second, although PTSD and complex PTSD are acknowledged in this book as important contributions in the field of clinical trauma in general and war trauma in particular, the analysis does not limit itself only to this type of approach. Since the main concern is the trauma of political violence, participants included in the study had to have suffered one or more traumatic events during apartheid. This aspect, however, is not necessarily inferring an assumption of direct causality between a traumatic event and the symptoms of trauma. Nor is this work seeking to develop a new clinical theory on trauma and recovery as advanced by the medical discourse. On the contrary, similar to Bracken (2002, 2007), it seeks to open up the way for a multidisciplinary approach to trauma in general and towards a contextual understanding of trauma and recovery experienced in the South African context in particular. The hermeneutical framework will be informed by contextual, psychosocial, anthropological and philosophical perspectives on trauma and recovery (Bracken, 2002; Bracken et al., 1995; Brison, 2002; Frank, 1995; Herman, 2001; Landau et al., 2008; Summerfield, 2002; Taylor, 1989). The analysis will also draw on important contributions to the field of trauma and political violence within the South African context (Foster et al., 1987; Manganyi & du Toit, 1990; Straker, 1992; Van der Merwe & Gobodo-Madikizela, 2007). However, as a characteristic of qualitative research, this work aims to create space for discussions, critiques and the integration of new elements that emerged during research, which are related to the historical, cultural, social and political context of post-apartheid in South Africa.

Third, any approach to trauma and recovery would have to make explicit its views on the human being and the world. Trauma due to political violence during apartheid is highly complex, affecting individuals, families and communities alike. Consequently, a predominantly individual clinical approach to understanding the phenomena under scrutiny would be insufficient if not reductionist. Human beings are relational beings and construct their identities in relation to others and the world in which they live (Bracken, 2002; Taylor, 1989). They are also autonomous and socially interdependent, "vulnerable enough to be undone by violence and yet resilient enough to be reconstructed with the help of empathic others" (Brison, 2002, p.38). In addition, the effects of long periods of repression cannot be understood in isolation from the characteristics of the social, political and cultural context (Antze & Lambeck, 1996; Danieli, 1998; Herman, 2001; Van der Merwe, 1999; Weine, 2006). Hence, the framework of the present study needs to be broad enough to allow space for the exploration of the complex interconnections between individuals, families, society and their sophisticated ways of giving meaning to intricate events in their lives. In this context, a systemic holistic approach to human beings and the world takes into consideration not only individuals but also their complex relationships with others in multiple contexts such as family, work, church, community, society and the world. Taking into consideration their relational, cultural and spiritual beliefs, will provide both freedom and structure to explore people's traumatic experiences and their ways of making meaning in their lives.

In order to illustrate the above-mentioned theoretical underpinnings, the discussion will begin with a section examining the postmodernist turn in psychology followed by the social constructionist approach to trauma and the narrative construction of the self. The following section will describe the main elements of systemic theories, which in recent years have been highly influenced by postmodern ideas. Finally, the chapter will conclude with an overview of the key theoretical assumptions used to shape the unfolding of this work.

3.1. The postmodern self and psychology

"We cannot but be postmodern." (Bertando, 2000, p. 85)

Postmodernism is a historical and philosophical paradigm, which paradoxically resulted both out of and as a reaction to modernism. Although a paradigm shift is often described as a visible change from an old to a new direction of thought, yet when required to produce definitions, characteristics and concepts, the discussion becomes highly debatable and full of contradictions (Kuhn, 2003). Defining postmodernism in general and its implications on human sciences in particular becomes therefore a difficult endeavour. However before describing the main theories of postmodernism, it is important to clarify the terms "modernism" and "postmodernism" as well as social and cultural perspectives of paradigm shifts in the transition from modernity to postmodernity (Harvey, 1993; Hassan, 1996).

Both terms refer to distinct historical stages in philosophical, social and cultural developments and different stances regarding the notions of knowledge, truth and the self. Regarding the historical stage, modernism is associated with the period of time following the radical transformations taking place in society through industrialisation, secularisation and the triumph of reason (Crossley, 2000). Roughly situated historically between the late nineteenth and early twentieth centuries, modernism challenges the romantic notion of compassionate thinking and proclaims the power of the human subject to create and develop through practical reason[1], technology, science and experiments. Knowledge is instrumentalised, standardised, rationally planned and in search of uniformity, harmony and balance (Crotty, 1998). The *Cogito ergo sum* dictum elevates human reason as the ultimate and universal truth. The human being is essentially a rational subject able to turn everything, including the self, society and history into objects of rational and experimental observation. Sociologically this resulted in the two faces of the same meta-narrative project based on human reason: the liberal Parsonian theory of economic development dominant in Western democracies and Marxism in all its concrete forms found in the Eastern side of the cold war divide.

By the late 80s the project of modernity with its grand rational metanarrative collapsed, creating space for a new phase, which as it was mentioned, is both a continuation and a profound rupture, moving into the opposite direction. To the belief in rational, linear and unlimited progress, postmodernism replied with suspicion towards universal claims, truth and ultimate reality. Hence, postmodernism brought to prominence ambiguity, heterogeneity, difference, multiplicity and asymmetry of perspectives about knowledge and what is truth. In fact, as the argument goes, there is no single truth but many voices and multiple truths constructed through language games and power. Meaning is elusive as the continuity of the

---

[1] see Kant's famous article *What is Enlightenment* republished in Eliot & Whitlock (1992).

self, development and progress is replaced by fragmentation and discontinuity (Crossley, 2000).

In the arts, modernism attributed the high art to specialists, whereas in postmodern times it is considered that *Tout est art* (Venturi, 1996). The modern artist, as a logical and rational being, was considered to be "the creator", while the postmodern artist is "the player" who is eclectic, repetitive and uses multiple styles as the style can be both important and meaningless at the same time. Imitation, collage, ambiguity and irony are all part of art's game.

As Crossley (2000) argues, postmodernism has a significant impact on psychological experience, cultural context and the self. In modernism the self was considered to be a coherent entity characterised by constancy and unity while the postmodern self is fragmented, variable and open to interpretation as the understanding of one's self depends inextricably on the multiple and often contradictory linguistic structures and the historical, cultural and social milieu in which the self exists. Consequently it becomes almost impossible to make universal claims about the nature of human selves since the postmodern relativist view on human identity emphasises the functional rather than the ontological and "tends to ignore attempts at identifying an ontological *sub-stratum*, or anything that would claim universality in an *a priori* way" (Rogobete, 2011, p. 272).

Hence, in order to understand the implications of postmodern theory in psychology in general and human identity in particular, it is important to explore its basic assumptions articulated in structuralism, post-structuralism and deconstructionism and represented by thinkers such as Michel Foucault, Jean Francois Lyotard, Jacques Derrida and Jacques Lacan (Kvale, 1992). However, since postmodernism is a vast topic, I will resume with the exploration of the above-mentioned currents of thought, views on the self and approaches on the concept of knowledge contained therein.

Structuralism and the functional self

One of the main assumptions of structuralism is that existence and the world in general cannot be represented through a single type of language. Knowledge and understanding should be built on the exploitation of multiple perspectives. Modernism's universal epistemology is replaced by *multiple perspectivism,* which inevitably leads to *relativism.* However, the new epistemology is still seeking to reveal what was believed to be *the true* nature of a complex foundation of reality. What prevails in this instance is the function and structure of things. The meaning of words is given by their relation to other words rather than by their reference to objects. Structuralists reject the idea that the primary function of language is to refer to things in the world. The elements of language acquire meaning not because of some connection between words and things-in-the-world, but only as part of a system of relations.

Structuralism has its roots in Saussure's (1916) linguistic studies, which claim that the word is a sign that consists of two aspects: a signifier and a signified (ex. traffic light sign-word-meaning system). Each signifier signifies by marking a difference or distinction within a system of opposites and contrasts. Underlying our use of language is always a system, and only because of the system is there any signification or meaning. In order to find the meaning one has to find the *grammar*, the *texture* of the text and the rules governing the system, as the meaning is determined by the system and not inherent to reality.

Structuralism could be also seen as the search for a new order, represented by Claude Levi-Strauss in sociological and anthropological studies and Jacques Lacan in psychology through his preoccupation with the structures of the mind. In terms of understanding the self and how knowledge is produced, hermeneutical analysis characterised by its focus on essence, analogies and linear story-telling and meaning is replaced by structural analysis represented by functionalism, multiplicity, differences, binary opposites, laws and structures.

However, a significant impact in the expansion of structuralist ideas has been considered to be Michael Foucault's (1979, 1980) concept of knowledge-power relationship. His thesis was constructed as a structuralist critique of modernist reason. The starting point of this project was the unmasking of structures governing the question of knowledge. His conclusion was that knowledge understood through the epistemological paradigm of universal reason is nothing more than a series of discourses of power governed by language games. In his books *Discipline and Punish* and *The History of Sexuality*, Foucault argues that professions such as psychology, psychiatry, biology and medicine are all imbedded in a discourse of power conferred thorough the particular knowledge and language used in a particular field (Gergen & Gergen, 2003, p. 36).

Poststructuralism and the de-centred self

As any post-theory emerging on the continuum of historical thought, poststructuralism is considered to be a response to structuralism. Since most poststructuralists started as structuralists and changed their ideas along the way, it is difficult to clearly distinguish between representative figures of structuralism and poststructuralism. However, writers such as Michel Foucault, Jacques Derrida and Julia Kristeva are often associated with poststructuralism (Crotty, 1998). The main criticism raised by poststructuralism claims that knowledge is based neither on pure experience as stipulated by phenomenology, nor on systematic structures as assumed by structuralism. Regarding the core subjects of the self, knowledge and psychology, there are several key assumptions of the postructuralist theory worth mentioning.

First, postructuralism rejects the rationalist dualist approach of the self in psychology, which perceives human beings as comprising of two separate entities – mind and body – in which the mind represents the mental system, the reason, the subject, while the body is the object, a vehicle for the mind or an extension of the mind. By emphasising the superiority of reason, such approach infers a modernist, universal view on achieving knowledge based on logical steps and empirical methods (Price, 2002). Consequently, the self is placed at the centre of human experience as a distinct, unique and coherent rational entity. Postructuralism considers this view as being illusory and claims instead that the self is torn between various conflicting knowledge positions related to race, gender, class and social status. As a result, such psychology is accused of being unable to integrate the contextual, contingent elements of the social world inherent in history and culture, thus missing the complexities of the situated self.

Second, the postructuralist critique challenges the objectivity, individualism and essentialism of scientific knowledge promoted by classical psychology (Gergen, 1973). In poststructuralism, the text does not have a single purpose and a single meaning. On the contrary, the act of knowing depends on a multiplicity of factors: the reader's perception of his/her own self, how this relates to her work, the positioning of the self, etc. The signification of a word cannot be fully determined but always delayed, being transposed into another signifier. Thus, there is no central meaning. On the contrary, there is a plurality and a multiplicity of *paths* of significance that can be traced from a text. Following a certain path of significance does not lead towards a centre but towards other interpretations and possible meanings. Implicitly, rejecting the idea of absolute truth and objectivity, postructuralism considers the possibility of many *truths* depending on the moral, political and ideological purpose of various discourses.

Third, within a postructuralist framework, language is considered fundamental in the construction of subjectivity, knowledge and social life (Foucault, 1972). Relationships and social links are established by language and not necessarily connected with a single thread, but rather constructed through the intersection of an undetermined number of language games. Since such multitudes of language games are not connected, it becomes implicit that there is no need or obligation to make stable combinations between these games or to make them understandable. Thus, the social subject seems to become not only de-centred but moreover dissolved into the dissemination of these language games. Social life atomises itself in these flexible networks of language games, each one of us being given the possibility to retreat in different sets of codes depending on the specific situation in which we find ourselves. Although this could be perceived as a pessimistic perspective or a loss, Gergen argues in fact that it should be celebrated as liberating from all the constraints imposed thus far by an objective perspective on reality and knowledge. On the contrary, he proposes a knowledge that is socially constructed and negotiated through language, culture and history. However, before examining social constructionism, the discussion will turn first to deconstructionism as promoted by the French philosopher Jacques Derrida.

The deconstruction of the self

First, it must be acknowledged that it is difficult to organise and put clarity into something that was not meant to have coherence, unity and consensus. Deconstructionism is a sceptical approach to meaning, which does not search for a holding centre but rather for various threads of discourse that comprise the text. In his writings, Derrida rejects primarily the logocentrism of the West and the structuralist theory of binary oppositions described by conceptual or theoretical opposites such as mind – body, male – female, white – black, private – public, individual – collective, rational - emotional and so on (Sampson, 1989). In his view, meaning is not grounded in metaphysics but rather is produced through language, difference and writing that is prior to speaking. As Carrigan (1996) argues, Derrida intended to demonstrate that "written words did not stand for spoken words, which did not stand for thoughts, which did not stand for Truth, or God, which were not referents of the metaphysical world. On the contrary, Derrida suggested the interpretation of a written text 'in a certain way'" (para 2).

Regarding psychology's self, Sampson (1989) highlights three main themes deconstructed by Derrida in his works: the person as "the centre of awareness", the person as "an integrated universe and distinctive whole" and the person as "a bounded entity set contrastively against other such entities" (p.13). It is not the context here to engage in the whole argument used by Derrida to deconstruct the self as described by these three characteristics. However, according to Sampson's analysis the main anchors of Derrida's thesis relate to the idea of self-consciousness, ideology, language and a symbolic system of meaning.

As the argument goes, self-consciousness is not a "direct and unmediated experience but rather is an indirect and always already mediated experience" (Sampson, 1989, p. 13). Although not aware of such experience, the social and historical context permeates and structures the consciousness and the self. As part of the language system, ideology becomes imbedded in the personhood, mediating and defining the subject. As a result, it could be said that persons are constructed through a symbolic system that places the subject in a certain space but outside the subject's mastery. Consequently, the persons are not "at the centre, fully aware and self-present masters, but have been decentred by these relations to the symbolic order" (ibidem, p. 14).

However, it is important to highlight Derrida's warning against regarding the *self* and the *other* as distinct opposites. Similar to Bateson (1972) who considers that both *organism* and *environment* are part of the same system, Derrida concludes that differences (not opposites) are part of the entity and describe the relations between the parts and not the parts themselves. Consequently, the subject cannot be separated from the multiple others, who are actually the self's very essence. Derrida considers that the idea of the *self* as being distinct and opposed to the *other* threatens their relationship and implicitly the very meaning and foundation of the *self*. As Sampson (1989) concludes "the Derridarian subject who would seek to oppose and enslave others can only suffer in kind for those others are elements of the subject's own personhood" (p. 16).

This perspective brings a positive note on the aspect of relationships and the social world, which are fundamental for the understanding of human pain, identity, meaning and reality. Following a deconstructionist discourse, one can claim that deconstruction and construction are both part of the same system and therefore the discussion will now turn towards the social constructionist approach to the self.

3.2. Social constructionism

Although social constructionism is considered to have multiple roots, its origins are primarily traced to the work of Mannheim (1936) and Berger and Luckman (1967). Prominent thinkers in this field classify social constructionism as "well established" in sociology (Sarbin & Kitsuse, 1994, p. 3), yet "not a singular and unified position" but rather as a continuous dialogue between people with various backgrounds, beliefs and ways of thinking (Gergen & Gergen, 2003, p. 2). It is often defined in opposition to realism and essentialism, which consider that phenomena are inherent to human beings, universal and not dependant on context. However, as Sarbin and Kitsuse (1994) argue, social constructionism claims that "social objects are not given 'in the world' but constructed, negotiated, reformed, fashioned and organised by human beings in their efforts to make sense of happenings in the world" (p. 3).

According to Gergen and Gergen (2003), although there is no fundamental set of commonly accepted assumptions, the ongoing dialogue of social constructionism revolves around three main axes: the communal origin of knowledge, the centrality of language and the ideological saturation of knowledge. In general terms, the social constructionist assumptions challenge the rational Cartesian view of the self, considering that the relationship instead of the individual is at the centre of knowledge. In other words, knowledge about the world and the self does not exist in the individual's mind but is co-created in relationships and shared in the context of a community that is rooted in history and culture. Furthermore, the concept of truth is defined within a given community that shares commitment to a paradigm that comprises of "the same rules and standards for scientific practice" (Kuhn, 2003, p. 7).

Regarding the centrality of language, another social constructionist assumption claims that understandings of the world, human experience, reality and facts are created within a linguistic context or through what Wittgenstein calls "language games" (quoted in Gergen & Gergen, 2003, p. 4). The linguistic milieu is defined by a set of rules that serve to give meaning to events, objects and experiences within a given community. In this context, it could be assessed that the social constructionist turn in psychology was introduced by a re-orientation within traditional psychology's concern with behaviours, emotions and traits towards a search for meaning (Sarbin & Kitsuse, 1994).

The aspect of ideological saturation of knowledge is of particular importance for the present study. Generally speaking, scientific theories in general and trauma theories in particular have been conceptualised by Western minds in Western social and cultural contexts. After PTSD's first official conceptualisation in the DSM III in 1980, an increasing number of researchers in the field of trauma have emphasised the importance of taking into consideration the characteristics of the historical and cultural context in which trauma takes place (Bracken, 2002; Danieli, 1998; Herman, 2001; Summerfield, 1998; Weine, 2006). Social constructionism challenges the universality and ultimate authority of theories of knowledge, arguing that such knowledge not only favours certain views over others but also "narrows the potentials of the science" (Gergen and Gergen, 2003, p.5). According to social constructionist assumptions, there is a diversity and multiplicity of stories, which can be both different and valid at the same time. However, as Burr (1998) argues, there is a potential danger in adopting a too relativist stance and "losing our critical edge on important social phenomena such as inequality or oppression, which threaten to become casualties of relativism and turn into just another story, just another way of interpreting the social text" (p. 15). Nevertheless, some researchers accept the idea of a social constructionist position, which does not necessarily entail relativism (Davies, 1998; Parker, 1998).

In conclusion, it can be summarised that the approach to knowledge as socially constructed is based on several fundamental assumptions regarding the interplay between scientific theory, reality, human interactions, social context and the production of knowledge. In Gergen's (2003) view, scientific theory does not reflect reality in a direct form but rather reality is co-created through human interactions. Knowledge from a constructionist position is the result of "an active, cooperative enterprise of persons in relationship" (p. 15). Constructionist inquiry involves the exploration of historical and cultural milieus in which social constructions take place as knowledge and understanding of the world is continuously negotiated through forms of social actions.

In the present context, a study on trauma due to political violence inflicted by the apartheid regime requires careful consideration of ideological, historical and cultural aspects related to human experience. The discussion will turn now towards the process of reconstructing meaning after trauma.

Reconstructing meaning after trauma

"The meaning of any past event may change as the larger, continuing story lengthens and grows in complexity. As readers we are continuously reexploring the significance of earlier episodes of the story in light of what transpires later, as we are caught up in the hermeneutic spiral of interpretation" (Antze, 1996, p. xix).

The view on recovery after trauma is closely linked with the theoretical perspective on the trauma concept as a whole. According to the particular type of approach, one is able to define the meaning of recovery and what it entails. Since in the previous chapter it was argued that an individualistic approach to trauma is insufficient, an approach to recovery that takes into consideration only the individual's inner world would also prove inadequate. Furthermore, it is important to consider that this discussion takes place in a multicultural context, which is obviously very different from the Western setting in which PTSD was conceptualised. Consequently, recovery after trauma due to political violence during apartheid may take different forms from those described by positivist and cognitivist approaches. Postmodern approaches consider recovery not as a cure or a complete disappearance of symptoms, but rather as a continuous process of "working through" which may often mean "accepting ongoing mourning and keeping the wound open" (Brison, 2002; Kaplan, 2005). Also since trauma is seen as the shattering of the self and the meaning of life, recovery would involve a process of reconstructing meaning and the self in the aftermath of trauma. While there is some consensus regarding the importance of such process, the ways in which the meaning-making process is developing differ greatly across paradigms and theoretical approaches.

A range of approaches to recovery after trauma have emphasised the importance of concepts such as "the human order of meaning" (Crossley, 2000), "systems and structures of meaning" (Polkinghorne, 1988), "the remaking of the self" (Brison, 2002), "the healing relationship and safety" (Herman, 2001), "the rewriting of the self" (Freeman, 1993), "healing connections" (Johnson, 2002) and "rebuilding a practical way of life" (Bracken, 2002) or in terms of transformation and growth (Pals & McAdams, 2004; Tedeschi & Calhoun, 1995). From a clinical and practical perspective, most of these concepts are fundamental elements of various therapeutic approaches to recovery after trauma used in individual, couple, family and group therapy (Bracken, 2002; Johnson, 2002). Interacting with Ehrenhaus and Christopher Lasch, Crossley (2000) engages in debates regarding the "therapeutic narratives that have become increasingly popular in contemporary culture" (p. 159) and the narrative psychology's project described as "one more manifestation of the 'profound subjection' inherent in a culture where psychology and psychologically related professions are increasingly coming to 'colonize' our experiences and understanding of ourselves" (p. 161). However, drawing on Giddens and Gergen's arguments, Crossley (2000) develops a more positive view of therapeutic narratives arguing that "all human agents stand in a position of appropriation in relation to the social world, which is to say that they respond reflexively and creatively to the changes going on around them. Hence, although it is true that modern social life may in some ways impoverish individual action, it is also true that it creates greater opportunities and new possibilities to individuals that were not even conceivable in previous eras" (p. 163).

Furthermore, Crossley (2000) brings our attention towards the "human order of meaning" which is closely related with the self, other human systems, human temporality and the multiplicity of relationships and connections taking place in the social world. In her view the construction of meaning takes place through language and the active exploration of "meaning systems and the structures of meaning that make up our minds and worlds" (p. 10). In practical ways, this process consists of creative agency, reflexivity and interpretation, talking, writing and relating to others in the cultural context. Emphasising the relational dimension of meaning, she argues:

> When we ask ourselves the question 'what does it mean?' we are asking ourselves (or others) how something is related or connected to something or someone else. It is the connections or relationships among events that constitute their meaning. Moreover such meanings are not produced subjectively by isolated individuals, rather they are formulated through cultural meaning systems such as language (and narratives) which reverberate with knowledge and connections and relationships across generations (p. 11).

In a similar vein, Gergen (2003) is against the traditional view, which considers that the source of meaning is in the individual mind. In his view, meaning is created in the context of relationships. As he argues: "Social understanding is generated from participation within the common system. In this sense, it is not the individual who pre-exists the relationship and initiates the process of signification, but patterns of relationship and their embedded meanings that pre-exist the individual" (p. 148).

In addition, arguing from a clinical perspective, Herman (2001) emphasises that recovery does not occur in isolation but in the context of a secure healing relationship, the therapeutic alliance between survivor and therapist being just one example. In her view, the process of recovery takes place in three stages: the first stage focuses on establishing safety, autonomy and empowerment of the survivor, the second stage consists of remembering trauma and mourning the loss and finally, the third stage targets the reconnection of the survivor with ordinary life.

Although Herman admits that the process of recovery does not follow a "linear, uninterrupted sequence" (p. 174), she nevertheless argues for a comprehensive treatment, which "must address the characteristic biological, psychological, and social components of the disorder" (p. 156). At each stage survivors take specific steps in the process of recovery, by focusing at the beginning on finding a safe context for the victims and on restoring their agency by achieving autonomy and control in their lives. In the following stage, the trauma survivor needs to undergo a reconstruction of the trauma story "so that it can be integrated into the survivor's life story" (p. 175). In the third stage, the survivor has to develop a new self and new relationships, previously shattered by violence, and restore a sense of trust in the self and the world. This meaning-making process involves reconciliation with oneself, reconnecting with others and participating in meaningful social actions.

In her *Afterword* to the new edition of *Trauma and Recovery*, Herman (2001) acknowledges the important contribution brought by collaborative working relationships with the trauma survivors to the treatment of PTSD. Although victims sometimes never get treatment, they still recover, developing resilience and strengths. As she argues: "To the extent that they recover, most survivors must invent their own methods, drawing on their individual strengths and the supportive relationships naturally available to them in their own communities. Systematic studies of resilience in untreated survivors hold great promise for developing more effective and widely adaptable methods of therapeutic intervention" (p. 241).

A stronger emphasis on a contextual dimension of the recovery process is brought by Bracken (2002). He argues for a "context-centred approach grounded in hermeneutic philosophy" (p. 207), in which the meaningfulness of the world is given by "the practical engagement of human beings with their social and cultural environment" (p. 211). While he admits that philosophy "cannot tell us what to do clinically, it can help to clarify what values are being used in the course of certain interventions" (p. 214). Based on his experience of working with people suffering trauma in Uganda, he provides an astute description of the dilemma facing professionals in the field of trauma. He expresses it as a contradiction between the need to understand and interpret the phenomena on the one side, and the restrictive and damaging potential of such interpretations on the other side. Helping others to rebuild their lives after trauma may involve a position of humbleness. As Bracken described it:

> I felt I had more to learn from them about endurance and resilience in the face of extreme tragedy. Individual psychological models, such as PTSD, seemed somehow inappropriate and did not fit with what I was hearing. Somehow it felt wrong to reduce the suffering I encountered – which had historical, cultural, religious, economic and sociological dimensions – to any sort of model at all. (p. 208)

However, in saying this Bracken does not advocate for the abolition of the PTSD framework but rather for a more tentative use of it and "only from a position of deep respect for local situations and ways of life" (p. 218). In addition, he argues for an alternative approach to the reconstruction of meaning after trauma which primarily involves "rebuilding a practical way of life", "a position of deep respect for local traditions of healing, local ways of life and local cosmologies" and "listening to local voices and learning the skills of what I shall call 'supportive non-intervention'" (ibidem).

Bracken's suggestions do not represent an attack on the PTSD concept but rather a call for respect and sensitivity for the suffering and particular ways of meaning-making of people from non-Western cultural contexts. The reconstruction of meaning after political violence and trauma may not be a well-defined organised and orderly process as described by cognitivist approaches. On the contrary a multitude of interconnected and overlapping processes may occur in which individuals reconstruct their selves while communities also rebuild their lives shattered by destruction. As Bracken argues, "it is in the regaining of an economy, a culture and a sense of community that individuals find a way of living in the wake of terrible suffering" (p. 219).

A commonality of the views presented in this section consists in the agreement that the reconstruction of meaning after trauma does not happen in isolation but is closely related to community life and the cultural context in which people interact every day. It is therefore imperative for researchers and clinicians working with trauma in various cultural contexts, to "recognize the importance of local contextual factors in shaping people's responses to suffering" (Bracken, 2002, p. 218) and to adopt a position of respect for people's practical ways of making meaning and relating to the world around them. The discussion will turn next to the ways in which people construct themselves through their relations and life stories which are interchangeably connected with their social context, their sense of morality and history.

Social construction of the self

In previous sections it was argued that an understanding of the self is closely intertwined with questions about the meaning of life. It was also argued that people experience trauma as the shattering of the self and the world in which they live. Although after such an experience they remain changed forever in the sense that they would never be the same again, yet this does not mean that they cannot be better off than before the trauma. As Brison (2002) argues, "when your life is shattered, you are forced to pick up the pieces and you have a chance to stop and examine them. You can say 'I don't want this anymore' or 'I think I will work on that one' (p.21). Yet, the ways in which people create meaning and how they interpret the *self* are complex matters and often mysterious as "the world is just too big and dense, too meaningful to be represented exhaustively" (Freeman, 1993, p. 10). Besides, the concept of the self cannot be approached without taking into consideration the theoretical assumptions that underpin the epistemological and hermeneutical framework of the discussion.

Unlike Cartesian individualist approaches, the constructionist paradigm understands the self as inextricably linked to others, language, history, culture and morality (Crossley, 2000). These complex interconnections have been conceptualised by various scholars who, among other directions of thought, have emphasised the relational and moral dimension of the self (Taylor, 1989) as well as the narrative and contextual dimension of the self (Freeman, 1993; Gergen, 1991; Ricoeur, 1992). A fundamental element of the social constructionist understanding of the self is language as a vehicle for the construction of the self. As Crossley (2000) put it "the experience of the self takes on meaning only through specific linguistic, historical and social structures" (p. 21).

In his book *Sources of the Self: The Making of Modern Identity* (1989), Charles Taylor argues that the self cannot be understood in the absence of a moral universe or what he calls "moral orientation" or "the good" (p. 31). In his view, it is impossible for us to imagine a stage of human existence in which people realised that they had to invent the meaning of right – wrong and good – bad. The good belongs to a moral realm and exists regardless of human decision. The meaning of the self therefore emerges in close connection to various notions of 'the good' and in relation to reflective processes in which we try to make sense of who we are. Commenting on Taylor, Crossley points out that "Taylor's main objective is to describe the way in which the modern concept of self is radically different from that of previous civilizations, a process facilitated by the interconnected development of new notions of 'the good', new forms of narration, and new understandings of social bonds and relations" (Crossley, 2000, p. 16).

In his eloquent analysis of the modern Western self, Taylor is critical of the "subjectivist expressivism" and "the cultural turn" or what he calls "the triumph of the therapeutic" (p. 508) illustrated by people's preoccupation with personal fulfilment and actualisation. If the meaning of good is understood only through the ways in which things bring fulfilment and realization to the self, then the result would be an "empty self" (Cushman, 1990). As Taylor (1989) argues:

But our normal understanding of self-realization presupposes that some things are important beyond the self, that there are some goods or purposes the furthering of which has significance for us and which hence can provide the significance a fulfilling life needs. A total and fully consistent subjectivism would tend towards emptiness: nothing would count as a fulfilment in a world in which literally nothing was important but self-fulfilment. (p. 507)

In Taylor's (1989) view, the modern self is characterised by a sense of inwardness (p. 111), which is similar to Augustine's understanding of morality as a turn towards the *self*. This implies a reflexive stance that includes self-control and self-exploration. The responsible engagement of the self in the world on the one hand, and the search for the self on the other hand, have become dominant themes in the modern culture. However, the way reflexivity is understood in the present days is very different from that of Augustine. In modern times, the reflexivity of the self was defined in the absence of a point of reference, which in Augustine's understanding was God. The self through inner reflection would position itself correctly in relation to God. On the contrary in the modern world, the loss of tradition, God and family life have led to the emergence of a "minimal self", characterised by "the individual's loss of a sense of history, continuity, feelings of belonging, morality and responsibility. This leads to a society made up of individuals who tend to feel that their responsibility is only to themselves and the sphere of their own self perceived interest." (Crossley, 2000, p.161). In this context, the self's reflexivity becomes a closed system or a vicious cycle which in the absence of a meaningful framework generates an ontological anxiety.
Analysing Tillich's concept of anxiety, Bracken, along similar lines, (2002) argues:

Concern about emptiness and meaninglessness are the central anxieties of our time. (…) Tillich relates these forms of anxiety directly to questions of 'spiritual self-affirmation'. Meaninglessness is the absolute threat of nonbeing to human spirituality, and emptiness is the relative version of this. The former is anxiety about the 'loss of an ultimate concern', the loss of 'a spiritual centre' that gives an ultimate sense of coherence, order and purpose to the world. In this, there is the loss of any answer to the question of life's meaning. (p. 173)

In Taylor's (1989) opinion, this type of anxiety, characterised by a sense of dislocation and loss of meaning which has been accelerated by the modern turn inward, is in fact the result of the self's efforts to define and reach the *good*. However, in order to reach the good and find meaning, selves need to adopt an orderly position in the world. As Bracken argues, "the restoration of meaning requires, as a first step, a focus on the practical world through which a sense of order becomes available to us. Meaning in this frame is something generated holistically through our embodied engagement with a social world. If meaning is broken, it will be through this social engagement that it will be restored" (p. 96).

The self's encounter with the *good* is not understood in functional or cognitive terms as mastery of good deeds and attitudes towards the world. On the contrary, this encounter has an ontological dimension as the self meets the good through 'being' not 'doing' or 'thinking' as in the Cartesian approach. It can be assessed therefore that Taylor continues the paradigm shift that started with the Cartesian 'I think therefore I am' and afterwards turned, in Bracken's view, by Heidegger into 'I am therefore I think'. Instead of human reason, Taylor considers that the foundation of the *self* and the *good* is *love*. An attempt at his dictum would probably be 'I love therefore I am'. However, Taylor's concept of love does not resemble the romanticist version of love – *eros*, and not even *fileo* – the love between friends. Taylor uses the *agape* connotation - the supreme sacrificial love, which in the Christian tradition, represents the divine love. In his view, "the original Christian notion of agape is of a love that God has for humans which is connected with their goodness as creatures (though we don't have to decide whether they are loved because good or good because loved). Human beings participate through grace in this love. There is a divine affirmation of the creature, which is captured in the repeated phrase in Genesis 1 about each stage of the creation, 'and God saw that it was good'. Agape is inseparable from such a 'seeing-good'" (p. 516).

In Taylor's understanding, the ethical and moral dilemmas of the self (conceived by Ricoeur (1990) as distinct) can be reconciled in the process of human participation in divine love through grace. In conclusion and using Taylor's own words, "high standards need strong sources" and failing to meet high standards leads to guilt and hypocrisy as "morality as benevolence on demand breeds self-condemnation" (p. 516).

Another outstanding contribution to the construction of the self was brought by Paul Ricoeur in his prolific works written during 1950 – 2004. His concept of the self is closely related to the understanding of fundamental abilities and vulnerabilities exhibited by people in their interactions with others and the world. From a methodological point of view, after the 60s, he brought a major contribution to the study of human reality by combining phenomenological description with hermeneutic interpretation. In Stanford Encyclopedia of Philosophy (2002), Ricoeur's understanding of the self, considered to be a *mature anthropology*, is articulated in connection with major themes such as discourse and action, selves as agents, narratives and time, ethics and politics.

In Ricoeur's (1992) view, selves are constituted of two types of identities that are inextricably connected. The first type refers to the concept of *idem-identity* that gives the self a sense of sameness shared with others in space and time. The second type, *ipse-identity*, represents the self's uniqueness and its ability to create, act and appropriate new dimensions of his of her existence. Since people exist in time and space in order to give expression to their present, they use discourse to describe past events, actions and contexts. They make sense of their present by remembering their past and also adjust their decisions in the present according to their expectations and anticipation of the future. Past, present and future are inextricably linked together in people's lives and the stories they tell about their lives.

This type of argument allows Ricoeur to conclude that personal identity is narrative identity as people make sense of their selves through their involvement with others and the stories that emerge through these interactions. Describing the complex connection between the narrative and identity, he states that "the narrative constructs the identity of the character, what can be called his or her narrative identity, in constructing that of the story told. It is the identity of the story that makes the identity of the character" (Ricoeur, 1992, p. 147 – 148).

Summing up, Ricoeur's understanding of the self is profoundly narrative, relational and ethical. Although identity is constructed through language, people understand themselves only through their engagement with others in action and agency. In these interactions, people realize that there are limits regarding their expectations from others and what they can change about themselves. What remains important is the ethical dimension described by the ability of the self to respond to others in a faithful and thoughtful way with the hope that "its responsiveness to others can and will bring about a better life for all of them, a life in which they all participate with and for others" (SEP, 2002, Narrativity, Identity and Time section, para 9).

In addition, Gergen (2003) highlights the importance of the social context, history and culture in shaping the understanding of the self. Moreover, he is critical towards the approach that begins at the level of the individual's subjectivity. He instead proposes to "begin our analysis at the level of human relationship as it generates both language and understanding" (p. 148). This is highly relevant for this study as it offers the broader relational context in which the self embarks in finding meaning after trauma. Moreover, in Gergen's (1991) view, the postmodern self is "saturated" with the multiple voices and discourses coming from various professional fields in society such as media, television, newspapers, computers, virtual reality and internet communication. All these voices have an impact on the construction of selves in society as "social saturation has the capacity to change our consciousness" and "it results in the fragmentation of our self-conceptions and relationships" (Crossley, 2000, p. 26 - 27).

However, taking Gergen's argument further, the self is not bound anymore to physical constraints as Ricouer argued, but is more fluid. Considering for example the internet type of communication, the self is free to adopt various positions and identities without having to assume responsibility for any of those choices and therefore is not bound by Heidegger's concept of "care" as "being-in-the world" or Ricoeur's notion of ethical responsiveness to others. Instead the self becomes dissolved into the many options of various appealing identities, a fact Gergen encourages us to celebrate rather than fear.

Another significant perspective regarding the construction of the self after trauma concerns the issues of forgiveness and reconciliation (Griswold, 2007, 2009; Gobodo-Madikizela & Van der Merwe, 2009). In Charles Griswold's view (2009), forgiveness is a "model virtue for reconciliation" and a narrative of forgiveness articulates "a view of ourselves as affective, embodied, vulnerable creatures" (p. 109). Brison (2002) argues that forgiveness, although not prescriptive, is a new way of relating to our traumas. Through forgiveness and reconciliation, the self is liberated from the captivity of his/her own feelings and able to "embark on a new journey of healing" as hate carries in time a strong potential for transgenerational transmission (p. 50).

Other important elements in the social construction of the self through narratives are gender and race. Gergen & Gergen (1993) consider that "each gender acquires for personal use a repertoire of potential life stories relevant to their own gender. Understanding one's past, interpreting one's actions, evaluating future possibilities – each is filtered through these stories" (p. 70). Regarding race, Foster (1993, 1995) argues for a dynamic and relational construction of identity, which changes throughout time. This is somehow in contrast with Ricoeur's understanding of "biological constraints" which in his view one cannot and does not need to change within the self or in others. However, narratives on life during apartheid of a group of women academics revealed "complex interactions between race, gender and sexuality" (Shefer, 2010, p. 393).

Furthermore, talking about the narrative turn in social sciences, Denzin argues that "persons are constructed by the stories they tell" as "material social conditions, discourses and narrative practices interweave to shape the self and its many identities" (in Andrews, Sclater, Squire, Trecher, 2000, p. xi). Similarly, Freeman (1993) points out that people continuously rewrite and reinterpret their lives through a process of remembering and telling stories about their lives. This is a dynamic process, which "involves significantly more than the mere reshuffling of words" (Freeman, 1993, p. 21). It requires imagination in using language to create new meanings about past events, ourselves and others.

In a similar vein, by exploring illness narratives, Arthur Frank (1995) brings a significant contribution to the understanding of the self as a *wounded storyteller* in search of new meanings. Through his own experience as a wounded storyteller and his encounter with other illness stories, he argues that there is "a need of ill people to tell their stories in order to construct new maps and new perceptions of their relationships to the world" (p. 3). In Frank's view, recovery becomes a search for "reclaiming the self" and "finding one's voice" (p. 71). He distinguishes three types of illness narratives: (1) the restitution narrative (stories depicting people's desire for restored health and body), (2) the chaos narrative (as "the opposite of restitution: its plot imagines life never getting better" (p. 97)) and (3) the quest narrative (stories that "meet suffering head on; they accept illness and seek to use it. Illness is the occasion of a journey that becomes a quest" (p. 115). As Frank argues, these types of stories are affected by the social and cultural context in which they are told.

As was mentioned so far, the construction of the self through narratives takes place in close connection with cultural context, power relations and knowledge, discourse and the notions of subjectivity and agency. Similarly, Andrews et al. (2000) highlights that "our stories are a cornerstone of our identity" (p. 77). She expands the complex relationship between narratives and the self by arguing that "the whole of our selves is bound up with the stories we construct about our past, present and futures, for these stories constitute the fundamental linkage across our lives. In this sense, our lives are the pasts we tell ourselves; through our stories, we indicate who we have been, who we are and who we wish to become" (p. 78). Such issues as social interactions, time, identity and culture represent fundamental elements of systems theory, which will be addressed in the next section.

3.3. A systemic approach to trauma and recovery:
Text and context

The discussion so far has pointed out that trauma due to political violence in general and within the context of post-apartheid in particular cannot be approached only through the unidirectional lenses of the individualist Cartesian framework. By bringing attention to other major contributions coming from philosophy and anthropology, this chapter highlighted the importance of cultural, historical and linguistic contexts that shape our understanding of human beings in the world, their suffering and their ways of remaking their selves after trauma. A systemic approach to understanding human existence will focus not only on individuals but also on their multiple and complex interactions with the wider system and subsystems in which they interact, make sense of their lives and continuously shape and are shaped in turn by their social context (Goldenberg & Goldenberg, 2008; Nichols, 2009).

The Systems Theory is not a unified set of assumptions but rather a collection of ideas centred on the concept of how systems work. Originating from Gregory Bateson's cybernetic conceptualisations of family communication patterns (Bateson, 1972; Bateson, Jackson, Haley & Weakland, 1956), the systemic approach claims that any action taken by an individual or family influences the entire system of relationships. New developments in the field of family systems theory created a new perspective for the understanding of human development, mental health and psychotherapy. The theory has been used in family therapy with the main assumption that "every family is significantly impacted by the relationships, rules and roles that are engendered within the larger social systems (neighbourhoods, schools and universities, workplaces, political institutions, the media, churches, economic institutions and systems) of which they are a part." (Ivey, D'Andreea, Ivey & Simek-Morgan, 2002, p. 394).

Through time, the systemic worldview has been greatly impacted by many approaches echoing thus the postmodernist influence in psychiatry, philosophy and anthropology. Although some postmodern family therapists have rejected the systems metaphor as too modernistic and positivist, the term should not be taken literally, as historically it represents a profound shift in thinking, from linear causality to a broader exploration of relationships and the context in which they occur. As Goldenberg and Goldenberg (2008) argue "systems language continues to provide a basic tool for thinking in interactional terms, expanded to emphasize the interaction between the individual, the family, and the surrounding society and culture" (p. 78).

From an epistemological point of view, one of the main assumptions in systemic thinking is the centrality of relationships as opposed to individuals, which has been the focus of positivist approaches to knowledge. From this perspective, individuals do not exist or define their identity in isolation from the *others* but they create meaning through complex interactions with various systems in which they live such as family, work, church, social clubs, community and society (Jenkins, 1986). Their values and beliefs are constantly shaped by these systems and in turn, individuals influence the outer world through their social interactions and the multiple discourses they use in the process of meaning-making (Hoffman, 1985; Pare, 1996). Families are seen as more than the sum of their members, thus including their complex and intricate web of relationships (Minuchin, 1974). Furthermore, in addressing the particular issue of recovery after trauma, clinical studies have emphasised the importance of family support and healthy relationships in overcoming the negative effects of trauma (Herman, 2001; Johnson, 2002; Weingarten, 2000).

Second, a systemic framework is not based on a linear type of causality but on a circular causality in which individuals, families and communities are interrelated and influence each other and their context. Symptoms therefore are not seen as 'residing' in a certain person or being the 'problem' of a certain family member. Re-framed and defined within the context of relationships and family dynamic, problems are viewed in a more manageable way, this fact having therefore a de-pathologising effect on individuals and families alike (Cronen & Pearce, 1985). In addition, in assessing family structure, we cannot talk about a 'typical', 'nuclear' or 'normal' family since the family structure and family dynamic is highly influenced by changes in the cultural, economic and political context. Consequently, families and their members are influenced and also influence values and beliefs about gender, roles, race, social class, expectations, norms and legal and political issues (Hare-Mustin, 1986; Hutnik, 2005; Rampage, 1994).

Third, a systemic approach is focused on the process rather than the content, thus understanding 'normality' or 'functionality' (if we can ever undoubtedly define such concepts) not as a rigid and static set of rules and desirable attitudes and behaviours. It rather considers that a healthy family involves openness and ability of the family system to change over time while maintaining continuity and support for its members to develop as individuals and in their relation with the outer world (Minuchin, 1974). In this context, trauma is seen as a horizontal external stressor (McGoldrick & Carter, 1982) impacting not only individuals but families and communities which experience trauma both directly due to political violence in their communities and indirectly by witnessing violence inflicted on family members and significant others (Weingarten, 2004; Weine, 2006).

Other important factors that influence individual and family life, and are highly relevant for the present study, are poverty, unemployment, lack of language skills and economically poor female-headed households. These factors operate together to weaken family relationships, to accelerate life cycle progression and to determine lack of education and unemployment. Under such conditions, some families "lead lives that are a series of crises, and others have forged family and social networks that are resourceful and workable. Above all, any efforts to equate poverty with psychological deviance first must take into account the harsh and confining social conditions usually associated with being poor" (Goldenberg & Goldenberg, 2008, p.75).

In conclusion, this work seeks to reconcile structure and text, thus agreeing with Bertando (2000) who considers that changes and paradigm shifts in theory and practice are not antithetic but complementary in the field of systemic thinking. Moving beyond the debate between structural-strategic and narrative approaches, which mirror in fact, the controversy between the modernist and postmodernist views, he argues that both *text* (narrative) and *context* (systemic) are important aspects of systemic studies as by using exclusively only narrative methods, researchers are in danger of dissolving the self into social and linguistic interactions, thus viewing the individual as a social and historical artefact (Cushman, 1995). He therefore proposes a common ground for the systemic approach, which is a synthesis of the two ways of thinking, arguing that:

> Text is useful in understanding the subjective dimension of experience, the meaning people find for themselves as individuals. Context is useful in grasping some idea of the supra-personal dimension of living, of all those parts of our experience we tend to be unaware of, because they come to existence somewhere beyond our knowledge. (Bertando, 2000, p. 100)

Such framework will provide a balanced approach to understanding the individual stories and also to gaining some insight into the collective dimensions of suffering by exploring how people reconstruct their traumatic past, their relationships with others and the meaning of their lives after trauma.

3.4. Concluding points

"We live in stories, and do things because of the characters we become in our tales of self. This narrated self which is who I am, is a map. It gives me something to hang on to, a way to get from point A to point B in my daily life. But we need larger narratives, stories that connect us to others, to community, to morality and the moral self, (…) we need new stories" (Denzin in Andrews et al, 2000, p. xiii).

The process of understanding human existence and suffering is utterly complex, and clear-cut responses proved to be inconsistent at times. Difficulties may result from inappropriate epistemological and methodological frameworks that function as blurred lenses seeking to explore an intricate and sophisticated reality. In this context, the PTSD framework informed by positivist and individualist approaches of Cartesian dualism is seen as insufficient for the understanding of trauma and the reconstruction of meaning and the self after trauma. The central concern of this study is not the elaboration of a new theory of trauma, but rather the broadening of the epistemological and hermeneutical framework towards relational and contextual dimensions for understanding trauma and recovery within the South African post-apartheid context.

Thus, the theoretical framework of this work is informed by postmodern approaches to knowledge such as social constructionism, contextual and narrative approaches and systemic views on understanding the self, the world and the reconstruction of meaning after trauma. Implicitly, the study challenges the linear causality, symptom evaluation, time perspective and the individualist approach of PTSD concepts. Experiencing trauma due to political violence under apartheid requires careful consideration of issues related to history, culture, race, gender, ideology, beliefs, agency and power. People respond in various ways to traumatic experiences and a predominantly Western understanding of trauma cannot be applied to a different cultural context without taking into consideration people's ways of making meaning of their lives in that particular setting. By proclaiming the PTSD framework as "the truth" bearing universal and infallible claims, there is a danger, as Foucault pointed out, to silence vulnerable voices. As will be further discussed, within the current South African landscape that asserts freedom of speech and human rights policies, this situation can become highly problematic.

Therefore, the hermeneutical key for interpreting peoples' life narratives takes into consideration contextual and relational dimensions of human suffering, identity and meaning as they are highly influenced by culture, language and social reality. From a systemic perspective trauma is understood to impact not only the individuals but also families and communities alike. The implication of such approach is that recovery defined as the remaking of the self and finding meaning does not happen only at the individual or intrapsychic level but most importantly in relationship with others.

From a social constructionist and narrative perspective, people reconstruct their selves through the stories they tell about their past and the meaning they ascribe to the present in anticipation of the future. They shape their stories through active and creative interpretation of their lives and are in turn shaped by these stories (Shotter & Gergen, 1989; Andrews et al., 2000). However, the self is not only a product of narratives (Parkes and Unterhalter, 2009). People are purposeful and moral beings, having the power and agency to change scripts, discourses and ideologies (Taylor, 1989; Ricoeur, 1992). Their ways of making meaning in life is profoundly rooted in traditions, religious beliefs and values. Therefore, in this study, the process of recovery is not understood in terms of symptoms' decrease or disappearance, but rather as an active and continuous engagement of the self with the world in which one lives (Bracken, 2002). Survivors of political violence rebuild their lives in various ways and their life trajectories after trauma will show both the struggles and the victories of such a dynamic process. The next chapter will describe the methodological framework employed by this work to examine survivors' narrative reconstructions of trauma and their journeys to recovery.

CHAPTER FOUR

UNDERSTANDING HUMAN SUFFERING THROUGH NARRATIVES

As I was trying to describe the approach, methods and decisions involved in the study process, Christopher Fisher[1]'s image of the labyrinth began to take shape in my mind. From my first step into beginning the research to the end line of analysis, the process has been far from linear, progressive or predictable. I entered the *labyrinth* with a vague mental map that proved at times to be fairly different from the actual *territory*. Besides the multitude of possible directions within the labyrinth, not every direction I took led to a fine path. On several occasions I had to find my way back to the previous turn, as the *path* I was following seemed to be a dead-end. Yet, false-leads and dead-ends are important elements of the journey (Alasuutari, 1995). As I reflect on my own experience of walking through the labyrinth, the process becomes what Silverman (2000) defined as "the natural history of my research" (p. 236). Similar to Fisher, I also hope that by the end of this journey, "there should be no trace that the maze ever existed, just a clear, well paved corridor" leading the reader towards the paths of my written thoughts.

As is often suggested in the literature, decisions regarding research methods have to be considered in close relationship with the research topic or theme (Bogdan & Biklen, 1992; Creswell, 2003; Ritchie & Lewis, 2003; Silverman, 2000). Since the topic of the present study concerns the trauma of political violence and process of recovery, I chose to use qualitative methods associated with a strategy based on narrative research. I considered that such a research topic could be better explored through qualitative methods, given the highly discursive, subjective and interpretive characteristics of traumatic experiences. Furthermore, the journey of participants to recovery, imbedded in their life trajectories is intertwined with complex processes, which could not be explored through quantitative methods that (usually) focus on statistical results. The

---

[1] Fisher, C. (publication year unknown). *Writing and the Labyrinth*

following sections of the present chapter will highlight some characteristics of qualitative and narrative research and describe the research study by presenting the participants, the interviewing techniques and the researcher's location in the process of analysis.

4.1. Qualitative research

New approaches in the field of research methodologies are endeavouring to discover ways to move beyond the qualitative-quantitative dichotomy (Ercikan & Roth, 2009; Hammersley, 1992; Kirk & Miller, 1986; Silverman, 2000). However, qualitative research inquiries are still often presented in contrast to quantitative methods (Creswell, 2003), emphasising different stances with regard to the use of words instead of numbers, a focus on the process not only on outcomes, and the centrality of the researcher instead of statistics in the interpretation of data. I will next highlight several assumptions and characteristics that emphasize the suitability of qualitative research methods for the present study.

Qualitative research is based on an assumption that such an approach can provide a more profound understanding of human experience and social interactions than that obtained through quantitative methods (Silverman, 2010). Since qualitative researchers focus on participants' experiences and the ways in which they make sense of their lives, the aim is to explore multiple ways of understanding reality (Lincoln & Guba, 1985) rather than making claims based on objective accounts. From this perspective, generated knowledge is fundamentally subjective and interpretive (Creswell, 2003), being continuously negotiated during the research process in which participants, researcher and the social world impact on each other (Ritchie & Lewis, 2003). In addition, Creswell (2003) argues that in qualitative research meanings and interpretations are negotiated through human interactions as the researcher attempts to reconstruct participants' realities. In other words, qualitative research involves interaction between researcher and participants, the researcher being concerned with capturing with accuracy people's perceptions and the assumptions they make about their lives (Bogdan & Biklen, 1992).

Regarding the nature of research design, qualitative methods use the natural setting as a direct source of data and the researcher as the primary instrument of data collection. This approach is based on the assumption that interactions are better understood when observed in the setting in which they occur and similarly, settings need to be understood in their historical and cultural milieu (Ritchie & Lewis, 2003). Consequently, qualitative researchers view human behaviour as highly influenced by the setting in which it occurs; they also continuously construct the meaning of that particular setting (Parker, 1998). The social phenomenon is viewed holistically, researchers using complex reasoning that is "multifaceted, iterative and simultaneous" (Creswell, 2003, p. 182). In terms of thinking strategies, qualitative research involves predominantly inductive processes although deduction is also part of the endeavour at various stages. Knowledge is generated from evidence variously collected, interconnected and grouped together. As Bogdan & Biklen (1992) argue, the process is not like a puzzle in which you put pieces together to assemble a pre-determined picture but rather like a picture that "takes shape as you collect and examine the parts" (p. 32)

Besides outcomes, which are the primary focus of quantitative research, qualitative methods explore the process in which patterns of understanding emerge. Meaning in itself is not as much about an outcome or an end product as it is about the ways in which one arrives at a certain type of understanding. Consequently, in qualitative research data is analysed in all its richness, details and small parts, which are taken into consideration during observation, collection and interpretation processes. Researchers use words and pictures rather than numbers, offering detailed and rich descriptions of their interpretations of complex processes taking place in social phenomena. Quite often, participants in this study placed more value on their journey towards a certain type of understanding than on the actual achieved end. Exploring participants' values, strengths, relationships and assumptions about life constitutes an integral part of this qualitative inquiry.

In addition, in qualitative studies, researchers involve themselves personally in order to connect in an empathic and collaborative manner with participants. An intensive and constant exchange between researcher and participants creates an appropriate context in which events can be explored and new meanings can emerge. Since researchers use their personal insight in the interpretive process, it becomes imperative for them to consciously reflect on their position and aspects of their identity that may impact their interpretations. It is therefore recommended that researchers acknowledge and make explicit their values, biases, preferences and interests; these aspects will be addressed at various points throughout this work, particularly in the last section of this chapter. As Creswell (2003) argues, this attitude conveys openness, honesty and personal responsibility in the research process.

Criticism and limitations with regard to qualitative research may refer to reliability and validity of findings (Silverman, 2010; Ercikan & Roth, 2009). However, the validation of accuracy in qualitative studies occurs in different ways from in quantitative reports and it plays a minor role in qualitative research. Validity refers to accuracy of findings from the angle of the participant, researcher or the readers and is suggested through concepts such as *authenticity* and *credibility* (Creswell & Miller, 2000). In order to assure accuracy of findings, qualitative researchers use different strategies such as triangulation, member checking, peer debriefing or external auditing of the project (Creswell, 2003). In the current study, these aspects are addressed in section 4.3, which describes the interview process and transcription of interviews.

In terms of research strategies, qualitative studies employ ethnographies, case studies, grounded theory, phenomenological research or narrative inquiries to study social phenomena. The present study uses narrative research as the main form of inquiry into the life experiences of participants. The concept, characteristics and steps of narrative research will be explored in the next section.

4.2. Narrative research

"There is a creative and formative tension between the ways in which stories are embedded in historical, political, economic, and ideological worlds and the ways in which narratives create those worlds." (Young, 1995, p. 25)

In contemporary times, narratives have been used in various forms in multiple research fields without claims of a unified meaning or definition of what they exactly entail (Riessman, 2008). Researchers have studied narratives from a broad spectrum of perspectives and disciplines such as literature, psychology, education, history, anthropology and medicine. The narrative is often used synonymously with "story" to describe experiences and events in a first-person type of account. In Aristotelian terms, narratives were moral tales representing experiences and emotions and having a specific structure with a plot enacted by characters (Riessman, 2008). Barthes claims the universality of narratives, considering that narratives are "like life itself" and are present "in every age, in every place in every society" (in Abbott, 2008, p. 2). However, Riessman (2008) argues that although narratives could be found everywhere, "not everything is narrative" (p. 4). In her book on narrative inquiry, she identifies several elements and functions of narrative analysis, which are at the core of this research method. These aspects will be discussed in the next sections.

Characteristics and functions of narratives

Riessman (2008) considers that contingency is the only common element in all types of narratives. The concept infers a meaningful pattern of linking events and ideas into a temporal or episodic sequence that has meaning for the speaker. Besides this characteristic, the elements that define narratives differ greatly. Regarding research in the field of psychology, narratives are usually used in the form of "extended accounts of lives in context that developed over the course of single or multiple research interviews of therapeutic conversations" (ibidem, p. 6).

An important feature of narrative is its constructive and performative character (Abell, Stokoe & Billing, 2000). Narratives do not convey unmediated facts and events since they rely fundamentally on language, memory, interpretation and human subjectivity. Consequently, narratives are not simple reconstructions of empirical past events, but ways in which past events are used by people in the present to make sense of their experiences and construct their individual and collective identities (Shotter & Gergen, 1989). Narratives are part of the collective through the way protagonists shape their stories and use language. According to Antze & Lambeck (1996), narratives also contribute to the construction of collective experience and meaning in the present.

The significant link between narratives and the self is emphasised by Paul Ricoeur (1992) in his book *Oneself as Another*. He argues that people define themselves as being distinct from others through a continuous narrative process in which past and present events are organised into actions, motives and situations (Antze, 1996). People construct identities through their stories, which fulfil multiple functions in the process. Riessman (2008) showed how narratives serve various purposes depending on who the speakers and the audience are. For example groups and communities make use of narratives to mobilize masses into action, to protest against injustice and to contribute to positive social change.

The interconnection between time and historical cultural context is another important feature of a narrative. Events, actions, experiences and feelings happen at a certain point on the temporal continuum and in a particular cultural setting. However, as Susan Brison observes, there is a gap between the event (which may be described in countless ways) and the experience of it (Brison, 2002, p. 31). Narratives contain both the interpretation of events and the interpretation of the experience of that particular event. How one shapes such representations into a narrative form depends significantly on personal values and beliefs, as well as on societal, historical and cultural processes.

Narratives operate in a linguistic universe in which structures of language confer coherence, order and meaning to representations of events, experiences, characters and actions. Although language is the vehicle of representations in narrative structures, the meaning of events is not restricted by inflexible linguistic boundaries. In this vein, Scott (in Riessman, 2008) argues that "experience is a linguistic event (it doesn't happen outside established meanings), but neither is it confined to a fixed order of meaning. Since discourse is by definition shared, experience is collective as well as individual" (p.34).

The political and cultural context shapes the narratives of individuals and groups in society. Narratives of war, genocide, mass-killings and refugees cannot be understood in the absence of a historical and political framework. Most studies on trauma have worked with life narratives of suffering, conflict and healing. Since this study uses narratives to analyse interpretations of past trauma and journeys to recovery, it is important to explore next the interplay between narratives, memory and trauma.

Life narratives, memory and trauma

Unlike career or educational narratives, trauma narratives face a greater challenge with regard to the act of remembering. Traumatic memories are not encoded in similar ways to other types of memories. Some traumatic experiences and events refuse to be remembered while others break unexpectedly into consciousness in the form of flashbacks or nightmares (Herman, 2001). Van der Merwe and Gobodo-Madikizela (2007), describe trauma as a struggle with memory, as "an impairment of the capacity to register events fully as they occurred". They argue that trauma consists of multiple losses: "loss of control, loss of one's identity, loss of the ability to remember and loss of language to describe the horrific events". The victims experience a tension between a "frozen state" of silence and the need to describe the traumatic events in repetitive, often identical ways.

However, by following this psychoanalytic prospective, one can implicitly presume that trauma narratives are used to predominantly diagnose the presence of PTSD symptoms or the degree to which cognitive structures are affected by trauma. In the same line of thought, it could be perceived that, since trauma is described as the "loss of ability to remember", the whole story and historicity of events may lack veracity. Moving beyond the medicalisation of trauma, Weine (2006) proposed an approach in which the trauma narrative, termed clinical testimony, is seen as a story of living history, imbedded with intuition and imagination. He places trauma narratives into a larger social context, by highlighting the importance of the story in revealing survivors' perspectives and their moral and ethical positioning with regard to their situation.

Antze and Lambeck (1996) made important assumptions concerning the role played by memory in the process of reconstructing trauma. They consider that memories are not raw descriptions of past events, as the process of remembering involves interpretations and is embedded in a historical, political and ideological context both in the past and present. Something important in this work, was to explore the way in which participants made sense of their memories by making links between past and present events and selecting to construct their narratives in a certain form. The selected parts of their stories are crucial for the meaning-making process in the present as well as for the rebuilding of the self (Brison, 2002).

Regarding the sense of directionality through time, trauma narratives are not essentially progressive. Since trauma is often defined as the shattering of a life narrative and the loss of language (Herman, 2001), descriptions of traumatic experiences are limited by the absence of adequate language to describe what Bar-On (1999) named, the "*indescribable and the undiscussable*". However, as Van der Merwe and Gobodo-Madikizela (2007) argue, "language offers the possibility of the transformation of trauma into narrative. The significance of narrative lies not simply in remembering trauma, but in its transformation through language." (p.25). In a similar vein, Brison (2002) considers that in the aftermath of trauma people rebuild themselves through narratives. She argues in fact that trauma is a "disruption of the narrative-building function of the self "(p. 39) and that verbal language is "the vehicle for narrative interpretation" (p.43).

However, the remembering of pain and the development of narratives out of the life events of victims does not provide them with a complete understanding of the meaning of life. Survivors continue to explore and discover new meanings of their traumatic past as their pain is continuously changing (Morris, 2003) and their self is reconstructed during this ongoing process of making sense of their experiences. Especially in the case of narratives of repression, Bar-On (1999) considers that human discourse after trauma carries a reminiscence of the "pure-ideological" and totalitarian way of thinking. In the reconstruction process, survivors experience an anxiety-provoking dilemma. On the one hand, they need to develop new skills in questioning facts contained in an indoctrinated discourse. On the other hand, they have to acknowledge facts that have been silenced by society, family and community. As Bar-On (1999) argues, "they now had to invent a whole new discourse, to replace the discourse which had dominated their life during the totalitarian, pure-ideological regime. This was not only an intellectual endeavor. It had emotional and behavioral components which had to be addressed simultaneously" (p. 5).

The abovementioned arguments have been significant in my decision to adopt narrative methods for this study. By exploring and analysing life narratives of people who experienced traumatic events under apartheid, the study aimed to broaden discussions on trauma due to political violence and its consequences as well as on the process of recovery and meaning reconstruction after the collapse of apartheid. Since trauma has the potential to create chaos in victims' lives, telling stories about suffering and pain may create "order and contain emotions, allowing a search for meaning and enabling connections with others" (Riessman, 2008, p. 10).

4.3. The research process

As an important element of a qualitative methodology, the design of the study needs to be placed within a broader methodological framework. The research process does not develop in isolation from the assumptions and interpretations made by the researcher. The study deals with memories of events, which represent interpretations of past events made by participants of the present time. In addition, the process contains the researcher's current understanding of the interpretations of participants. In other words, this study becomes the researcher's story about doing research on narratives of trauma and recovery in South Africa, almost twenty years after the collapse of apartheid.

The historical framework of the study is closely linked, on the one hand, with my personal experience of repression under totalitarian communism in Romania, and on the other, with my encounter with the South African experience. Soon after my arrival in South Africa, following my husband (who, although an academic at that time, received a governmental appointment as Consul General of Romania in Cape Town), I became aware of the unique experience of reconciliation in South Africa through the Truth and Reconciliation Commission. While we were actually flying to South Africa at the end of 2006, our Romanian president Traian Basescu was publicly condemning communism as a totalitarian, illegitimate and criminal regime, thus becoming the first president in history to officially condemn communism (Raport final, 2006). Within this context, the South African political discourse felt radically different. The differences did not only regard the use of psychological language (Moon,

2009) emphasising forgiveness, reconciliation and healing but also the significant contribution to truth-revealing processes which in Romania had been silenced for a long time (Tismaneanu, 2008).

However, my initial interest to do research was triggered in the context of a bilateral cooperation on scientific research between South Africa and Romania. Since doing my masters studies and later as a psychologist and family therapist, I have been preoccupied with the impact of repression on individuals' personal values, attitudes and social interactions (Gavreliuc, Bozian, Gavreliuc, Rogobete & Vochin-Bartl, 2006). Also, by reading Danieli's (1989) book on the multigenerational legacies of trauma, I realised that the dialectic of trauma continues and it has an impact not only on the individuals who suffered severe trauma but also on their families, communities and even the next generation, if the previous generation does not deal appropriately with the effects of traumatic experiences. Both Romania and South Africa have in common a long history (almost 50 years) of repression and gross violations of human rights inflicted on its people.

Another important experience contributing to my decision on the research topic was my happening to meet Charles Villa-Vicencio, former National Research Director in the Truth and Reconciliation Commission of South Africa. Informal discussions and the opportunity to be part of the group who organised his visit to Romania were real learning experiences. Listening to one of his debates in the Romanian context on "Beyond Condemnation: Towards dialogue and reconciliation", I understood, if only partially, how societal attitudes towards victims and perpetrators can influence the process of reconciliation acting either as a facilitator of positive dialogue or a hindrance in the nation's process of transition from a repressive totalitarian state to democracy. I also understood that the dialogue with former victims about their past and present situation would never be enough. Archbishop Desmond Tutu, at the Truth and Reconciliation Commission's opening address in 1995, acknowledged that the nation as a whole needs healing as "every South African has to some extent or other been traumatised".

In the early stage of the study, I realised that trauma of repressive regimes has specific characteristics and particularities that I could not define exactly at that stage, nor did I have a clear picture of how I was going to explore it. My further interactions as a family therapist with the Counselling Department at St. James Church, Family and Marriage Association of South Africa (FAMSA), Ubuntu and Amy Biel Foundation helped me connect with South African people in a more meaningful way as I realised how much their past traumas still play an important role in their present stories. Despite positive political and economic changes in post-conflict societies, human interactions are often contaminated with suspicion, corruption, prejudice, discrimination and violence. Patterns of belief developed under repression are deeply rooted in the collective memory of the nation, hence making the process of healing quite a lengthy one. Thus, the research topic gradually narrowed down from the general issues related to the impact of repression and the transgenerational transmission of trauma to the more specific topic of a retrospective construction of trauma due to political violence and the process of recovery after the collapse of apartheid.

The first stage of the study consisted mainly of reading theory and collecting data. The research theme concerned the trauma experienced by victims during apartheid and their journey after traumatic experiences to the present times. The decision to use narratives to explore the reconstruction of political trauma and the *self* seemed appropriate for the type of qualitative study I had chosen. Each story brought new elements into the study, helping to focus the process of analysis on the impact of trauma on individuals, families and community, as well as on coping and meaning-making strategies involved in the process of recovery.

Reflections on and interpretations of the data took place both during the interviewing process and after all interviews were completed. It has been helpful to write down after each interview the personal reflections on my interaction with participants and their stories. It was during this stage that I realised the importance of maintaining a balance between the wholeness of each narrative and the common patterns that may emerge across the entire sample. Consequently, I decided to add a thematic component to the narrative analysis, which as Braun and Clark (2006) argue is both theoretically flexible and rigorous. Thematic narrative analysis, as it was termed by Riessman (2008), fits a broad range of contexts and narrative texts, thus offering researchers the possibility to explore not only meanings constructed by individuals but also elements of group identities and social phenomena.

As Riessman (2008) described it, data collected through participants' stories were interpreted "in the light of themes developed by investigator (influenced by prior and emergent theory, the concrete purpose of investigation, the data themselves, political commitments, and other factors)" (p. 54). Thus, from a theoretical perspective, the study builds on previous research in the field of war trauma and the process of recovery in the aftermath of trauma. However, the current approach moved beyond the medical discourse on trauma to explore the uniqueness and complexity of multiple voices in the interpretive process as well as the importance of historical, political and cultural context in shaping survivor's experiences (Bracken, 2002; Frank, 1995; Weine, 2006). Therefore the methodological approach could be placed within a multidisciplinary context, roughly at the intersection between psychosocial approaches to trauma and recovery, and social constructionist perspectives on meaning-making processes in the present. The next section will explore the role of the researcher as an active protagonist involved in the research endeavour.

The role of the researcher

As a feature of the qualitative research and as a result of the poststructuralist emphasis on subjectivity, the researcher's interpretations are viewed as representations of human experience in the meaning-making process (Price, 2002). Since the narrative methodology involves an intensive interaction with participants, it is important for the researcher to identify her values, interests, experiences and potential biases and how they may impact the research process. Following Riessman's idea (2008), I will reflect on some relevant past and present experiences that have shaped my identity, thus providing some background information for the story of this study.

I briefly mentioned above how my professional identity as a psychologist and family therapist helped me become sensitive to the challenges families are facing in South Africa. I was thus able to understand how much people's historical past is part of their current realities and that, quite often, current broken relationships, mistrust and violence are deeply rooted in the experience of humiliation, marginalisation and injustice of the past.

In addition, my national identity as a Romanian living in South Africa for the last four years provided me with, what one of my trainers conceptualised as a "systemic insight" (Nabarro, 1992). This is defined as the ability to adopt a position of being both *inside* and *outside* (meta to) the system, thus consciously experiencing being part of the complex web of relationships and at the same time being outside this web, observing with relative objectivity the intersubjective reality of participants in the study. This also served as a significant benefit in my relationship with participants. My neutrality to the context, as I could not be categorised either White (Afrikaans) or Black, made them feel comfortable in the interviewing process, helping participants to explore aspects, which in a different context may not have been revealed.

Furthermore, I need to acknowledge that my perceptions of political repression are shaped by my personal experience of living under totalitarian communism until the age of 23 years. My childhood memories include vivid images of food shortage, crowds of hungry people waiting in long lines, cold apartments and my almost fainting in the summer heat during school rehearsal for yet another megalomanic ceremony in honour of the dictator. Later on, as a university student, I remember the fear and terror of being reported to the secret police for my involvement in an underground student movement or for complaining against the status quo. However, such involvements represented forms of resistance and ways of finding meaning in a rather meaningless repressive context. It also made me intensely perceptive to ideologising and manipulative discourses. Moreover, I realised how my reflexivity, creativity and critical thinking abilities were repressed, denied and forbidden during my formative years. The educational system under the totalitarian communist regime used brainwashing strategies aimed at producing obedient individuals who would reproduce information infused with the communist ideology.

Having gone through these types of experiences, my encounter with the historical South African context and culture felt quite familiar even if the nature of the conflict and ideology were different from those experienced by totalitarian communist countries. I believe that my experience of repressive times, my education and the opportunity to experience the South African context first hand enhanced my understanding, global awareness and sensitivity towards participants' lives in South Africa. However, as Sprenkle and Piercy (2005) correctly conclude "prior knowledge of context has to be evaluated in the light of new learnings just as new information must be integrated into prior knowledge" (p. 73). I will therefore turn next to describe the participants in the study.

Participants

The research sample consisted of twenty participants, all victims of political violence and gross violations of human rights during apartheid between 1960 and 1994. The group emerged in accordance with Silverman's (2000) indications for theoretical and purposive sampling. The method consists of selecting categories of people on the basis of their relevance to the research questions, theoretical position and the explanations developed by the researcher. As Jennifer Mason argues, "theoretical sampling is concerned with constructing a sample, which is meaningful theoretically, because it builds in certain characteristics or criteria which help to develop and test your theory and explanations" (quoted in Silverman, 2000, p. 105).

Consequently, since the research topic concerned the study of trauma due to political violence under apartheid, the sample comprised former victims of the particular context. The inclusion criteria were based on the status and the age of the victim when the traumatic events occurred. The status of the victim was established during a pre-interview and was defined according to Section 1 of the TRC Act from July 1995. According to this description, the term "victims" includes "persons who, individually or together with one or more persons, suffered harm in the form of physical or mental injury, emotional suffering, pecuniary loss or a substantial impairment of human rights, as a result of a gross violation of human rights, or as a result of an act associated with a political objective for which amnesty has been granted".

The age of the participants was defined by the time at which the traumatic event took place during repression in relation to the ability of the individual to recall memories about the traumatic event. Research has shown that political thinking is developed in adolescence, teenagers tending to be more vulnerable when confronted with political trauma (Danieli, 1998). Therefore the traumatic event should have occurred in the life of participants after the age of ten. Regarding the type of traumatic events, participants selected in the study had experienced forced displacement, detention, torture, imprisonment, interrogations, beatings, being shot at and teargased, life threats, the loss of a family member and witnessing killing or violent acts inflicted on significant others.

Participants were selected through the Institute of Justice and Reconciliation, Khulumani Support Group in Cape Town, St. James Church and Families South Africa (FAMSA). Interview meetings were scheduled with the assistance of coordinators of these institutions, through phone invitations or a written invitation sent to potential participants by email. Signature of informed consent and permission was obtained from each participant to report the findings and use participants' real names or a pseudonym, according to their desire. Since the interviews referred to serious traumatic events, I wanted to assure myself that participants felt free to remain anonymous if they wished so. However, eighteen participants (out of twenty) decided to use their real names. On the one hand, their decision was based on the fact that some of their experiences and opinions had been already quoted in previous publications and their names were already known, thus bearing a historical significance for the South African context. On the other hand, some participants in the sample wanted to use this opportunity to purposefully express their views, in the hope that their voices may be heard or as Frank (1995) described–"to find their own voice".

The total number of people interviewed was twenty-five. However, not all participants could be included in the sample for the following reasons: three persons did not satisfy the inclusion criteria of the study and two did not complete the interviews. Regarding their location, eleven participants lived in black settlements around Cape Town in Nyanga, Crossroads, Gugulethu KTC, Philippi and Khayelitsha and nine lived in Cape Town and the surrounding areas. All interviews took place in English excepting five in which a translator was used to translate from Xhosa into English. Even in this situation, participants were able to understand English but felt more comfortable to express themselves in their home language. The following tables show descriptions of the sample in regard to race, gender, age, education, living conditions, number of children and type of traumatic events experienced by participants in the study.

Table 4-1: Sample Profile

Race			Gender		Age			
Black	Coloured	White	Male	Female	30-40	41-50	51-60	61+
12	6	2	11	9	2	5	5	8

Table 4-2: Education level

Education level	Black	Coloured	White
Standard 2- 4	2		
Standard 5-7	2		
Standard 8-10	2		
Matric	4	2	
Higher education	2	4	2

Table 4-3: Living conditions

Living conditions	Black	Coloured	White
Poor	9	1	
Moderate	2	1	
Good		3	1
Excellent	1	1	1

Table 4-4: Number of children

No. of children	Black	Coloured	White
No. with children	12 (highest = 8 children)	5 (highest = 4 children)	1 (highest = 1 child)
No. without children	0	1	1

Table 4-5: Traumatic events

Traumatic events	Black	Coloured	White
Torture	6	2	
Solitary confinement	6	3	
Prison	9	3	
Beatings	9	4	
Police harassment	17	4	1
Being shot at	5	2	
Lost a child, parent or a close friend	6	4	2
Permanent disability as a result of political violence	4		1
Forced removals	4	5	
Witnessing violence inflicted on significant others	12	6	2
Massacres (St. James massacre)		2	1

The interview process

Bogdan and Biklen (1992) consider that interviews are used "to gather descriptive data in the subjects' own words so that the researcher can develop insights on how subjects interpret some piece of the world" (p. 96). However, the information during the interview process does not flow only from the interviewee to interviewer but is rather developed within the context of the interaction between participants and researcher, leading to new constructions of meaning (Silverman, 2000). Research studies have emphasised the importance of helping participants to feel at ease before the interview begins. In the context of the present study, the friendly and informal atmosphere began at the start when I introduced myself, informing participants where I came from. Our interaction soon met on common ground since participants felt free to ask me: "You also went through some tough times in your country, isn't it?" This situation created a safe context in which participants felt free to talk about their traumatic stories and helped us develop a collaborative type of relationship based on trust and respect for each other's experiences.

The interviews took place in participants' homes, workplaces or at the institutions mediating the selection of participants. Interviews with participants living in townships I mostly conducted in their own homes where I was taken by a representative of the organization that set up the meetings, and who could translate from Xhosa into English if need be. I had already some idea about townships from my volunteering experience of training community counsellors and from attending public events in churches and organisations located in townships. I remember my first shock at discovering that in a 15-20 minute drive, I could move from one of the most luxurious areas of Cape Town to the poorest places in Gugulethu and Khayelitsha. These are areas where seven people sleep in the same room and rape and extreme violence are part of everyday reality. However, entering the actual *home* of my participants – a shack - was a different experience. Their perceptions of their own space mirrored their attitude towards their own *self* and *others* in many ways. I was, therefore, able to observe that in the middle of coarse poverty and chaos, some people display and hold dear pictures of family members and friends, religious symbols and objects that give them a sense of belonging and stability. Although the space was small, one could see the effort put into finding the right place for each object and the sense of pride on people's faces for being able to achieve this. Yet I also encountered empty rooms with only a broken sofa and a chair where one felt only the presence of participants' complaints and disappointments filling the air around us. I would not have been able to access such realities in any other circumstances, realities that allowed a deep human encounter between myself and my fellow human beings.

Therefore, the form and nature of the interviews were shaped by this human encounter taking place in the context of remembering pain, suffering and struggles in the process of rebuilding the self after trauma. Although I clearly explained to participants the nature of the interview as being research, not oriented towards therapy, I did not exclude the possibility of therapeutic outcomes resulting from this authentic encounter (Lum, 2002; Satir & Baldwin, 1983; Yalom, 1989). However, I informed the participants about the main subject of the study and the procedures for the interviews, assuring them of confidentiality and my interest in their well-being. Hence I explained that they could stop at any point during the interview or withdraw without any consequence.

The interview process began with a pre-interview with the purpose of verifying participants' suitability for the study regarding inclusion criteria. Permission to audio-record the interview and report findings was obtained for each participant in the study. Knowing that such devices were used by repressive organs to gather data during interrogations, I had some anxiety related to asking participants to have the interviews recorded. However, I was proved wrong, since none of the participants objected and soon after they began their stories, the audio-recorder was completely ignored. The average amount of time spent for an interview was approximately two hours. In addition, written messages and telephone conversations were part of the follow up process in which I wanted participants to feel supported and appreciated for their openness.

Each interview started with a general question – "What is the story of your suffering during apartheid?" – encouraging participants to talk freely about their past experiences. As my aim was to get a good understanding of participants' subjective realities, I did not ask questions at this stage but mostly made notes of important clarifications I wanted to make after respondents finished. In the first stage of the interview, I did not intervene much as I purposely intended to observe the way participants organise their stories. Therefore the first part of the interview consisted of participants' narratives told in their own words and structured as they intended. The discussions focused on the repressive context of apartheid, various types of traumatic events, political violence and the impact on themselves, their families and communities.

I paid close attention to the way they chose to construct their narratives, the language they used, non-verbal communication, gestures, the way they began and ended their stories, characters, actions, evaluations and interpretations they used in order to make sense of their stories. As expected, participants had different ways of putting their memories into narratives. Some developed long and detailed accounts about their trauma under apartheid, organising the events chronologically or thematically. Other participants talked about an event and then stopped to wait for a question. In such situation I asked a question, thus helping the participant to continue his/her story.

When participants reached an end to their stories about trauma during apartheid, I asked them to continue their stories in order to find out what their journey was after their traumatic experiences. At this stage the interview was oriented towards what happened after the trauma, meaningful events, family life and relationships, sources of support, difficulties and achievements on the journey to recovery and perceptions about the present context. At the end of the interview, I asked each participant if there was anything else they would like to add or comment about. I also thanked them and expressed my appreciation for their willingness to share their experiences with me. Since some participants had longer stories than others, when necessary, I scheduled further meetings in order to continue the interview. Three participants needed two interview sessions each in order to complete their stories.

The transcription of interviews was challenging not only in terms of the amount of cognitive effort invested in the process but even more so in an emotional way. During the interviews, my exposure as a witness to participants' trauma was limited to a single story each time. However, during transcription I became immersed in the multitude of stories, experiencing vicariously the summative effect of participants' traumatic memories. Supervision sessions during this stage were essential in helping me to avoid burnout, process the traumatic cognitions and regain clear boundaries in my interaction with data.

When transcripts were finished, some were sent to participants for accuracy check. However, in some situations this was not possible due to the inability of some participants to read in English. In these cases, the checking was done with the translator who was the same person for all cases that needed translation. Through all interactions with participants, I emphasised my commitment to listen to their feedback, disagreements or further clarifications. This openness and collaborative attitude was not unidirectional by any means. It was particularly rewarding to receive phone calls and e-mail messages from participants showing their care and encouragement which often came at the most needed times in the research process. As complex webs of relations develop naturally in human interactions, I will comment in the next section on issues of power relations during the interviews, related to cultural background, profession, gender and age.

Relations of power in the interview process

Oscillations within the equilibrium of power in the interview process are explained by Bhavnani (1990) through the concept of "researching-up" and "researching down" described in terms of the researcher's subjective experience of the relation shaped by her view of the self, the other and the context. I had several concerns regarding the way participants would receive my invitation to share their traumatic experience with me, given the fact that I am not a South African. Their complex stories of pain and loss together with their resilience and ability to find meaning even in the most staggeringly difficult contexts provided me with an invaluable learning experience and, more importantly, fuelled my own strengths as a purpose-driven human being. With these considerations in mind, I felt that my experience of working with former victims of apartheid was researching-up.

Nevertheless, my professional role and possession of a certain type of knowledge that was unfamiliar to participants would theoretically place me in a superior position of power. According to Foucault, knowledge conveys power and all disciplines of knowledge such as psychiatry and psychology "not only keep their participants under control but also order the minds and actions of those who come to learn" (quoted in Gergen & Gergen, 2003, p. 36). Not only my profession but also my social status, when compared with participants living in townships, would definitely place me in a higher position. During the interviews that took place in the black informal settlements, I was often overwhelmed with my participants' helplessness regarding the poverty and crime they were facing daily. My genuine interest in them as persons and my respectful and appreciative attitude hopefully contributed - at the interpersonal level - to restoring the balance of power in our relation.

As a woman researcher working in the field of trauma, I connected well with women participants, resonating with their stories. Being a wife, I could listen empathically to women's narratives about their husbands being beaten and arrested by the police. Furthermore, having myself two teenage sons, I could sense the despair and pain of the mothers who had their sons tortured or killed in the political struggle. Grief and tears coming both from participants and the researcher alleviate a victim's loneliness and become symbols of communal sharing of suffering. My witnessing of their pain, thus acknowledging their trauma created a context of healing and integration of loss (Frank, 1995; Weingarten, 2000). In similar ways, my interviews with male participants were marked by meaningful interactions and a degree of personal disclosure. However, I was aware that a man might not feel comfortable disclosing his pain to a woman, as this would place him in a vulnerable position, which could be perceived by him as a weakness. Yet, men participants felt free to disclose significant aspects of their suffering, whether these were related to loss in their families or to individual experiences of torture.

Finally regarding age, since I interviewed both younger and older participants, it is difficult to clearly identify how age influenced the balance of power during interviews. I appreciated the care, wisdom and dignity of the older participants in their stories but I could also sense disillusionment and defeat in the situation of people who still struggle with poverty and illness in old age. The younger participants were closer to my age. They displayed more vitality and energy and also were more passionate and vocal about present injustices. Overall, participants expressed willingness to revisit their traumatic past and considered the process as being beneficial both for themselves and for future generations of South Africans. Since only four participants had an encounter with the Truth and Reconciliation Commission, other testimonies given in the context of the present study represent participants' contributions to the collective memory of the nation and, perhaps, one more step towards healing.

Finally, having described the main coordinates of the research method in terms of the study outline, participants, interviews and role of the researcher, the discussion will continue in the next chapter by describing the form of analysis chosen for this study – thematic narrative analysis.

CHAPTER FIVE

NARRATIVES, LANGUAGE AND MEANING

5.1. Thematic narrative analysis

It is commonly acknowledged that narratives can be analysed in a variety of modes (Riessman, 2008; Silverman, 2010). The purpose and particularities of the research study are crucial for the decision to adopt a certain method of analysis. Recent studies analysing narratives have implemented a combination of methods in order to create space for more complex interpretations in the process of analysis. Given the type of narratives as stories about suffering and the extensive amount of data imbedded in the twenty individual narratives, the analysis process in this study uses a combination of narrative and thematic analysis. This type of combination has been conceptualised at an earlier stage by Riessman (1993, 2008) under the term thematic narrative analysis. Such approach is using both case-centred analysis and category-centred models. The thematic analysis has been further developed and clearly described by Braun and Clarke (2006) by identifying the particularities of this method compared to other qualitative research methods.

The focus of the investigation concentrates on how victims of political violence during apartheid reconstruct their trauma and their journey after the collapse of apartheid up to the present time. As Riessman (2008) reflects, there is a "complicated relationship between narrative, time and memory, for we revise and edit the remembered past to square with our identities in the present" (p. 8). Participants' narratives consist of their current representations of past traumatic experiences and their ways of reconstructing the self in relation to others and the world after trauma.

Both local and societal context are important aspects of narrative analysis. An understanding of the political, historical and social context is vital for an appropriate interpretation of participants' narratives. Stories of apartheid trauma lose their meaning in the absence of a context. Participants gave extended accounts of the micro and macro context in which their stories take place both in relation to the past and in the present time. However, contexts as well as narratives need interpretation and impact each other in sophisticated ways (Brison, 2002).

Furthermore, the analysis in this study pays attention to how stories are constructed in terms of the sequence of events, plot, time and chronology, language and meaning as well as to the way participants reconstruct themselves through narratives. Trying to capture both the specific within the wholeness of each narrative as well as the common elements across the sample, the analysis shifted continuously between general and particular aspects of the narratives. The twenty core narratives presented in Appendix B were derived from a process of repeated listening to the recordings, and readings of the transcriptions. These summaries are presented in alphabetical order according to participants' names, and numbered in the list included in the Appendix. Also each name is followed by a significant quote from the participant, which I found relevant for the context of the story. With the exception of two names marked by an *asterisk* (*), all the other names are real, as this was the choice of most participants. The core narratives summarise the basic content and plot line of each story and comprise only the core elements, essential phases of the life trajectory, information about the type of traumatic events and, when relevant, significant expressions from transcriptions. Detailed descriptions and evaluations are not included in the core narrative. The size of the core narrative (number of words) parallels the size of the content of the full narrative.

Besides these major foci, I need to acknowledge my own involvement as a researcher in the interpretation process "simultaneously mediating and interpreting the *other* in dialogue with the self" (Riessman, 2008, p.17). A preliminary clustering of data was observed around two main elements: (1) the type of political violence and (2) progress and recovery after trauma. Major differences were observed between the narratives of victims of state repression living in black settlements and those of victims of violence inflicted by liberation movements. By further examining the use of language structures and the intent of the stories, a second cluster was revealed around the topic of progress after trauma. Some narratives highlighted significant progress in the lives of survivors after trauma while others, on the contrary, showed less progress or even decline. Each narrative was analysed by describing the following aspects: (1) the chronology of events, (2) the plot and characters, (3) the beginning of each story, (4) time orientation and (5) content. Results at this stage of analysis showed major differences between narratives of victims of state repression and those of victims involved in the St. James massacre. The next chapter will highlight some characteristics of the two types of narratives in terms of content, chronology, language structures and meaning.

5.2. Narratives of state repression

Narratives of serious trauma do not follow characteristics of prototypical narrative forms. The effort of bringing to memory traumatic times and experiences is associated with a high degree of confusion, ambiguity and disorientation. The format of the interview was in a sense a chronologically organising influence, since I invited the participants to share their stories of suffering during apartheid and their journey after trauma. However, the narratives did not always follow a chronological sequence of events. Survivors often move back and forth through time in their efforts to retrospectively describe and discuss what, in Bar-On's (1999) words, is *indescribable* and *undiscussable*. The plot of the narratives takes sudden turns, containing repeated and prolonged tragedies, which create tension and suspense for the reader. Current evaluative and moral statements are often inserted into micronarratives of past traumatic experiences. In so doing, the narrators seem to continuously shift between two realities: (1) life during repression and (2) current assertions about past experiences.

A possible intention behind the shift between the two temporal frameworks is to create continuity between past identity (as a hero, victim, survivor, freedom fighter, etc) and present identity (as a successful person, able to overcome past difficulties, resilient or as somebody who is still struggling, is still a victim and is still suffering even in the present). It could even be asserted that this narrative function is more important for those who are still suffering in the present, to reconstruct their past identity as freedom fighters and heroes. It shows the intention or the need of the narrator to assure the listener and maybe even himself/herself that "it is the same *me* who did that in the past", almost waiting for others to openly confirm this fact. In support of this idea, Colvin (2006) argues that traumatic storytelling "is the only intervention that confers a politically valuable identity on sufferers. It is the only one that distinguishes certain traumatised individuals and their claim for recognition from the rest of the suffering poor who populate post-apartheid South Africa" (p. 175).

With regard to the beginning of narratives, it is common for trauma survivors (in general, not in this sample) to reconstruct their stories by beginning first with memories about the traumatic event (Straker & The Sanctuaries Counselling Team, 1987). Surprisingly, victims of state repression did not begin their stories by recollecting memories about detention, torture, beatings or losses they experienced during apartheid. They chose instead to begin their stories with the earliest memories they could access about feelings of fear, injustices, discrimination and humiliation that they experienced as children. Patrick recalls his experience of humiliation when, as a child having to rush to hospital in an ambulance with his sick grandmother, he was not allowed to enter the hospital because his skin was darker than his grandmother's. As he recalled: *"She was rushed in there and I had to go through the non-white section of the hospital and so... it made me feel almost less human because you associated fair or Caucasian with acceptance."* Thembi also begins the story of her suffering with memories of pain related to growing up without her parents:

> *The story of my pain is that of a little girl who moved from the country where I was living with my grandmother and who could not see my parents. And I could not live with my mother because she was living in the back of white people's house and she had no space for me to live there. As far as I know, I lived with my grandparents. My grandmother always was saying "your parents are coming to see you at Christmas" and I would spend all my time thinking when is Christmas. Is in June Christmas, is in July Christmas, when is Christmas coming so that I could see my parents? And time was never enough as they would stay only for two weeks and they were gone. The minute they leave, the minute they say goodbye and the minute I see them disappear behind the mountains, my next thought is when is the next Christmas so that I can see them again. So my pain starts there and continued.*

Even as children, participants registered the impact of repression on the extended family. In this vein Sipho, beginning his story with early memories as a child, said: *"I grew up in Eastern Cape. My uncle was in jail but I didn't know what was the problem. My mother was harassed by the police. Since I was about seven, I remember about these things. Later on as I grew up I learned that the Whites, the Afrikaners, were dominating the Black people and that my uncle was in jail because he was against apartheid."*

Monica had a traumatic beginning at a very early stage in her life. Her mother and younger sister disappeared when she was still a baby and the mystery of their disappearance has never been solved. This is how she begins her story:

> *I grew up without a mother. I've never known who my mother was. I was told that my mother was harassed by the police because she was against the government. I didn't attend the school because I was suffering.*

Sometimes I couldn't get books and I didn't even have clothes to go to school. I grew up with a single parent who was my father. He even took us to Eastern Cape because he was suffering himself. I was in and out from school because I had to look for work because even my father didn't have a permanent job himself because he had to hide from the police.

Such narrative beginnings point to the fact that trauma under apartheid was not caused by a single traumatic event but developed gradually from an early stage in people's lives, due to the inherent characteristics of the repressive ideology of apartheid. Moreover, victims' stories do not contain only a single traumatic event followed by a typical aftermath and recovery, such as in the case of accidents or catastrophes. On the contrary, their stories convey continuous threat, emotional intensity and prolonged terror. The chaos and complex blend of multiple traumatic events can even seem unreal to those estranged from these realities. Continuous harassment from police, detentions, beatings, shootings, torture and killings occur one after the other in the same story at such intensity that the reader has the sensation of being in a thriller or a horror movie. The plot of the stories contains multiple actions and no resolution following their climax. It usually has the following line: "I was taken by the police… and then I was beaten… and then my son was arrested…. and then…" This form of expression has the function of creating more tension for the reader. This is clearly reflected in Zitulele's story: *"I was arrested many times and beaten. My wife didn't have a pass and was arrested all the time. Later on, my son got involved in the PAC. Police would come in the middle of the night and arrest him. If you didn't open the door immediately, they would kick you and beat you. They really didn't care if you were a woman, if you were naked. They would just come in."*

A specific characteristic of the stories told by victims living in townships is the absence of a recuperative aftermath of trauma, a safe space in which the survivor can embark on a process of healing. Due to continuous harassment and political violence, survivors lived under constant terror, having to hide and always be on the run. Alfred described it in the following way: *"I remember all those times when I was arrested and tortured during apartheid. In 1988 when things got really bad, I was being harassed by the police. I've never had time to rest as I was always harassed by them."*

Another important characteristic is a lack of chronology, hierarchy and order, the victims beginning their stories at a particular point in their life, but then going back and forth as they are trying to recall memories and make sense of them. Possible reasons for such temporal oscillations are related to victims' cognitive efforts to make connections between what happened in the past and the implications for present or future reality. The regular evaluations inserted into the narratives (*"That was the life we were living"*) suggests an active meaning-making process between the present reality, the arguments coming from the past and the recreation of new meanings for their life in the present and future. These facts point towards a specific type of coherence, which is not fixed or rigid but dynamic and flexible in supporting the narrative structures and the reconstruction of one's self through storytelling (Antze, 1996).

The middle part of participants' narratives is marked by the collapse of apartheid and the aftermath. Although the stories describe the joy of freedom and high expectations, some life trajectories depict the perpetuation of apartheid legacies of poverty, violence, lack of education and unemployment. The content of some narratives in this category is more weighted towards past times, anger and disappointments with the current situation. The greater the number of trauma memories, the shorter the narrative content about recovery after trauma. These types of narratives are also more dominated by negative stories and the continuation of trauma through time even up until the present, due to poverty, crime, illness and the continuous threat of township life.

However, some victims of repressive violence depicted different images of their life trajectories after the collapse of apartheid. In spite of their previous underprivileged socio-economic context, they were able to recover by pursuing higher education and moving out of the township. They developed healthy relationships with their families and community and currently have good employment and a stable financial situation. Patrick assessing his journey through life, has declared: *"I am different in my way that I have set up goals and directions for myself, accomplishments, things I wanted to accomplish because I didn't want to be a product of my legacy. I wanted to establish a legacy. And I wasn't going to accept things the way they were. I was going to challenge my identity because my identity was not going to be determined by my past"*

In addition, the content of these narratives comprises broader descriptions of present reconstructions of the self, recovery, meaning and issues of forgiveness and reconciliation. In terms of movement through time, they have the characteristic of progressive narratives. Although they include interruptions, difficulties and failures, there is a continuous effort to deal with contextual difficulties and commitment to search for new alternatives in the process of finding meaning for the self, others and the world.

A rather particular case is Fr. Lapsley's narrative which highlights the fact that a different race identity does not modify the reconstruction of trauma under state repression. Although Fr. Lapsley is White and was born in New Zealand, his identity as a fighter against the injustices of apartheid in South Africa caused him to reconstruct his trauma in similar ways to the Black participants in the study. Instead of beginning with the letter bomb (sent by the state repressive structures) he received at home, which left him blind in one eye and missing both hands (see Fr. Lapsley's core narrative in Appendix 2), he chose to begin his story with a chronological account from his birth. He answered the first question of the interview in the following way:

> I: *What is the story of your suffering during apartheid?*
> Fr. Lapsley: *I was born in New Zealand and I was brought up there until I was 17 years old. I went to Australia to become a priest of the Anglican Church. I was transferred to South Africa to study. I was a student in Durban to study Mission and Psychology. I became Chaplin of the campus and of another two black campuses. One was of Indian-African coloured background and the other of Indian descent.*

Similar to other narratives of state repression, Fr. Lapsley shows how his trauma is profoundly linked with the historical, social and political realities during apartheid. As he recalls, *"In 1976, I was the national Chaplin and just after the Soweto uprisings when many school children were shot, I was expelled from the country. I went to Lesotho and joined the ANC and spent 16 years there as a member of the ANC and the ANC's Chaplin".*

Finally, it must be said, there are also differences between Fr. Lapsley's narrative and other stories of state repression, with regard to his choice to identify with the oppressed, while the black population had no choice in this respect. For the latter, their status as "the oppressed" was a given that they inherited with the colour of their skin. In addition, Fr. Lapsley's narrative shows a different trajectory of recovery described by *"good treatment in Zimbabwe and then in Australia for seven months"* and *"more important (…), the prayer, love and support of people from around the world"*. On the contrary, the narratives of Black victims living in townships show the absence of a safe context in the aftermath of traumatic experiences and a continuity of more traumatic events following the previous ones.

5.3. Narratives of St. James Church massacre

The second category of victims – victims of reactive violence or violence produced by liberation movements – was involved in the St.

James Church massacre from 25 July 1993, in which four young Black men from the Azanian People's Liberation Army (APLA), one of the major anti-apartheid movements, opened fire and threw grenades into St. James Church during the evening religious service, killing eleven people and injuring over fifty-five. The three survivors involved in this study, besides their personal traumatic experience, also suffered the loss of a family member and/or a close friend in the massacre.

Their narratives begin with the traumatic event itself and continue by describing the devastating impact of the massacre on themselves, their families and the congregation. Events are chronological and linked through a sense of directionality and causality. The narratives contain well-defined plots that, compared to previous narratives, focus more on the resolution aspects in the story. This is clearly reflected in the long descriptions and evaluations of the impact of the massacre both in terms of the immediate aftermath and at various stages throughout their life trajectories.

These narratives contain features similar to those of victims of natural disasters, accidents, rape and loss, characterised by a single traumatic event and a distinct aftermath in which the victims, according to Herman (2001), are able to find a safe context and social support to embark on a journey to recovery. The stories begin with memories about the physical and temporal context *("it was a stormy night")*, continue with descriptions about their perceptions of the massacre, the impact, coping mechanisms on the journey to recovery, issues of forgiveness and interracial reconciliation, and end with representations about themselves, others and the world in the present.

In reconstructing the traumatic event, participants reported similar perceptions related to the time length and speed of actions. Although in reality the event lasted only for two to three minutes, everything happening very rapidly, all three participants felt it was like being in a slow-motion movie, which lasted for a longer time. Mandy, who lost her mother in the massacre, remembered the event in the following way:

> *It was in the beginning of the service. We were listening to a couple singing. As they were singing the song, the front door opened with a bang. One guy came up the aisle and threw a grenade. My initial reaction was that this is a skit. It didn't seem a reality. Although it happened very quickly, it seemed like in a slow motion.*

Such experiences support the argument that traumatic memories are "not encoded in the same way as normal experiences", as victims usually struggle simultaneously both to remember the traumatic event and "avoid the images of the traumatic experience" (Van der Merwe & Gobodo-Madikizela, 2007, p. 25).

Another important feature of the massacre narratives is the victims' vivid reflections and effort to make sense of trauma in the particular context as defined by the setting, and the politics of segregation. Although the members of the St James Church, being an Anglican church, were predominantly White, yet compared to other Anglican churches, the congregation had more members of other races and ethnic backgrounds as well. Questions related to race, God and theology rapidly rose in people's minds. Ross Anderson who was leading the service during the massacre, recalls his efforts to assist the wounded congregation in the immediate aftermath and reflects upon these types of questions:

> *I remember I was very busy visiting all those who were hurt, busy planning all the funerals, lots of media attention, lots of interviews, so it was a very, very busy time. In a way, I suppose that helped me a lot to process everything. Crying with the bereaved, doing many of the funerals, going to visit extended family members... and they all had lots of questions: Why God let this happen? Where was God?*

Another specific feature of the massacre narratives is the large number of characters and actions that give life to the stories. Although these narratives talk about horrendous pain and death, they nonetheless seem to convey an implicit message about the continuation of life, even while "going through the valley of death". Mandy remembers people's support after the massacre: *"There were lots of phone calls and the following days lots of people coming and offering to help. After my mother's death, my aunt became a very important person for me. My aunt and my cousin started to become my family"*

The largest amount of space in the narratives is given to the participants' journeys up to the present time. They all experienced post-traumatic stress symptoms in the aftermath of the event. However, according to their accounts, some symptoms reoccurred at significant developmental stages in their lives, for example, in Mandy's case. She is pregnant with her first baby and admits how difficult it has been for her to face the idea of motherhood in the absence of her mother. She started having nightmares, sleeping difficulties and symptoms of anxiety: *"It's a process in life, you work through it again and again and it gets easy with time. I had two months of going through very tough times. I prayed to the Lord to take my fears and gradually I began to feel excited about this baby coming."*

Finally, the narratives of the St. James Church massacre are stories of profound loss. Not only the victims lived the horrifying experience of the massacre, but they lost people in their families, and good friends. "Survivor's guilt" and minimizing their suffering were common strategies employed by survivors to cope with their pain. As Liesl shared: *"You know, I feel so strange... I didn't really grieve... I thought I didn't lose somebody from my family as my husband or others in the congregation... I thought my pain should be smaller."* In addition, it can be easily noted how participants were especially concerned with others and the communal loss. The abundance of characters and the dynamic of relationships described in the narratives highlight the importance that survivors attribute to their families and community support in the aftermath of the massacre. Furthermore, they placed these aspects within a spiritual framework, which opened new avenues for the reconstruction of meaning in the aftermath of trauma (Ogden et al., 2000), aspects that will be further developed in Chapter Six and Seven. Gradually progressing towards more specific aspects of the narratives, the discussion will continue next to explore particularities related to intention and language structures used by participants in order to reconstruct their life experiences.

5.4. Language and meaning

Silverman (2000) suggests that while performing the narrative analysis, researchers should move beyond their data in order to find explanations. This means to move from "commonplace observations to a social science analysis" (Silverman, 2000, p. 133). It is also what Braun and Clark (2006) defined as a search for *latent meanings,* a process considered to be more than a mere description of phenomena. Important questions to bear in mind at this stage would be: "What is the purpose of participants' descriptions in this study and what are their intentions in structuring their stories in a certain form?" and "What is the meaning of these stories and why are people telling these stories?"

By examining survivors' narratives with a focus on these particular questions, the analysis process was able to access new and multiple levels of meaning in which social expectations, cultural values, language structures and identity constructs interact in sophisticated ways to shape the structure and meaning of narratives. Observing closely the life trajectories of survivors, clear differences were distinguished in the area of survivors' journeys after trauma up to the present time. Some narratives follow progressive pathways while others, on the contrary, show stagnation and regression which may point towards a condition of *continuous traumatic stress* following previous experiences of trauma (Eagle, 2011; Straker, 1987). Participants actively use language structures and metaphors to interpret and construct various meanings about their selves and the world in which they live (Rogobete & Rogobete, 2014). Thus, some participants in this study reconstruct themselves as survivors, heroes, successful, able to cope with challenges, resilient and in control of life events. Others, on the contrary, describe themselves still as victims, helpless, angry, bitter, defeated and disillusioned. The next two sections will discuss some of these features comparatively.

Stories of success and disappointment

The use of language in the form of passive or active verbs, the use of personal pronouns as well as metaphors and symbols suggest a means for understanding intention and meaning in narratives (Silverman, 2000; Riessman, 2008). For example, in success stories, one can easily notice the extensive use of the "I" pronoun, active verbs and detailed descriptions about achievements and personal efforts. Such stories do not talk to a great extent about trauma and its psychological impact, but rather describe positive coping mechanisms and how survivors succeeded in overcoming the negative effects. Through the construction of these stories, the self emerges as being in control of his/her life, as an agent of change and being engaged with social realities.

In Patrick's narrative on only one page of transcript, the pronoun "I" is used over 50 times and the pronoun "my" 26 times. The following paragraph shows how the language he uses is shaping the narrative form:

*And so this great fear almost apprehended you and these things welled up on the inside and **I** needed to deal with those things because **I** couldn't allow **my** greatest fear to restrict what **I** thought **I** needed in order to make a contribution. And so in dealing with this **I** needed to create within **myself** the opportunity to explore and internalise this great hope that whatever **I** went through had an expiry date. That is, it will end. That was **my** greatest hope. **I** just couldn't determine when it would end. But this hope was inside of **me** and so part of **my** answer to the solution was **my** hope. Hope is a fickle thing and very often disappoints you. Because of the struggles that **I** went through and the fact that **I** was born out of struggle as it were, **I** felt **I** had endured enough struggles to be able to carry on hoping this would be better. And **I** said to **myself**: this was only a transitory phase in **my** life. **I** am destined for greater things. That is what kept **me** alive, that is how **I** kept sane amidst all the insanity.*

The quote shows how the use of active verbs (deal with, create, explore, internalise, determine, endure) and metaphors ("*I was born out of struggle*") create the idea of agency and control, which are important elements of progressive narratives.

On the contrary, the majority of Black participants who still live in townships and continue to struggle with poverty, unemployment, illness and crime have used a different type of language structure. They also considered it more important to talk about their past, their suffering under the apartheid and the impact of their sacrifice for the good cause. They expanded on the impact that multiple types of trauma had on themselves as individuals as well as on their families and communities in which they lived. Their language reflects extensive use of verbs used passively (taken, put, beaten, carried) and of the pronoun "they". Thulani's torture narrative shows these features:

> **They** *caught me and put chains around my legs. I was full of blood on my face.* **They** *threw me in the back of the van and took me to John Vester Square in Joburg at the 10th floor, room 1026.* **They** *tortured me, beating me and asking me all sorts of questions.* **They** *put a handkerchief in my mouth, cover my mouth with a plaster, put my hands at the back with handcuffs and* **they** *chained my legs. Then* **they** *covered my head with a wet bag. While I was struggling breathing* **they** *electrocuted me. I don't know how many times. When* **they** *cool it out, I was very numb...*

Participants make extensive use of metaphors in their stories. This is highly visible, especially when they try to reconstruct their pain and negative feelings. Metaphors, comparisons and personifications become useful tools in participants' attempt to find the right language to describe their suffering. For example, Ethel describes herself in the light of past and current victimisation through a powerful metaphor: "*I'm a vandalised person by the apartheid*". Benyi describes himself in the present as a "*mental wreck*", "*a laughing stock*" and "*a joke*". Similarly, when talking about his recovery after trauma with regard to his family, Alfred concludes: "*We cannot be recovered... we are just mingling around in mist*". In addition, when talking about current attitudes of people in black communities, Sindiswa uses a powerful comparison: "*It is such a sense of poverty and our people is nesting it like a baby. Poverty is their baby. They should say, no! Go out! Don't stay with me! You are not my friend! I'm fighting with you! You are the devil!*"

All these elements point towards what Silverman (2000) termed the puzzle, arguing that it has to be assembled piece by piece in the process of analysis. A major task at this stage was to find explanations for the intention behind the use of language in the narratives. Within this context, Silverman's indication is to search for data outside the confines of the study. Therefore, I complemented existing information with findings from similar and broader social contexts by searching deeper with regard to the moral and cultural worlds of the two types of narratives, whose protagonists were former victims of repressive structures of apartheid. On the one side, it is the universe of those who "have made it" or who "are climbing the mountain" and are at various levels of height. On the other side are those who "are still struggling" or have not made much progress in climbing the mountain. The metaphor can go on with regard to why the second category of people were not able to climb the mountain, whether because of lack of the right equipment (education and personal resources) or fear of difficulties (lack of skills and social support) or because of trying to find an easier way around the mountain (avoidance/passivity). However, although such presuppositions may carry with them some psychological truth, there is a need for a more profound analysis and interpretation both in the context of the study's further findings and previous theoretical concepts. These issues will be further explored in the next chapters, when the analysis process will look specifically at how survivors reconstruct their life trajectories after trauma.

Latent meanings: Two polarised worlds

In any young democracy, polarizations in society are inevitable. South Africa makes no exception; on the contrary, for many years it has been considered to be the most unequal country in the world, having a Gini coefficient of 0.68 in 1991, 0.77 in 2001 and 0.65 in 2011 (Business Report, 2011; Human Science Research Council, 2004; World Bank, 2014). After Mandela's election as the country's president in 1994, former freedom fighters and political detainees started to climb the social ladder, eventually becoming the new political leaders of the country. Obviously not all former victims of apartheid were able to occupy important governmental or parliamentary positions. As a result, a new polarised reality has developed, this time not according to race identity (between Blacks and Whites) but inside the category of "comrades", between the *rich* political elite and former *freedom fighters* who still live in conditions of radical economic poverty. Polarities were also signalled by Colvin (2006) who argued that "through traumatic storytelling, South Africans were encouraged to challenge the old borders of race and construct new borders – temporal borders between past and present, social borders between the healed and unhealed, and political borders between the new state and the old" (p. 166). However, as Van der Berg (2014) avows "high inequality probably will remain a feature of South African society for decades to come, at least until education and services radically improve and their benefits are felt in the labour market" (par. 15).

The group of participants in the study who are currently well established, emphasised the idea of agency, internal locus of control, perseverance and success which are fundamental values of a Western democratic society, a society to which they want to belong and identify with. In such a world, it is the individuals' responsibility to pursue higher goals and work hard to achieve them. The temporal orientation of these narratives focuses on the present, current personal development and continuous positive change. On the contrary, survivors who still live in poverty and are disappointed with their present situation reconstruct extensive narrative accounts about their struggle for freedom during apartheid. Micronarratives of past traumatic experiences allow them to portray themselves as heroes who showed courage, *"fought for freedom of this country"* and *"preferred to die instead of suffering injustice"*. There is not much evidence of personal reconstruction in the present, as the present image is deprived of dignity and they feel humiliated again, this time by their own communities (*"I am a laughing stock in my community"*, says Benyi). Their continuous complaints about the government's lack of care towards them are founded on external attributions and the belief that it is the state's responsibility to take care of its heroes, a belief which is rooted in cultural values of a collective type. Moreover, such a belief is coherent with the *Ubuntu* values, which political leaders claim in their speeches to adhere to but which is absent at the grass roots level, in townships where former victims continue to be victimized.

A discourse based on the values of Ubuntu creates space for former victims to develop high expectations of social care and support from the government. The Ubuntu values are described in *Zulu* as *Umuntu ngumuntu ngabantu* ("a person is a person through other persons") or as Desmond Tutu (1999) defines it: "My humanity is caught up, is inextricably bound up, in yours. (…) What dehumanises you, inexorably dehumanises me" (p. 31). Within such a cultural context, they feel a sense of legitimacy in having these expectations since they risked their lives and are currently carrying with them physical and psychological wounds they suffered in the fight for freedom and democracy. In other words, the new political leadership is in power because of their support. Former victims feel confused by the political leaders' discourse, as they do not act according to their cultural values. This dichotomy is clearly reflected in Sipho's statement:

People in power just look after themselves thinking where can I put myself now? What can I get out of this thing? So people are focusing on themselves and forgetting about the masses. They are disloyal to the organisation, cheating... That's why there are problems in this country and in the ANC. If you want to be a president, you have to do that and that, suppress that one, pull those strings; you must support that one and be loyal to that one... they become indebted to all these people... What about the country?? The loyalty should not be towards your friends... so these are the problems we are facing...

This could be a possible explanation (among other complex interpretations) of why all narratives of survivors living currently in poverty end up with extensive descriptions of their disappointment with the government, complaints that they *"are not helped"* and they *"are not listened to"*. They feel ignored in their attempts to engage with the authorities and oscillate between defeat and anger. From a psychological point of view, these attitudes point towards the presence of external attributions or external locus of control, which regardless of their validity, do not provide an explanation of why individuals tend to have such attitudes, unless one starts to explore their relationship with the cultural context in which people live. As the process of looking more closely at the narratives continues, it becomes clear that the way people construct themselves through narratives is complex and involves multiple levels of meaning. Thus, the next chapter will examine survivors' life narratives by highlighting the means through which they reconstruct their traumatic experiences during apartheid in South Africa.

CHAPTER SIX

DIMENSIONS OF SUFFERING
DURING APARTHEID

The process of remembering the past is selective with regard to the ways in which events, characters, actions and emotions are described. Forgetting is as much part of the process as remembering. Survivors become actively involved in a process of interpretation, presenting their stories in a certain order, using specific language and defining their identities in a particular manner through the narrative process. According to Bruner (1991), the narrative is not merely a vehicle of social representations but a way in which people construct reality and organize human experience in their effort to create meaning. Memories are complex constructions that involve ambiguities, symbols and the continuous struggle of human beings to make sense of themselves and the world in which they live (Cassey, 1987). In addition, Antze and Lambek (1996), warning researchers against a too literal reading of memories, consider that "when memories are taken as clues to real events, one runs the risk of becoming deaf to their subtler symbolic meanings. Memories visit us unbidden, not simply as records of the past, but as responses to our ongoing needs, hopes, predicaments" (p. 10). Furthermore, regarding the relationship between stories and contexts, there is a creative tension between "the way in which stories are imbedded in the historical, political, economic and ideological worlds and the ways in which narratives create these worlds" (Young, 1995, p. 25).

The period of time remembered by survivors goes back to 1960 but most of the traumatic events took place during 1970-1993, when they were teenagers or adults. There are major differences between narratives of victims of state repression and those described by victims of violence coming from liberation movements. Although they are not representative of the whole population of South Africa, the stories of state repression share many similarities with findings revealed in previous research studies such as Straker's (1992) study on 60 youngsters from Leandra township during 1986-1989 and the report on trauma in the Western Cape produced by The Trauma Centre for Victims of Violence and Torture in 1998 (Skinner, 1998). This chapter reveals new reconstructions and meanings of apartheid trauma twenty years into the transition to democracy as well as perspectives of three survivors involved in the St. James Church massacre perpetrated by representatives of one of the main liberation movements in South Africa. The results of the thematic narrative analysis have been interpreted in the light of the broader contextual approaches to trauma, by analysing the characteristics of the traumatic context and the impact on the individual, family and community.

6.1. Victims of state repression

The events described by victims of repressive structures of apartheid took place in the context of black settlements near Cape Town area such as Nyanga, Gugulethu, Khayelitsha, KTC and Crossroads. Participants' ages during this particular period were between 15 and 30 years old, most being activists in the struggle against apartheid oppressive practices. In dwelling on the stories about life in townships during this particular time, the aim was to understand how participants subjectively reconstruct the trauma of apartheid and its impact - a quarter of a century after the historical events, in the new political milieu of contemporary South Africa. The eyes of the participants have seen many changes since the collapse of apartheid. Negotiation between the two sides of the conflict as opposed to bloodshed, a new political leadership, the Truth and Reconciliation Commission's efforts towards forgiveness and interracial reconciliation, Black Economic Empowerment strategies and new developmental projects in education and economy are just a few of the major assets of the new democracy. Nevertheless, as in any process of transition, the South African society has also experienced shortcomings in the form of high levels of crime, continued poverty, corruption and socio-economic inequality.

Accompanying socio-political contextual changes, participants themselves have also undergone identity changes throughout this time period. Achievements and failures, success and defeat, meaningful and destructive relationships, all have contributed to the way they reconstruct themselves in the present and thus influence the way they interpret their past trauma. However, since trauma is subjectively experienced and not all people involved in the same traumatic event end up experiencing similar psychological effects (Herman, 2001) it is important to explore first what language and particular words participants use to convey their suffering. Building on findings discussed in the previous chapter with regard to language structures and metaphors, the next section will particularly discuss the ways in which victims of state repression describe their suffering.

Through the eyes of the oppressed

"The pedagogy of suffering means that one who suffers has something to teach"
(Frank, 1995, p. 150)

Looking for terminology that describes suffering and traumatic experiences, it was noticed that most participants used words and concepts like "pain", "wound", "I've been traumatised", "that was very traumatic", "it was a big trauma" and "I've been vandalized by apartheid". However as the stories unfold, one can sense the psychological discourse intertwined with metaphors and symbols throughout narratives. This apparently confirms Moon's (2009) assumptions that the TRC public hearings in South Africa have created a national culture of reconciliation and healing in which words such as trauma, pain, healing, forgiveness and reconciliation have become part of everyday vocabulary. Even before the TRC, if we read the forward by Mamphela Rhampele to Straker's (1992) book, the metaphors used are powerful ways of conveying the dramatic effects of apartheid's political violence on the South African society: "Violence has become as a festering sore in the body of South African society. It has undermined the fabric of our society. It burst forth, pouring pus and blood just as we begin to have hope that temporary calm will become a true harbinger of peace" (p. ix). Participants in this study have used metaphors, words and expressions in similar ways to convey their traumatic memories. Ethel recalling her experiences says:

> *When I'm thinking about it, I have a wound that has not been healed. I had physical problems, heart problems because of that time. I lost my child Bishop. He was shot. I'm now a person that has lots of sicknesses. I'm still traumatised. This gives me all kind of sickness. I'm a vandalized person by the apartheid.*

Benyi, before beginning his story admits his difficulty of entering the process of remembering past traumatic events: "*Even as I speak now, I have to adjust myself as it is very traumatic*". The use of present tense suggests that not only were the events traumatic then, but even the present process of revisiting the past becomes challenging for him. Frans, although he does not use the word trauma, he indirectly conveys the traumatic effect of the loss of his son: *"One thing that affected me the most was when I lost my son and that changed my life completely..."*

Thembi describes herself as *"the voice of the voiceless"* in order to define her identity as an actress, using the stage to speak against injustices on behalf of disadvantaged people in society. Throughout her story, she uses the word "pain" to establish contingency and connection of events, showing how these events together contributed to her suffering:

> The story of **my pain** is that of a little girl who could not see her parents
> *(...).* So **my pain** starts there and continued *(...)* And **my pain** goes on and
> on when I went to see my mother at work. *(...)* Time went by and I ended
> up having my own child... *(...)* And this is not my **only pain**. This is the
> **pain** of every Black woman... *(...)* Every family was affected. But there
> were people who didn't even know what struggle they were fighting. They
> were not politicised. They knew there was something wrong and they
> wished somebody to take away **their pain**. Every person was **traumatised**
> by apartheid. *(...)* So, I use the stage to relief **my pain**. I was doing this and
> it became as a therapy for me. To see that you are **not alone in your**
> **pain**...

It becomes obvious how the language of trauma in Thembi's narrative creates the connection not only between various chronological events in her life but also between her pain and the collective suffering of many others. *"My pain"* becomes gradually not *"the only pain"* but *"their pain"* as well and even *"your pain"* in the witnessing process.

The preliminary analysis highlighted that survivors of repressive political violence reconstruct their trauma as an engulfing process, affecting both the individuals and communities as well. Within this context, the analysis process revealed the following major themes: (1) the traumatic context of repression and (2) its impact on individuals, (3) families and (4) black communities which are going to be discussed next.

The traumatic context of apartheid: Ideology and identity

It is common for trauma studies to concentrate on events that cause trauma and the symptoms individuals develop as a result of the traumatic event. Although at various times in history, paradigm shifts brought attention to the political context in which traumatic events took place, yet the impact of ideologies has been largely overlooked (Foster, 1991). While this is not the context to explore the reasons for such fact[1], it is however important to articulate the need for taking into consideration the impact of apartheid's ideology within the South African context characterised as it is, by a long history of oppression and intergroup conflict. According to various social theorists (Miles, 1989; Therborn, 1980; Thompson, 1984), ideology is closely related to language, meaning, human subjectivity and agency (Giddens, 1979) and has a powerful emotional component (Foster, 1991). It becomes clear therefore that there is a large overlapping area between ideologies as practice and the impact such practices have on individuals and groups. Foster (1991) describes the ideology of apartheid as an instrument for domination of Black people, which was built on the previous ideology of segregation, spanning from 1910 to 1948.

The Black participants involved in the study described their experiences during apartheid as a continuous process of living under terror, suffering constant humiliation, violence, marginalisation, poverty and lack of freedom. These characteristics had profound psychological effects on people's identity and their relationships. The overall image created by participants' narratives revealed not just distinct individual traumatic events but rather a traumatic context defined by continuous repressive practices rendering the victim hopeless and helpless in finding safety or escape.

Comparing various studies on war trauma, Holocaust survivors, rape and child abuse as well as trauma's intrinsic relationship with the contextual aspects in which it developed, one can notice that the traumatic context of apartheid repression had many aspects in common with a range of types of trauma, but also many differences. While there is research, although limited, on the psychological impact of apartheid repressive practices (Gibson, 2004; Hamber, 2004; Simpson, 1998), yet findings have not managed to map the complex elements and characteristics of trauma suffered by various individuals and groups within the South African society under apartheid. It is thus the aim of this section to analyse the particularities of participants' traumatic experiences under apartheid as they are recalled through their narratives.

In many ways, the context of apartheid was experienced as war, but also different from it since there were no clear descriptions of an enemy identity or a coherent strategy of the conflict (Straker, 1992). Through detention and torture practices, the trauma of apartheid resembles the

---

[1] Foster (1991) argues that the neglect of ideology is mainly "ideological". The concept of ideology has been virtually assigned to social sciences as it refers to societal processes, while it has been assumed that psychology deals only with individuals.

traumatic experiences of dissociation, depersonalisation and despair of the Holocaust victims, although the purpose of apartheid was not the mass extermination of Black people. The helplessness and depersonalisation of rape victims was also experienced by apartheid sufferers through mutilations and cruelty, in which victim's sexual organs were part of the torture practices in solitary confinement. Comparisons can indefinitely continue, yet as Herman (2001) correctly underlines, "the severity of traumatic events cannot be measured on any single dimension; simplistic efforts to quantify trauma ultimately lead to meaningless comparisons of horror" (p. 34). However, the description of multiple characteristics of traumatic events is important in order to understand the severity of trauma and its psychological effects.

The repressive ideology of apartheid and its practice was built on a continuous series of traumatic events and was inflicted by human intent. It had high intensity, long-term exposure, and was experienced by a large mass of people (Hirshowitz and Orkin, 1997). The types of traumatic events described by Black participants refer to at least three main categories: (1) repressive practices of apartheid ideology in the form of racial segregation, oppression and excessive control, (2) detentions, solitary confinement and torture and (3) lateral violence (inter-community violence between black communities).

a) Politics of segregation, oppression and control

The repressive methods of apartheid were in many ways similar to practices of other repressive regimes such as totalitarian communist regimes from Eastern European countries and the former Soviet Union. Still, the essential elements regarding human beings and their social interactions were radically different. While under the totalitarian communist ideology the emphasis fell on people "being equal with each other", the apartheid ideology was based on exactly the opposite, namely being different, and furthermore one group being overtly superior to the other. The contrasting positions were based on a purely deterministic characteristic of human beings,that of skin colour. Through the practices implemented it was inferred that people with white skin were superior, thus enjoying superior benefits, while those with darker skin were separated geographically and socially in isolated and underdeveloped areas. The Registration Act issued in 1950 requiring all South Africans to be separated into racial groups induced new dilemmas for people's individual identity, group identities and family dynamics since appearance, social acceptance and descent were major classification criteria. Living with a constant reminder of their racial inferiority and enforcement strategies of segregation, Black people perceived themselves as being inferior and, according to some of the participants in this study, developed low self-esteem. Since the most important element in their identification as human beings was the colour of their skin, their identity incorporated feelings of rejection, humiliation and worthlessness. Also the fact that there was nothing they could do about it, made them feel helpless and not welcomed into the world, as this world valued only the white skin. Patrick recalled childhood memories when for the first time he started to make sense of racial segregation: *"It made me feel less human. I associated fair with acceptance and black with rejection."* However, in order to achieve a desirable identity, fantasy became both an escape and a something of a solution for positive identification. Talking about her dreams of being white, Thembi said:

> *When I found that I could not go to the same school as the White children... we had our own school which was inferior. This is when I learned about segregation, when I moved to the city. There I learned that White people are different from us. Why they are different and superior? So, I grew up thinking "I wished I was White" I wished I could dress as a White person, do everything as a White person, anything white was better... The person didn't matter, only the colour.*

As part of the oppressive structures, the Black population was economically deprived and forcedly uprooted from their families in order to work for the White privileged class. Their children were left at home in the care of grandmothers or other relatives, a situation that opened the doors for neglect, abuse and violence inflicted on the unprotected children. This was the situation of most Black people who lived in Eastern Cape and were taken to work in the Western Cape (De la Rey et al., 1997). In the absence of parental models, especially a maternal figure, some children developed feelings of abandonment and mistrust of the world. This is reflected in Thembi's story depicting her "always" waiting for her parents to come home and wandering *"when is Christmas? Is Christmas in June, July? When is Christmas coming so that I could see my parents?"*

The effective implementation of racial segregation was often enforced by oppression and excessive control over the black population. With the introduction of the pass law by which all Black people were forced to carry a passbook with them all the time coupled with the Bantustan inferior education and hard labour, it became increasingly difficult for the Black population to endure discrimination and injustice. The breaking of the law attracted repressive actions from the apartheid state in the form of arrests, shootings, detentions and even killings. Describing the way in which police used to harass people in their houses Thelma said: *"Because sometimes they would come in the middle of the night to ask you were is your pass and then they would harass you and arrest you... they arrested my husband in the middle of the night. I couldn't go to work. I had to look for him to see where he is. I found him in a police station in Nyanga. I've got him and I had to pay his fine."*

At the beginning women were not allowed to have passes and not supposed to follow their husbands into the areas where they were taken to work. Still, some men brought their wives with them, so in this way were subjects of continuous harassments and arrests. Zitulele described how police would constantly arrest his wife even if she had a baby:

> *It was an inspector, a white man who would come any time and arrest my wife. I had to go and pay to get her back. I remember, they used to kick the door and enter by force. If I told them, "my wife is in bed with our baby", but they would care if it was a woman, or a child... they didn't care. Lots of men brought their wives from Eastern Cape. They will be arrested and you had to get money and pay to get your wife back. We kept on paying. They made lots of money from us.*

Being taken by surprise by a traumatic event, increases the psychological harm of the persons involved (Herman, 2001). Taking into consideration all the unexpected brutality imposed on Black people, it may be said that their identity was continuously undermined and invaded without any notice. This was a deliberate strategy to induce more terror through violence inflicted on victims without the possibility of their being able to anticipate it. To illustrate this, Zitulele continued his story: *"Police would come any time to your house, 1, 2, 3, 5 o'clock, any time they would come and do what they liked... they would kick you, if you didn't open the door immediately, they would kick you and beat you. That was the life we were living. They really didn't care if you were a woman, if you were naked. They would just come in."*

Individuals were reduced by the repressive state to worthless objects whose most basic human needs were completely denied. Lack of consideration for privacy and constant humiliation was degrading for the self-image of Black people, thus significantly damaging their dignity and self-worth. In addition to this strategy, forced removals and deportations were further means to uproot Black individuals and families from their communities in order to be under stricter control in especially designated areas. Thelma recalls such memories, which as she emphasised, are difficult to forget:

> *One of the problems was the forced displacement. I used to live in Retreat*
> *but we were taken away without notice. We were brought here in Nyanga*
> *West. They took our things in a big truck and just dumped them here. They*
> *said to us: "This is your home". Then, it so happened that my husband was*
> *working for (company) and he was able to build a house here but when it*
> *came to winter, it was raining and one morning we woke up like in a dam,*
> *full of water everywhere. Everything was flooded. So my husband had to*
> *bring up the floor. That's how we were left. But even now, they said we will*
> *be compensated but I've never got anything. That stayed with me. I had*
> *young children, two at that time, one was five and the other was two. I*
> *would always remember that.*

In areas where people refused to move, houses were burnt and people were arrested and beaten. Frans recalls feelings of bewilderment when he arrived at the place where his house used to be:

> *In 1986 I was living here in KTC but I was in Worcester building an*
> *elderly home. I was on the roof and I was called and asked where I was*
> *living. I was told they were burning the houses in KTC and when I heard*
> *that I started panicking. When I got here in KTC everything was burnt*
> *down, I didn't even get a piece of my house. I only got my dog. It was my*
> *dog that took me where my family was hiding in Gugulethu. We ended up*
> *staying in some churches in town.*

Deportations and forced removals had negative psychological effects on families and communities, aspects that will be discussed further in the following sections. The increasing weight of oppression and injustices determined Black people to join protests of political liberation movements. As a result the repressive state increased violence, responding with even more hostility and aggression.

b) Detention and torture practices

"Torture is a grotesque piece of compensatory drama" (Scarry, 1985, p. 28)

Another important characteristic of the apartheid trauma was the politics of detention and torture practices (Foster et al., 1987). Participants reported detentions in various situations ranging from regular raids performed by the police randomly in the community to specific attacks and harassments on people in their own houses. During political protests, boycotts and attacks on administrative buildings, people were arrested and kept in solitary confinement where they were severely tortured. Thirteen participants from the study experienced the effects of captivity through arrests, detention in solitary confinement and imprisonment for long periods of time ranging from three months to eleven years. Within this sub-group, six participants were survivors of severe torture.

Participants in the study were arrested at home, on the streets or in demonstrations. Some were beaten, shot and wounded and were not offered any medical care. Dehumanising conditions, invasion of privacy, interrogation and torture were some of the major characteristics mentioned in the narratives. However, the most disturbing experiences were those recalled by victims of torture during solitary confinement. All survivors who were detained in solitary confinement were active in the political struggle against apartheid and were held by the security police without trial (Skinner, 1998). During this time they were interrogated and tortured with the purpose of extracting information about other political fighters and also to be punished for their involvement.

The conditions in solitary confinement were more difficult than those in prison. The brutality of physical and psychological torture, aimed at destroying the identity of the victim, had a devastating impact on the detainees. The methods of psychological torture mentioned by participants were: sleep and food deprivation, silence and lack of communication, being forced to stand naked for a long time, showing of the gun, making threats to family members and being moved through various prisons. Physical torture involved the use of mechanical devices such as metal or wooden sticks used to kick the prisoners' feet, electric shocks, plastic bags, burning cigars, electrocution and suffocation with a wet plastic bag. Sexual assaults were common practice meant to cause the ultimate destruction of any form of human dignity and will. The continuous combination of these practices produced confusion, psychological disorientation and overwhelming feelings of terror and helplessness.

The process of remembering torture was associated with intense emotions and feelings of sadness. Participants were often unable to continue their stories due to the inability to bear the high levels of pain evoked by these types of memories. Still, most of them were able to describe the horrors and confront the despair and helplessness from a stronger position now in the present. Benyi has described his experience in the following way: "*I was for six days brutally tortured, my teeth were kicked out, I was electrocuted, I was blindfolded, I was made to take off my clothes and stay naked. They handcuffed me, they put electric wires around my fingers and the electricity was switched on. I nearly died.*" In Thulani's case, after describing repeated torture through beatings, suffocation and electrocution, he continued to be tortured:

There were two policemen with two dogs. My hands were handcuffed behind my back. One dog... they just loosen up the chain and one dog came up to me and ripped my pants apart. I didn't fall but after a minute I started to feel warm in my pants and when I looked, I was bleeding. They took me up on the tenth floor and when I got there they were sitting in a circle. One of them, I always feared that guy. He had a big moustache and a bit red. He came to me. He said something in Afrikaans and pulled down my pants. He had a cigar in his hand and pushed it down in my testicles. The pain was just too much... I can't remember anything afterwards...

Such experience of physical pain confirms Scarry's (1985) opinion of intense pain as "language-destroying" (p. 35) and "world-destroying" (p. 29). In her view, torture is the destruction of language and interrogation represents the "deconstruction of the prisoner's voice" (p. 20). Furthermore, such pain creates chaos thus becoming "suffering left in its own uselessness" (Frank, 1995, p. 179). It can be asserted that detention and torture bring new dimensions for trauma constructs. Besides feelings of terror and helplessness, the context of captivity brings the victim and perpetrator into a special type of relationship characterised by coercive control, destructive proximity and lack of escape (Herman, 2001).

Many prisoners were killed in solitary confinement and those who survived were put on trial and sentenced to many years in prison. Thulani was only seventeen years old when he was sentenced to 18 years on Robben Island. However, when moving from solitary confinement to Robben Island, he said "*I felt like a president going to the palace*". Indeed, his testimony is supported by Mandela's statement that Robben Island was in a sense "the university of political struggle". In prison, detainees developed a sense of solidarity and group identity. They also learned life skills and coping mechanisms for survival. Thulani remembered how younger prisoners received advice from older political prisoners:

The older prisoners started to teach us the younger ones. They said "don't fight with the guards". So we started to be nice and talk to them about our families. We opened up and they became a very important source of information for us. My former guard is still here and we are good friends. We had good smugglers. You know Tokyo Sexwale, his wife Judy... she was so good. She was bringing everything. They did let us mix with other sections. We built a nice trophy out of an ostrich egg. We would keep busy among ourselves. Some of us were very young. The older ones would teach us how to wash our clothes, put them straight under our bed. The pants were straight.

Keeping their minds busy and establishing patterns of activities helped the prisoners gain some sense of order, coherence and control in their lives. These were important coping strategies aimed at enabling them to achieve more emotional balance and meaning in captivity. On Robben Island political prisoners had the opportunity to recreate the microcosm of political resistance and moreover to continue planning and dreaming about freedom. In their efforts to draft a constitution, Thulani recalls:

> We planned our future as a country here. We were thinking what kind of South Africa we want. We even drafted a constitution in this prison. So, now when we compare, we see there are lots of similarities. Another thing was that each one was given a leadership role. We never thought, "oh, you are not Mandela, then you are not a leader. We were many Mandelas having a leading role. We said we must be an example of leadership for our communities.

However, while in prison, detainees often heard about violence inflicted on their families and communities as well. The inability to do anything about it increased their feelings of disempowerment and helplessness.

c) Lateral violence

Suspicion of betrayal was a common strategy used by repressive regimes to divide communities and increase control over the oppressed population. By undermining group unity and cohesion, the oppressors intend to destabilize and conquer. Similar with the old roman dictum, "Divide et empera", the repressive structures of apartheid have induced suspicion of collaboration of Black people with the oppressive state (Straker, 1987, 1992). The security police used various strategies in order to disseminate among black communities the fear of betrayal and mistrust of their own people. Conflicts between different anti-apartheid movements were exploited by the state to turn people's attention from the real cause of violence. In situations of inter-community violence, the police would not intervene or would be selective in their involvement with the purpose of creating more terror and despair inside the community as well as depicting a tribal image of the Black people to the outside world (Straker, 1992).

Although there was only one participant in the sample that had witnessed the effects of lateral violence in her family, it is however worth mentioning it, given its pervasive nature in the family and the country as a whole. Thembi, still horrified by her memories, recalled the panic she and her mother experienced when they heard that her younger sister was going to be necklaced[2]. This profoundly traumatic event had a devastating impact on her sister and their family as well. Thembi struggled to put into words, memories that the whole family has tried to silence and forget:

> My younger sister was nearly necklaced in the '80. There were lots of problems with the UDF, INKATA and everyone was suspected to be a spy. My sister was going out with a boyfriend who had a job in the police service and the other boy in the streets named my sister a spy. I was in Joburg at that time. They grabbed her and said they were going to necklace her. My mother called me and she was hysterical. I went to the UDF in Joburg and went to a guy called (name). He was in a high position in the UDF. I called my mother to talk to her and support her. He called some UDF people from Durban and asked them to rush to that area. They had took my sister to a deserted place and were going to necklace her but they got there in time and saved her. It was a miracle...

Asking Thembi about her sister's recovery from such trauma, she replied:

> I don't think she ever recovered. She never wanted to talk about it since then. She is still living with my mother. She is 35 now and is a very sick person. She never got married, she doesn't have any relationship... This experience destroys you as a person. You stop loving yourself, stop loving other people, you stop loving anything. She was never able to keep a job, she keeps moving from one job to the other, from one relation to the other.

Trauma shattered not only her sense of self but also her sense of the world and others. Existence becomes meaningless and life, people and relationships are mere reminders of an unredeemable hostile world. This is a hopeless and lonely space in which the safety of the present context and the supportive relationship of her mother are just not enough for recovery to begin (Herman, 2001). The ability to remember, to mourn and to rebuild a new *self* is of the utmost importance. Yet, for those in the family and community, witnessing the suffering and continuous degradation of the person is also traumatising.

It becomes clear that an important characteristic of apartheid trauma was the relational dimension of suffering. Trauma was not only experienced individually or privately as described by earlier studies on trauma (APA, 1980, 1987, 1994). The impact of oppression affected families, communities and the whole black population. Even in situations

---

[2] A tyre soaked in petrol was placed around the individual's neck and set alight (Straker, 1987).

in which perpetrators could be identified, all participants found it difficult to distinguish individual perpetrators responsible for causing their pain. Most of the participants connected their trauma with a deep and painful feeling of injustice and helplessness. Betrayals by collaborators with the apartheid structures and lateral violence (Foster et al., 2005) highly complicated the situation, making it very difficult to distinguish between victim and perpetrator. The discussion will analyse next the ways in which participants reconstruct the multidimensional impact of apartheid repression on the individual, family and communities.

Individual trauma

At an individual level, participants felt the effects of trauma as a profound psychological disorientation in the process of defining one's identity, physical and emotional pain and shattering of trust in self and others. Although all participants who experienced torture mentioned having recurrent symptoms of posttraumatic stress, only two participants have been continuously under psychiatric treatment. The trauma of the individual under apartheid, as it is socially constructed in the present, lays greater emphasis on the injustices and damage done to the self as part of the collective. In their narratives people construct their experiences and identities in relation to others. This is not to minimise the impact of trauma on the individuals. On the contrary, it is important to consider that trauma of individuals during apartheid is not a mere collection of symptoms as defined by the Diagnostic Statistical Manual IV. While relating their narratives, participants constructed mental and bodily symptoms as a significant aspect of their suffering; however, their experience of trauma was yet more complex. Trauma was gradually constructed as a process rather than as a traumatic event followed by an aftermath as defined by the concept of PTSD.

Individuals experienced the impact of discrimination early in their childhood as Black youngsters becoming aware of injustices regarding racial segregation and questioning their personal identity and race. The hostile reactions received from the outside world made them feel inferior ("*it made me feel less human*") and rejected ("*I associated fair with acceptance and black with rejection*"). Disorientation continued with questioning one's identity on earth. As Patrick said: "*What was the purpose of my birth? Why have I come into the world to experience this?*" In the process of struggling to find answers to these questions, the fantasy of being White, as mentioned earlier, became both an escape and a way of coping with the painful reality. As Thembi remembered: "*I wished I was white, I wished I could dress as a white, do everything as a white person, anything white was better... the person didn't matter, only the colour".* The sense of inferiority was perceived as almost being inherited as it defined the ways in which people understood their reality and relationships with others: *"So when you meet people, you almost have this chip on your shoulder"* (Patrick). Some participants highlighted how their feelings of inferiority related to their insecure attachments in relationships, individuals assuming the victim's role *("I was needy, almost like needed to be taken by hand and led to a direction")* or the saviour's role *("I find myself automatically in that spot. If I see someone on the road begging, I'll drive to the shop and get him something to eat").*

Experiencing torture and witnessing cruelty inflicted on significant others have the most devastating impact on the individual. All participants in this category reported symptoms of posttraumatic stress, anxiety, depression, flashbacks, nightmares, fear of annihilation, suicidal ideation and somatic illness. Most participants were simultaneously confronted with various types of trauma, experiencing the overwhelming summative effects. Recalling the multitude of her traumatic events, Ethel symbolically stated: *"I'm a vandalised person by apartheid".* This is an indication that for some survivors the suffering has continued and it is still vivid in various forms even in the present. An intriguing question concerns the interpretation of survivor's present perceptions of their suffering in relation to past traumatic experiences and current social realities.

a) Diagnosis and meaning

Six participants in the study were severely tortured. Their micronarratives include not only descriptions of torture practices but also the impact on themselves during torture, afterwards and even in the present. In order to illustrate the meaning of events and symptoms for the survivor, this section will analyse a case of severe torture and highlight how perceptions of psychological impact and a strict diagnosis of complex posttraumatic stress disorder as conceptualised by Herman (2001) (and presented in Chapter 2) are open for debate and interpretation.

Benyi was introduced to Steve Biko and joined the liberation movement in March 1973 at the age of eighteen years. Three years later he was arrested, badly tortured and suffered permanent mental damage. He was diagnosed with amnesia and depression and has been under psychiatric treatment since 2002. Describing his struggle with suicide ideation and attempts he said:

I even had suicide thoughts and even attempted to take my life after all the trauma I went through but when I was about to push, I had a gun, a 9 mm Berretta, an Italian gun and I put the bullets in. Instead of blowing my brain out, I got scared. It was late in the evening and I got so scared of taking my life but I do still think of doing it, but not as before. Maybe the medication is helping me. When I tried the second time I stood over the roof of a building in Sea Point. I wanted to jump head on over the hills. Again, I got scared. Then I took myself as a coward and I said to myself "You are a coward, why don't you do it? You lost your father; you've been in prison. You've done nothing wrong but you are suffering. So, I thought life is not worth living. I am nothing in society, I am nothing... but the psychologist from the trauma centre used to say that I'm a strong person for the mere fact I didn't take my life.

According to Herman (2001), individuals with a "history of subjection to totalitarian control over a prolonged period (months to years)" are prone to develop complex post-traumatic stress disorder (p. 121). This being the first condition among seven other types of symptoms, the next one refers to alterations in affect regulation characterised by recurrent suicidal preoccupation and fluctuating anger. Talking about his inability to control his anger, Benyi said: *"I still have anger, a never ending anger, flashbacks. Sometimes I get angry over nothing. When I'm in that mood I want to become violent and I always think that violence is the only solution to solve things."*

Alterations of consciousness were present in the form of his already diagnosed amnesia, dissociative episodes and depersonalisation. His disappointment and helplessness in the present situation make him regret his investment in the political struggle. He feels stigmatised and disrespected by others. These elements are described by Herman as alterations in self-perception illustrated through Benyi's following statement:

In a few days I'll be 55. It is disgusting; it is so disgusting for all who fought for the country. Until this age you have not achieved anything, but what you have done was a lot... I end up sometimes hating myself, sometimes I think that if I had stayed with my hands crossed and not do anything, it would have been better but I couldn't, I had to do something... I have no answer when I ask myself why did you do it...

Broken relationships, lack of trust and inability to have a steady job were also described by Benyi as having a long term negative impact on his life:

B: I wasn't able to support myself. I was working and then I got fired... this company.. I work for them for 10 months. In one year they made one

billion rand. One day at 1.00 o'clock the unit manager called us all and said we are very happy with your work and are thankful to you and we were given a packet of biscuits each, a pack of assorted biscuits. I tried to mobilise workers to ask for their rights and I was fired...I was always fired from wherever I was working...
I: Why was that happening?
B: Because whenever I saw injustice and ill payment, I would speak up. I couldn't tolerate this. Even today in Cape Town. There are so many divisions. Coloured persons get better jobs and salaries, better privileges. Apartheid is in full swing. It's still in people's minds and they are practising it full time.

The sense of helplessness and despair associated with a loss of sustaining faith could be distinguished as an overall feature of Benyi's narrative. This is termed by Herman under the seventh diagnostic criteria labelled as alterations in systems of meaning. The following quote from Benyi's narrative could be interpreted as such. The context and the ways in which his evaluations are connected together are very important for the interpretation of the text. This is the reason for providing the quote with the possible indications of the symptom within the context of his story. Trying to link his past experiences with his current situation, he made the following statements:

*I was incarcerated in solitary confinement for 6 months: from January to July, without talking to anybody, whistling or singing. They wanted a deadly silence, which was enough to drive one off the wall. It was enough to drive one crazy and besides being beaten and electrocuted, that also played an important role in my health situation... Solitary confinement...that quietness... it was quiet as the grave. You are all by yourself in the cell... solitary confinement... It played a role and I would never reconcile with the perpetrator, because even today they live such a posh life, they live a good life. Look at the victims, all survivors of torture like myself. We are still struggling to eat meat, but we can't. Believe me, I used to walk from Langa to this office and if I need something to eat I would go to the soup kitchen... This is **the man who fought for democracy... Isn't that a joke?** When we look at them, the people with whom we fought together in the struggle, they forgot that we were with them.*
I: You were talking about this never-ending anger. Who are you angry at?
B: I'm not angry because their life is much better than my life but because of the conditions I'm living now, the perpetrators... We wanted to repair the country. Unjust laws must be abolished. It is not the colour of your skin...Justice to all. Now it's the opposite.
I: Where do you think that things went wrong?

B: Today our country is run by elites. They are the ones who are controlling the economy of the country now like during apartheid. The vast majority has nothing to say against injustices. Even today you cannot voice out against the government but you will be in trouble.

Listening to Benyi and interpreting his statements through psychiatric lenses, it is easy to consider that (using Herman's complex PTSD conceptualisation) he experiences many forms of psychological alterations including some paranoid elements. Indeed throughout his story one can distinguish the majority of symptoms that sum up the diagnostic criteria for complex posttraumatic stress disorder. Nevertheless, his fear of "getting in trouble" seems to be more than mere paranoid elements if we consider the recent statement of the COSATU general secretary - Zwelinzima Viva – proclaiming "corruption-busters have been assassinated" in Mpumalanga and North West provinces (Du Plessis, 2010). However, the concern at this point is not so much to do with the process of establishing a correct psychiatric diagnosis but more with what is happening with Benyi's discourse in his interaction with the social world. A closer look at this process shows that while Benyi is talking about being stigmatised and marginalised, blaming himself and expressing self-disgust, professionals can see alterations of self-perception, relations and systems of meaning. His "never ending anger" becomes in this context an alteration in affect regulation. The next question is how is anyone going to listen to or hear his unhappiness and feelings of injustice without labelling it as "alterations in systems of meaning" or any other type of alteration?

b) Psychiatric diagnosis: Another brick in the wall

From a strictly medical perspective, I agree with Herman's (2001) assumption which considers that "naming the syndrome of complex post-traumatic stress disorder represents an essential step toward granting those who have endured prolonged exploitation a measure of the recognition they deserve" (p. 122). This is extremely useful for victims of child abuse, battered women and victims of trauma due to long time exposure to oppression. However, the context of political oppression involves new dimensions, which need to be taken into consideration both in the process of defining trauma and in the process of recovery. There are several reasons for which a complex posttraumatic stress disorder diagnosis is not a sufficient answer for the current challenges facing former victims of apartheid.

First, Herman's statement is not universal, as it operates on a Western view of the world as being coherent and orderly, a place in which the victims have the benefit of a safe and nurturing context and an opportunity to enjoy the care of compassionate others after they have been diagnosed. Such a context has very little relevance, if any, within the socio-economic context of victims of political violence still living in townships in contemporary South Africa. A new psychiatric diagnosis will not bring much recognition to those who have been exploited by apartheid or by any other political system. From their perspective, what will bring them recognition is a sense of justice described in reparative terms through an improvement in their present socio-economic situation that is shattered by poverty and crime (Baker, 2010; Chapman & Van der Merwe, 2008; Colvin, 2000; Skinner, 1998; Van der Berg, 2014).

Second, not only complex posttraumatic stress disorder but also any diagnosis of mental disorder is socially and culturally open to stigmatisation and marginalisation. Victims in black communities do not feel "the recognition they deserve" (Herman, 2001, p. 122) through the psychiatric diagnosis attached to their person. On the contrary, such a diagnosis associated with their current economic struggles undermines their dignity, thus increasing their sense of helplessness and isolation. It also confirms their sense of the world as hostile and unsafe. Benyi describes how he and other former victims are treated as "laughing stocks" due to their present economically deprived situation.

Third, an overmedicalised attitude towards former victims would impede the listener hearing their story (Young, 1995). If their complaints are labelled in society as various forms of psychological alterations, the former victims find themselves unable to express their ideas and to present their discourse in a coherent way. Being ignored and abused by others they become again victims of the present injustices, thus perpetuating the cycle of victimhood. To illustrate this feeling, Benyi was saying:

> I have the experience that whenever I talk about my rights, I'm not listened to, it's like talking to a concrete wall. Whatever I talk, nobody wants to listen to me. I rather resort to violence as the last alternative and I think even today of taking up arms again… it is not an easy decision to make, but I have that feeling that it will happen one day. Because there are thousands of people like me that are marginalised and ignored. We are laughing stocks in our communities. I can't even ask for something from anybody.

Finally, Benyi's discourse against injustice, although coherently constructed in terms of facts, contains fundamental elements that threaten the image of the new political ideology constructed on the notion of *Ubuntu* and national reconciliation (Moon, 2008, 2009). In this context a psychiatric diagnosis represents an easier solution to the problems he raised since such a diagnosis can be treated through medication while dealing with poverty and crime is almost insurmountable at this stage in the South African transition. He stated the following:

> *Look today... poverty, diseases among black communities, theft – it is now an usual thing... We got so used with somebody dying all the time...it's a common thing. The political situation destroyed Ubuntu and relationships, our customs. About perpetrators... church ministers, everybody told us to reconcile with those perpetrators. I'm so reluctant to reconcile with them. Even during the TRC, they were never called in my case. If I said to the statement taker at the TRC, ok I want my case to be shared in a private hearing, but they were never called in. And even if they were, I would have never reconciled with them. Because today I'm not what I was and I'm not where I wanted to be in life. When I was at school, even before I reached Matric, I wanted to become a lawyer. I'm now a mental wreck. It never happened. My ambitions, my dreams collapsed... because the torture I experienced...*

If the shattering of the self and personal goals are labelled as indications of alterations in systems of meaning, the problem becomes intrinsically individual, thus residing in the victim and being the responsibility of psychiatric services to deal with it. Furthermore, trying to understand the social implications, if these symptoms are not fitted into a psychiatric category, they have to be interpreted and dealt with within the larger social system, whose institutions have been largely unable to find suitable solutions.

In conclusion, the dilemma of the dialectic of trauma persists with regard to the bi-directional relationship between the interpretation of perceptions and the social context in which they are constructed. As a result, are the symptoms of complex posttraumatic stress disorder evidence of trauma or are they socially constructed through the process of labelling the victim with a mental diagnosis? Are symptoms helping professionals to establish a diagnosis when the very presence of a diagnosis attracts the hostility of the social system in which the victim lives, thus causing the victim to display the psychological symptoms conceptualised as such? In other words, is Benyi's "never ending anger" an alteration in affect regulation or is it a natural response to the marginalisation and condescension with which society treats him? A balanced post-modernist view would argue for a space in which both options can exist together. However, it is noteworthy to highlight the potential danger of labelling victims' sense of helplessness, despair and frustration at not being heard in society as "alterations in systems of meaning". This approach can become just another brick in the wall separating victims from the outer world with which they desperately try to engage and connect. The danger consists in interpreting their discourse against injustice as a symptom of mental illness and therefore easily ignored and discarded as being "not real and not true". Unfortunately, this has been the experience of many members of the Khulumani Support Group who have been given various diagnoses as a result of psychological damage suffered during apartheid, but who are constantly struggling for their social rights, and are therefore still subject to abuse.

Summing up, individual trauma as constructed by participants in this study is experienced as helplessness and as shattering of the self and the world (Herman, 2001). Although their multiple symptoms may fit the diagnostic criteria of complex posttraumatic stress disorder, participants' narrative constructions show that these feelings are more rooted in the injustice experienced in the present rather than in past traumatic events experienced during apartheid (Eagle, 2011; Kaminer & Eagle, 2010). On the one hand, they are disappointed with the current government for not offering them any reparations for their investment in the political struggle. On the other hand, they are thwarted by derogatory attitudes of people in their communities who "laugh at" their hopeless situation. Their psychiatric diagnosis tends to isolate them even more as their complaints are interpreted as being caused by their mental illness and therefore should not to be taken into consideration. Their trauma becomes the impossibility of sharing their story with an empathic other (Etherington, 2003; Frank, 1995). Similarly, in Brison's (2002) view, their trauma is a "disruption of the narrative-building function of the self" (p. 39) in which the victims become "the prison of their own memory" (p. 43). Moreover, as mentioned previously, the psychological effects experienced by individuals reverberate at the level of the family and community, leading to further traumatic experiences.

Family trauma

Individual traumas have inevitably affected relationships and family dynamic due to multiple challenges coming both from an internal and external context (Weingarten, 2004). Although the analysis is based on the narratives of individuals, the content is profoundly infused with collective memories of experiences impacting participants' families (Straker, 1987). One type of family trauma was experienced through the terror and instability of the repressive context. Another type referred to a bi-directional vertical transmission of trauma due to a family member's trauma (parent/child) or murder. However, families living in a township during apartheid were confronted at the same time with multiple traumatic events. Just by reading the core narratives of the participants in the study, it is easy to notice how the same family would experience many types of trauma at various intensities. For example, in Monica's family, she recalls her mother and sister's disappearance in the struggle, her beatings and arrests by the security police, her daughter's permanent disability because of being teargased at a very young age, her own permanent neurological disability because of being hit with a gun during an arrest, her husband leaving her and the trauma of divorce and continuously struggling with illness and poverty since those events up to the present time. The overwhelming amount and nature of the traumatic events suffered is a common characteristic of families who lived in black settlements during apartheid.

The experience of losing a child or a parent, or witnessing the gradual degradation and death of a family member due to permanent injuries, had the most devastating impact on the family (Cairns & Lewis, 1999; Felsen, 1998). Trauma within families during apartheid was explored, through the eyes of mothers who lost a child in the political struggle or were severely tortured, and through the eyes of participants who, as children during apartheid, either lost a parent or grew up without any parent due to murder or the politics of labour displacements (Hamber, 1995).

a) Parentification and injured parental selves

Narratives of forced displacements and work practices during apartheid revealed traumatic developmental experiences and dysfunctional patterns of interaction, beliefs and values within the family structure (Simpson, 1998). Participants in the study experienced the trauma of growing up with relatives or grandmothers, as parents went to work in Western Cape and were able to come home only once a year. Thembi's story is particularly relevant to illustrate the impact of repression on families and the transmission of life patterns to the next generation. As she recalls:

I would spend all my time thinking when is Christmas. Is Christmas in June, in July, when is Christmas coming so that I could see my parents? And time was never enough as they would stay only for two weeks and the minute they left, the minute they said goodbye and the minute I saw them disappear behind the mountains, my next thought was when is the next Christmas so that I would see them again.

Some families were able to bring their children with them to Western Cape to live in Nyanga and Langa townships. However, as parents went to work, especially mothers who lived in the *"back houses of the White people"*, children were left alone, being with their parents only two days over the weekend. Uprooted from their communities and without protection, the children had to face loneliness, neglect, abuse and role reversals (De la Ray et al., 1997). Most families consisted of a single mother and several children and therefore it was common for the older children to assume parental roles. Thembi remembers assuming a parental role in her family from a very early stage in her life: *"I was a kind of a mother in the family at a very young age. I became the mother of my brothers as my mother was working"*. Parentification in the family is often a helpful aspect in maintaining the family homeostasis as long as it is well-defined and has clear limits (Minuchin, 1974). However, if the child is assuming the role of the parent for an extended period of time, this situation can become a barrier for the child's personal development (Carr, 2006; Haley, 1967).

Most participants had vivid memories of witnessing the humiliation and oppression of their parents, which in Weingarten's (2004) view, doubles the risk of traumatic impact. Following Thembi's story of her pain while witnessing the humiliation of her mother because she, as a nine-year-old child at that time, used the master's toilet instead of using the servants' toilet prompting the master's outrage. As she recalls: *"I saw my mother crumbling down, becoming like a little child, and this whole woman that I always looked upon as my queen, as my everything and to see her crumbling down on the floor just because her little child used the white toilet..."* The experience of the mother as a "little child" is overwhelming for a child who does not have the necessary emotional resources to provide shelter for the mother's injured self. In response, the mother who carries with her injured self-images becomes emotionally unavailable in her relationship with her child who, in turn, finds it difficult to differentiate correctly and establish his/her own self (Weingarten, 2004). In this process some may embark on various strategies to "repair" the past others remain stuck in a certain stage of their development, unable to find solutions to move on (Volkan, 2009). In Thembi's case, she found herself after a few years in an almost identical situation as her mother:

> *Time went by and I ended up having my own child and again as my mother, I could not be with her because I became a domestic worker myself playing with the White kids which I wished they were mine and my own child was playing in the dusty streets in the townships. There was no one to look after her, as I was looking after my boss' children so that my child*

would have something to eat... and this is not only my pain. This is the pain of every Black woman. Today even if we have Black doctors and Black lawyers, they all come from the same place where their mothers were scrubbing floors to get food for them. Every family was affected...

b) Lack of emotional bond and couple disintegration

Families experienced the trauma of apartheid in terms of high levels of disorganisation, diffuse boundaries, lack of rules, role confusion and couple problems (Simpson, 1998). Most men got involved in extra-marital affairs and eventually left their families. Due to police harassments, arrests and detentions, it was difficult for families and especially couples to develop and build an emotional bond. There was a destructive parallelism between the socio- political instability and family instability, depicted by chaotic dynamic and broken relationships. Due to political violence and oppression, families had limited contact and were unable to provide a nurturing environment for their members. This had a negative impact on child development as well as on the couple relationship. Monica recalls how difficult it was for her to develop and strengthen the affective bond with her husband while having to hide and be on the run from the security police. The longer excerpt from Monica's narrative illustrates how multiple contextual stressors overlapped in the life of the family producing devastating effects on family members and the family dynamic (McGoldrick & Carter, 1982; Nichols, 2009):

I've never had a time in which I stayed with my husband because of the struggle. We used to attend meetings but after the meeting, he didn't get back home. He took his own way. The situation was very chaotic until we divorced. I never had a time in my life when I stayed with my husband and did things together, sharing at home... We never had that time. In the end he decided to take his things and went to another woman. I've never had a cent from him. He lives now in Khaelitsha. My older daughter is helping me a bit but because she doesn't have a permanent job she cannot help much. The other one is disabled because of the teargas... she was just a baby and I used to run with her in my arms, but the teargas damaged her because she was too little.

Contextual stressors determined by various forms of political violence had a destructive impact on this family through lack of mutual support in the couple's relationship and the permanent disability of the younger daughter. The family system in this context experiences a high amount of pressure in the process of continuously striving to survive and protect its members. The natural life stages of family development are affected by lack of resources and flexibility to adapt and find new options to preserve the unity of the family in the process of change (Landau et al., 2008). In the absence of a functional couple relationship and the stress of caring for a disabled child, Monica's husband decided to leave the family. As a single mother, Monica had to find the strength to continue to care for her family, developing coping strategies that enabled her to maintain family functioning and attain a new level of homeostasis.

Moreover, Monica's case is not unique as many other women living in black settlements during apartheid went through similar experiences. As described by other women in the study, a single mother often experienced a chaotic type of family dynamic with children *"overstepping their boundaries"* and *"questioning her authority"*. In addition, young mothers who were involved in the political struggle faced often overwhelming difficulties, having to deal both with police harassments and with raising their children. However, as their stories unfold, most mothers and women in this study were able to developed strength, good coping and resilience when faced with apparently insurmountable challenges (aspects further developed in Chapter 7). These findings reveal Black women's complex positioning with regard to where their multifaceted identities as wives, mothers, daughters and freedom fighters interact (Price, 2002; Shefer, 2010). Similar to Sideris' (2003) research on Mozambican women refugees, in this study too, one can affirm that Black women during apartheid were "an integral part of the battlefield" (p. 713).

c) Complex loss and 'unfinished business' from the past

A difficult aspect in dealing with family trauma caused by apartheid repression is the loss of a child or parent and the *unfinished business* involved in the working through complex grief, regrets and guilt. All participants involved in the study experienced a type of loss in their families plus a long-term psychological impact that is continuing to reverberate in the present and maybe will for the rest of their lives. As most of them expressed it, the loss of a dear one is "a pain that never goes away", a pain that changes the other members of the family forever. Asking Frans in what ways the loss of his son changed his life *"completely"*, he replied: *"By this I mean that I became very angry. Then and afterwards, I always aligned this with the White people who never gave me the money for my work and who now killed my child. I became so angry that I could not control myself."* Also, trying to express the engulfing effect of multiple trauma, Ethel stated the following: *"When I'm thinking about it, I have a wound that has not been healed. I had physical problems, heart problems because of that time. I lost my child Bishop. He was shot. I'm now a person that has lots of sicknesses. I'm still traumatised. This gives me all kind of sickness. I'm a vandalized person by the apartheid"*

The traumatic loss experienced by families during apartheid has a specific component compared to families whose loss has different causes. The analysis shows a connection between family trauma due to the loss of one of its members and feelings of guilt, regrets and the unfinished business of the grieving members of the family. In order to explore more closely this relationship, this section will discuss first the situation of the mothers who lost a child in the political struggle and then those who lost a parent due to political violence of apartheid.

All seven Black women in the study experienced either the loss of a child (Cyntia and Ethel), torture or violence inflicted on their child (Fowsia, Monica and Thelma) or violence inflicted on a family member (Thembi, Thelma, Monica and Sindiswa). Cyntia is one of the mothers who lost their sons in the "Guguletu 7" killings on the 3rd of March 1986 when seven boys were killed and many more were injured by the police in Gugulethu. Her story of forgiveness is well known due to the TRC hearings in which Mbali, the policeman who killed her son, came to ask for forgiveness. The trauma of loss in Cyntia's case is not confined by the family boundary but becomes a trauma shared by the community. Other mothers lost their sons at the same time and the common pain they share creates a new type of subjectivity and group identity. They are the mothers of the "Gugulethu 7". Their sadness continues no matter what they do; their sons will never come back (Kgalema, 2002). Reflecting on her experience of forgiveness, she said:

So, I said I forgive you because I can see you are almost the age of my child and is of no use holding on the revenge because my child will not come back. He is gone, he is gone... So that is the end of the TRC. Bellingham never came to ask for forgiveness himself. This was the end. Nobody was prosecuted. These are the stories that make us sad. You know being a mother... everybody was so sad.

In Ethel's situation, her son was shot during a protest and suffered permanent mental and physical damage. Due to his disability, he became totally dependent on others to look after him. As the family did not have the necessary resources to provide continuous care, he died at the age of 38 hit by a car close to his home. Ethel's trauma narrative is about witnessing the gradual degradation of her son's life, the shattering of her future goals and the guilty feelings related to her inability to prevent his death. As she recalls, her son (as the first born), represented the hope of her future: *"There was one thing that really killed my life because I had a vision that he will be the breadwinner of the house. I'm not working now, especially that I'm suffering all sorts of illnesses. He was the eldest child."*

In Monica's case, family trauma is constructed around her mother's and sister's disappearance as she begins and ends her story on this topic. Although she experienced multiple traumas in her life such as her daughter's and her own permanent disability, and her divorce, the emotional tension revolves around the *unfinished business* of the past which cannot be put to rest by the family. Her suffering related to the disappearance of her mother and sister was transgenerationally transmitted from the traumatised father to her, since she was very young when her mother and sister disappeared and has no memories of her mother. The other members of the family in their attempt to process their grief have tried to find closure in practical or symbolic ways. Monica remembered the legacy left by her father and younger sister before they died:

> *When my father was about to die, he said to me that I must try to do everything I can to look for my mother but he died and we still don't know anything about her. Even my younger sister, before she passed away, she told me what she tried to do in order to find out what happened to our mother and sister. She went to a traditional healer to ask about our mother and the healer said that she is deep under the ground but she couldn't say where. My sister also could not understand why our mother left her so young as she was then and, after she said that, she died."*

Monica's narrative highlights the *liminal* social space in which the family has been living for such a long time (Hamber &Wilson, 1999). According to Hamber and Wilson, "the personal perplexity and incoherence of the trauma is extreme in the case of political disappearances" (Liminality and reintegration, para 1). As highlighted in Monica's description, their bewilderment may be rooted in the traditional beliefs of some black communities that the dead (or the disappeared) person's body keeps haunting the people in the community until the mystery is solved or until a certain form of symbolic recognition and reparation is performed (Ramphele, 1996).

In addition, Volkan (2009) argues that the mourning process involves the "burying" of mental representation of the lost person. From this perspective, Monica could be considered a perennial mourner, as she cannot bring her mourning process to a practical end due to the absence of mental representation of her lost mother. Not only has she nothing physical to bury but also her memory cannot recall any mental image of the lost person. In the context of disappearances, the entire process of grieving is problematic since there is no person to reflect on and no image of her non-existence. A disappearance cannot be integrated, as the mourner is still preoccupied with solving this problem, a situation defined by Edwards (2009) as complicated or traumatic grief.

Communal trauma

An important component of trauma, highlighted by the majority of participants who lived in black communities, was the communal dimension of suffering under oppression. Although this study was based on individual interviews, each narrative reconstructed trauma in relation to its wider impact on communities. The language structures used by most participants reveal significant forms of identification of individuals with the communities in which they lived or with the liberation movements in which they acted. For example, right from the beginning of his story, Shaheed feels the need to mention the following: *"I think there are various levels of my story. Even if I talk about me, generally as activist, I'll use the plural because we never acted as individuals but we were part of the collective. In fact, it wasn't only the activists that were suffering but the whole population"*. People's individual trauma is closely related to the suffering experienced by communities. As mentioned by participants, the major constructs of communal trauma concern: (a) the continuous terror and control inflicted by the state repressive structures and (b) witnessing trauma and loss in communities.

a) Between terror and solidarity

As described by participants, black communities during apartheid were shattered by political violence, security police raids, pass control, detentions, shootings, lack of medical care, street fights and lateral violence (described in section 6.1.2.). This conglomerate created a paradoxical situation in which people felt both terror and a sense of solidarity in specific situations. Involvement in protests and liberation movements gave people *"a sense of belonging"*, it helped them feel *"less inferior"* and increased their sense of agency by being able to *"contribute to the greater cause"*. Sean recalls the solidarity among students and academics at the university: *"Yes, there was a lot of loss and sadness but there was also the excitement"*.

A particular case of community trauma was the situation of the mothers whose sons were arrested for their involvement with anti-apartheid structures, badly tortured during solitary confinement and condemned for twenty years imprisonment on Robben Island. Fowzia Lowe remembers her efforts to organise and prepare the mothers in case they were arrested:

> *It was Quinton Michael's mother, Ashley Forbes' mother... quite a few of them and as I was arrested before, I told them what was gonna happen. I told them: "They are going to arrest us, make sure you take your drugs, soap, toilet paper and a face cloth with you as there is no place in the cell where you can...They put us all in one cell. You could hardly breathe as that place stinks.*

Mothers and fathers in the study lost sons or witnessed helplessly the gradual destruction of their youngsters due to the effects of torture and physical wounds. Reflecting on her pain, Ethel remembers: *"He was 19 when he was shot. He grew up with the bullet in his body but he became paralysed on the right side and mentally disturbed. He died later hit by a car as he had to have somebody looking after him all the time"*. Feelings of guilt and anger for not being able to provide the necessary care and protection complicate the trauma of mothers in the community. Friends and family members of those involved in the struggle became targets of threats and intimidation (*"they said they will abduct me and nobody will know where my body is"*, *said Fowzia*).

Lateral violence experienced as a result of suspicion of collaboration with apartheid structures devastated individuals and their families. Still horrified about the event, as noted earlier, Thembi described how her sister was almost necklaced by some youngsters in her community who believed her sister *"was a spy"*. Sean also has been deeply affected by the death of his best friend who died as a result of betrayal by one of their comrades. The fear and extreme type of political violence, this time coming from within the community, increased the state of terror and despair in black communities already shattered by apartheid repression.

b) Witnessing trauma

Witnessing torture and killings was exceptionally traumatising. All participants in the study witnessed violence in their communities and even now, some still live with a family member that has partial or permanent damage. Witnessing the pain of a family member, or even worse, watching helplessly someone's continuous physical and mental degradation is particularly traumatic for all people involved (Weingarten, 2000). Moreover, the process of witnessing trauma becomes the transmission mechanism for the emotional impact of traumatic events, thus extending the communal effect of trauma. The language used in most narratives illustrates the widespread aspect of suffering in black communities. As Thembi evaluates, *"there were people who didn't even know what struggle they were fighting. They were not politicised. They knew there was something wrong and they wished somebody to take away their pain. Every person was traumatised by apartheid"*.

According to Weingarten (2004), the position of the witness is defined by two important concepts: awareness and empowerment. Awareness refers to the ability of the witness to have knowledge about the context and the event he/she is witnessing. Empowerment defines the ability of the witness to act in the given situation. Through the combination of the two dimensions (awareness and empowerment), we obtain four witnessing positions characterised by specific elements and emotional challenges for the *self* of the witness and the others involved in that particular situation. The most distressful position for *the self* of the witness is the situation in which the witness is aware of the suffering but is helpless and powerless to do something about it. This is the position experienced by most Black children, youngsters, women and men during apartheid in South Africa, witnessing injustices, humiliation and cruelty without being able to do anything about it. Most participants had vivid memories of witnessing the humiliation and oppression of their parents. Others have witnessed their comrades being beaten or tortured. Fowzia, while being detained for her political involvement and protests, witnessed the torture inflicted on a detainee woman from her group:

> *They used to do all sorts of things... for example, you go on duty now with me and in two hours after having the satisfaction of being cruel, you go off duty and the next person comes and carries on... and they do not let you sleep... they carry on right through the night. Another girl that was also on trial...they had their office on St. George's Street and it was raining that day. The cops said to her: "Take off your clothes, it's hot", No, she said, I'm cold!" She had huge bust. They asked her to lean onto the desk and they put her breast into the drawer and they shut the drawer into her breasts... you know how a woman's breasts are... very vulnerable and tender. They didn't care if you were a girl, a woman, a man or a boy. Tutu is able to forgive and Mandela also. He had no anger when he was released, no vengeance and I admire him for that but somehow I can't... I will maybe forgive but will never forget.*

The witness in such a context becomes the victim of psychological torture, crushed by the double-bind tension (Bateson, 1972) between empathy for the victim and the feelings of helplessness resulting from the impossibility of changing the situation. Empathy moves people naturally towards being caring and supporting, while in a torture-witnessing context these very concepts become meaningless. The impact such an experience has on the witnessing person is made explicit through the last phrases of the quote, which construct an evaluative ethical judgment in regard to gross human right violations and the ability to forgive. Fowsia is specifically talking about the witness's ability to forgive, not about the victim. As a woman, she identified with the pain of the woman who was tortured, taking upon herself her suffering. The gender identity becomes the common ground on which pain can be shared in the witnessing process, allowing both the victim and the witness to experience togetherness and closeness. Being a woman myself, I felt the power of the witnessing dynamic and the words drawing me close – *"you know how a woman's breasts are... very vulnerable and tender"*. Identification with and imagination of the victim's pain takes precedence, as the witness's body becomes an extension of the victim's body by trying to bear and share the physical and emotional damage. A return to reasoning and individuality is confusing for the witness who tries to make sense of her experience while also struggling with the moral dilemma of vengeance and forgiveness. Yet, the transformative power of national moral pillars such as Tutu and Mandela could overcome the revenge by opening space for possible forgiveness while preserving traumatic memories.

Another witnessing position is the one in which the witness is unaware of the situation but has the authority and power to act in the name of a certain ideology. This is considered by Weingarten (2004) to be the most detrimental position for *the other*. For example, within the South African context, White people in particular, as beneficiaries of the apartheid system found themselves in this category. Most of them claimed they were unaware of the political violence inflicted on black communities and therefore some were mere bystanders who remained passive. While this may be valid with regard to the extent of the repressive acts and atrocities carried out by the apartheid structures, still in Ross's view (survivor of the St. James massacre), this argument serves as a justification, a rationalisation and an unwillingness to assume responsibility on behalf of the White race. Commenting on White people's attitudes, he boldly states: *"For those who are guilty of social evil, to say "oh, we weren't aware" it does not help the situation at all. You need to be bold enough to say "we messed it up, we messed it really badly". There is actually no excuse. There are reasons, it was a very complicated thing, but we were wrong".*

White people involved in the repressive structures of the apartheid state became the perpetrators responsible for the unilateral violence inflicted on the Black population (Foster et al., 2005). In the light of the witness theory, they also claim a "not aware" position but this time the so-called unawareness is due to indoctrination of the apartheid ideology (and theology), turning an appalling act into a commendable one. This particular witnessing position became extremely dangerous due to the empowerment and authority to act in the name of the erroneous ideology of apartheid, deliberately created on the basis of ignorance (Simpson, 1998). The Whites' position was characterised by power and, supposedly, lack of awareness regarding the further implications of their actions. Whether some were prevented from knowing (or it was just a conscious 'blindness'), such a position facilitated the development of the perpetrator's identity, allowing them to wield power in the name of an ideology that made them blind to moral and ethical reasoning (Foster et al., 2005). A more or less similar mechanism could have facilitated the behaviour of those responsible for the St. James Church massacre in which the perpetrators representing the APLA/PAC liberation movement claimed they were not aware that they were going to open fire on people attending a church service. The next section of this chapter will analyse the narratives of three survivors of the St. James Church massacre, looking at the major elements of their trauma reconstruction, and remarking on some possible differences between their subjective experiences and those of victims of state repression as discussed so far in this chapter.

6.2. Victims of liberation movements

As was mentioned in the previous chapter, the presence of the three narratives told by survivors of the St. James Church massacre induced an internal sample comparison and highlighted important differences between survivors of state repression and survivors of liberation movements. The preliminary analysis revealed major differences both in the ways in which trauma was experienced and in the various ways in which the two categories of survivors tried to rebuild their lives after trauma. This section will discuss only the aspects related to the experience of trauma and its impact among the massacre survivors. The next chapter (Chapter 7) will deal with the process of recovery and the survivors' life trajectories in the aftermath of trauma.

Memories of the massacre

No matter the magnitude of a political conflict, the thought or anticipation of a brutal attack when people go into a church, would seem utterly absurd. Yet, on the 25th of July 1993, during the period of intense negotiations between the two poles of the interracial conflict in South Africa, four armed Black men opened fire and threw grenades into a defenceless congregation of 1400 people in St. James Church. Three participants in the study (two Coloured women and one White man) were in the church that night and survived the massacre. They have tried, during the interviews, to revisit their past by recalling memories, images and feelings associated with this horrific event. Yet, especially at the beginning of the interviewing process, the language to express the horror and devastation of the aftermath of this tragic event became limited, lacking the necessary linguistic structures to illustrate "the indescribable and the undiscussable" they experienced that "stormy night" as all of them described it (Bar-On, 1999).

The first feeling remembered by all three participants was the sense of disbelief and unreality they experienced when hearing the first sounds in front of the church. Their immediate cognitive reaction followed a logical path, connecting the noise with the spatio-temporal environment in which a couple was singing a worship song in front of the church. Consequently, one participant though "*oh, is the youth putting out some drama show*" and another was thinking, "*this is a skit*". Ross Anderson, one of the church ministers, who was actually leading the service that night said that his first thought was "*ahh... I can't believe it! Our neighbours were so sick and tired of our parking problems that they have come to disrupt the service with firecrackers*".

Although bombings and shootings were happening quite often during that period of time, the possibility of an attack in a church could not fit any logic or sense of reality. Even if the next emerging cognitive associations would point towards an attack, the logical censors of consciousness would completely reject this possibility. Ross described this mechanism in the following way: "*When I realised it was an attack, my first feeling was of total disbelief. I couldn't believe it was happening. If someone would have said to me, St. James would be attacked, I would have thought, never... Police stations – maybe, army barracks – maybe, even a civic centre, but not a church!*"

Besides the sense of disbelief, participants also reported a perceptual crisis in the form of temporal, spatial and visual distortions. As Ross described it "*I wasn't really aware of time... Looking back, it seems it happened very quickly. It didn't go on and on, although it wasn't an instant either*". Also Mandy reported that although "*it happened very quickly, it seemed like in a slow motion*". The compressed time and slow motion type of actions intensified the feelings of unreality and shock.

These perceptual distortions could be explained in a context characterised by unpredictability and a victim's inability to make sense of his/her reality.

Participants' accounts clearly support the idea that their trauma was related to the shattering of basic assumptions of safety and benevolence, as invoked by Janoff-Bulman (1989, 1992). However, these assumptions were more related to their then current context rather than to a universal notion of trust in the world as a safe and benevolent place, as was previously conceptualised by Janoff-Bulman. Their specific assumptions of safety were theologically constructed, and developed in close relation to their Christian values and the space in which trauma took place. The church and participants' spiritual beliefs created an atmosphere of safety in which nothing wrong could happen. Even an explosion could have been interpreted as a show or a firecracker, while a deliberate human-inflicted attack was beyond comprehension within this particular framework.

It could be also argued that in contrast with victims of state repression who lived in townships, the victims of the massacre who were living in safer areas projected a different sense of predictability and control over life events. During apartheid, people's identities and experiences were profoundly shaped by geographic separation, this being an integral part of the segregation ideology. Within this particular social environment, the St. James Church massacre could be considered as a traumatic event *outside the range of usual human experience,* which resembles Western conceptualisations of trauma in the form of PTSD. Yet survivors' subjective experiences of trauma and their subsequent meaning-making process are profoundly shaped by idiosyncratic experiences and beliefs. The next section will explore the impact of the massacre on the wounded congregation, as remembered by the three participants in the study.

A wounded congregation

In situations of extreme suffering and pain, victims become short of words and linguistic structures to express their feelings (Scarry, 1985). The survivors of the St. James Church massacre sensed hardly definable emotions and even after seventeen years, memories were still painful and confusing. The narrative reconstruction of traumatic reality in the aftermath of the massacre is shaped by survivors' identities and roles in relation to their family, friends and congregation. The widespread extent of injury and distress contributed to the immersion of individual suffering into the collective pain, victims channelling their first reactions towards the needs of others.

Participants' narratives conveyed the idea that their individual trauma made sense only in relation to the others involved in the massacre. Their language and the content of their memories highlight the collective dimension of the traumatic impact. This is clearly illustrated through narrators' preoccupation with long descriptions about the others around them, with little attention given to their own suffering. Immediately after the perpetrators left, some survivors even assumed that members of their families were all right and ran to help the injured people in front of the church. As Mandy remembered "*we got out and heard people screaming. I just assumed that everything was ok with my family and as I was looking I saw one of my best friends killed on the floor with a bullet in his head... (crying)... and it was then that I turned to my mom. She was lying on the floor struggling to breathe*". Also Liesl talking about Mandy's brother said:

> *My husband who was my boyfriend at that time went in front of the church to help other people who were injured. He somehow assumed that all people from his family were all right. Unfortunately his mother had a shrapnel in her heart and died on the way to hospital. I went to find him to tell him that his mother was hurt.*

Ross Anderson, as one of the ministers of the church, started to organise the congregation, giving instructions in order "to limit the damage". He was concerned about the elderly and the injured people who "*might have got trampled on*" if people had started running to the exits. With more than 1000 people trying to make their way out, the situation could have become easily chaotic. Instead, Ross had a moving experience in which the congregation, at the sound of his voice, acted as a single individual. As he reported:

> *I went back to the pulpit and said: "Don't run to the exits, just lay down flat on the ground and start looking for the elderly and the wounded... and the moment I spoke, it was like a wave that suddenly stopped. It was the most incredible thing, which shows you, I guess, that even in the situations like that, you've got to have someone in the lead, someone to hold together and a familiar voice that can be trusted. So, that was quite remarkable and people did lie down.*

The overall view Ross must have had at this time from the pulpit must have been overwhelming, as he was the first one in a position to grasp the extent of the tragedy: "*the blood all over the place, grenades going off and people wounded*". However, he could not spend time in contemplation as urgent aspects had to be taken care of. These images were going to haunt him in the form of flashbacks and nightmares at later stages in his life. At that moment, his immediate reaction was "*a huge sense of anger*" towards "*the perpetrators for coming and doing such a thing to innocent people. Of course they would say "they are not innocent". Even then to slaughter defenceless people made me very very angry and still does*". Subsequently, his anger was channelled constructively by "trying to limit the damage" and assisting families who lost loved ones: "*I remember I was very busy visiting all those who were hurt, busy planning all the funerals, lots of media attention, lots of interviews, so it was a very busy time. In a way, I suppose that helped me a lot to process everything*".

Those who did not lose immediate family members adopted a supportive role towards others in the congregation, thus minimising the extent of their own trauma. Liesl described her dilemma as a witness: "*I feel so strange…I didn't really grieve…I thought I didn't lose somebody from my family as my husband or others in the congregation*". Such a belief leaves little space for the witness to attend to her own pain and process her own loss, as she constantly thinks, "*my pain should be smaller*". This aspect highlights the fact that the collective dimension of trauma is woven in the context of complex interactions between wounded individual subsystems and their multiple ways of experiencing the shared traumatic reality.

However, when analysing communal trauma, one should avoid the risk of losing the individual inside the community. As is clearly illustrated in survivors' narratives, the massacre had a devastating psychological impact on individuals as well. Yet, in the immediate aftermath, survivors were more preoccupied with those wounded or those who lost loved ones. The present reflection on the traumatic event helped the three participants to interpret their reactions and develop new meanings for their symptoms, coping mechanisms and their identity as they journey through life. All three survivors reported symptoms of PTSD such as: difficulty in sleeping, nightmares, flashbacks, anxiety, startled reactions to noise, avoidance, dissociation, sadness, paranoid reactions, depression and difficulties in relating to others. Some symptoms were experienced in the immediate aftermath, some after a few months or even after a few years.

However, what is important to notice is that throughout their stories, survivors place less emphasis on these symptoms and more on the context in which they happen and the particular stage of their life trajectory. Furthermore, the meaning they give to these symptoms is far from describing dysfunctions or abnormalities and is rather understood as part of a natural process of re-making the self and the world in which they live. For example, Mandy who lost her mother in the massacre talked about her nightmares, anxiety and depressive symptoms when she became pregnant with their first baby. Particularly moved by a recent dream, she recalled:

> *In my dream, it was this baby whom I was supposed to take care of, to give me good practice for the time my baby comes... and I try my best, I'm sort of panicking and nobody is helping me out. I turn to my mom and say ... (starts crying and sobbing for 3 minutes)... 'please, can't you see I'm going through the most difficult time in my life' and she is not helping me out and my aunt is not helping me out. I tell my husband about it... people were busy and could not really be there for me...*

These findings support the arguments regarding the importance of close human connections and a family life cycle approach for the understanding of trauma and recovery (Herman, 2001; Johnson, 2002; Landau et al., 2008; Weingarten, 2004). Furthermore, they highlight the fact that individual and collective trauma cannot be separated or understood in isolation from each other. As conceptualised by Bracken et al. (1995), they are interrelated and shaped by social, political and cultural reality. In the context of the St. James Church massacre, cultural reality mainly depicted through "spiritual and religious involvement, basic ontological beliefs and concepts of self, community and illness" provided survivors with a contextual framework in which trauma was understood as part of the political and spiritual reality at that moment. This is clearly illustrated in Ross' reflection on the traumatic event:

> *So, for me things were clear: first, we all live in a fallen world. Secondly, South Africa at that time was a very politically violent country on the brink of civil war. Although some major steps have been taken for the good and the ANC being unbanned but nonetheless... that was the reality in SA. It felt in some sense almost immoral to ask where was God, when horrible things have been happening all over the country for many years and no one ever asked where was God then in our circles. So, it almost sounded immoral to ask this now that it suddenly hit home. Why we suddenly worry about that when for 40 years we weren't worried about that? That for me is more of an issue... The theology didn't trouble me. I didn't doubt that God was with us; I didn't doubt that God loved us; I didn't doubt that God couldn't stop it if He wanted to, but that was the reality in South Africa.*

This shows how his experience of trauma is profoundly shaped by political reality and his theological beliefs, in which the meaning of the horrific event gains ontological coherence. Assuming his social position as a White middle class man, Ross is able to take on the role of a prototype by acknowledging the social injustices of his race and see trauma in the larger historical context. Within this conceptual framework, trauma is understood as a result of the perverted fallen nature of human beings and political systems, which could turn *"three young men into murderers"*. As Ross recalled:

> *That made me very angry and I remember thinking to myself: if our roles were reversed and I were in their situation, I may as well have done the same thing, unless by God's grace I was converted, I may as well have done the same thing. So, it forced me to look at human nature, it really showed me the massive consequences of politics.*

Ross's complex identity and understanding of contextual realities creates the grounds for his honest reflection and mirroring exercise. His extreme identification with his perpetrator allows Ross to enter the world of the perpetrator and even to have the possibility of redeeming it. His words clearly show how an understanding of political and spiritual context can change perceptions about self, others and the world, including human suffering. Such a contextual framework plays an important role both for the understanding of trauma and the process of recovery. It is fundamentally related to the ways in which people and communities interpret their traumatic experiences and reconstruct the meaning of life, while continuing to deal with the impact of trauma. This finding echoes Heidegger's concept of the self as "being in the world" and Charles Taylor's "moral universe" as a context for defining meaning (Bracken, 2002; Taylor, 1989).

In trying to summarise the main points of this section, it can be asserted that results of the thematic narrative analysis show clear evidence that survivors' experience of the St. James Church massacre go beyond clinical conceptualisations of trauma. In saying this, the purpose is not to minimise the traumatic impact of the massacre, the intensity of PTSD symptoms or the importance of support and counselling in the aftermath of trauma. On the contrary, the three participants in the study reconstruct their trauma in relation to the event of massacre (as opposed to victims of state repression who experienced trauma as a prolonged continuous process). Furthermore, survivors of the massacre admitted they experienced PTSD symptoms and benefited from trauma debriefing, counselling and group healing workshops at various stages after the traumatic event. From this perspective, their understanding of trauma resembles the PTSD concept. However, the difference consists in the meaning attributed to these symptoms and the contextual, spiritual and social processes that mediate the understanding of suffering within this particular context. As it was argued previously, throughout their narrative reconstruction of the traumatic experience, survivors rarely talked about symptoms as being abnormal or that they made them dysfunctional. They rather considered them as part of human existence in a 'fallen world', which is not governed by 'good' and 'right'. In such a world, suffering is part of the ordinary and, thus, a consequence of the perverted nature of human beings. Most importantly, the support of other believers in the congregation and the faith in a coherent God, open new avenues for the understanding and transformation of suffering, a process supported by several constructionist theories (Lutz, 2003; Gergen & Gergen, 2003).

Finally, as was mentioned before, the understanding of trauma and the process of recovery cannot be separated, as they are closely interrelated, influencing each other and overlapping in the process of reconstructing the self after trauma. However, for reasons related to a clearer presentation of data and results, this chapter has dealt primarily with narrative understandings of trauma illustrated by victims of two types of political violence: (1) repressive state violence and (2) liberation movements' political violence. The next chapter will focus mainly on participants' recovery and narrative reconstruction of their life trajectories after trauma. However, the interplay between participants' present interpretations, past traumatic experiences and future aspirations will accompany the narrative analysis throughout the whole process, aiming at linking past, present and future. Before moving further though, it is important to draw some conclusions regarding the experience of trauma within the context of political violence in South Africa.

6.3. Concluding points

This chapter has focused primarily on analysing participants' narrative reconstructions of their trauma during apartheid. The main areas of investigation regarded: (1) the understanding and the impact of traumatic experience and (2) dimensions and meanings participants ascribed to their suffering. The results of the thematic narrative analysis highlighted some differences between victims of state repression and victims of liberation movements, in the ways in which they interpreted their traumatic experiences. Consequently, for clarity and ease of presentation, the findings were described in two distinct sections within the chapter while inserting linking comments along the process when necessary.

Regarding the experience of traumatic events, victims of state repression described their trauma as an engulfing process, not as a result of a single traumatic event as conceptualised in the PTSD. This could be explained by the ways in which the repressive apartheid ideology affected all areas of life for people living in black communities. They felt their whole life and the entire context in which they lived was traumatic. Most survivors of state repression reconstructed their trauma under apartheid as a continuous process beginning when they were born, growing up without their parents, living under constant terror of the police, suffering humiliation, poverty, detention, torture, losing dear ones and witnessing suffering in their families and communities.

In the case of the St. James Church massacre, although survivors experienced trauma as a result of a single traumatic event, their reconstructions did not focus merely on symptoms but were profoundly shaped by political, spiritual and social processes. In addition, even if at an individual level, people experienced symptoms of PTSD, the experience of trauma was more complex and it was further mediated by communal experiences, spiritual beliefs and meaning-making processes. These aspects will be further analysed in the next chapter, which will focus primarily on participants' recovery and narrative reconstruction of their life trajectories after trauma.

CHAPTER SEVEN

LIFE TRAJECTORIES AFTER TRAUMA AND PERSPECTIVES ON RECOVERY

In searching for a relevant metaphor to symbolise participants' experiences of suffering under apartheid and their journey towards healing, Arthur Frank's (1995) metaphor of the shipwreck seemed most appropriate for at least two reasons. First, most participants mentioned in their stories the idea of being wrecked or vandalised by the apartheid. Second, it fits well with local histories that describe ships that have been wrecked by the stormy waters of the Atlantic Ocean and shattered in many pieces on the Western coast of South Africa. The stories of apartheid trauma bear comparison in many ways with the troubles and drama of ships sailing through storms and being wrecked on the Cape of Storms, which paradoxically was also named the Cape of Good Hope. Could this contradiction represent the context that "both produces the wreckage and provides the resources for the reclaiming" of the self (Frank, 1995, p. 69)? Would this very paradox, born out of the coexistence of storms and hopes, be the nurturing cradle helping people to move from suffering to hope? For some people in this study it proved to be, for others it did not.

Participants' subjective experiences and interpretations of their life trajectories were diverse, and therefore, attempts to define the process of recovery turned out to be highly debatable and full of ambiguities. One of the main reasons is related to the multiple ways in which human beings create meaning and reconstruct their reality in the aftermath of trauma. People continuously reflect, create, revise and transform their perceptions about their *selves* and the world according to their values, beliefs, intentions and social realities (Adhikari, 2009; Bracken, 2002). All these facts emphasise the multidimensional nature of recovery and the need for a conceptual framework that will encompass both the commonality and the diversity of human experience.

The theoretical framework for understanding the process of recovery (as described in Chapter 2 and 3), has drawn on several approaches that validate the importance of relationships, resources, social context and culture in healing after trauma (Bracken, 2002; Herman, 2001; Landau et al., 2008; Luthar et al., 2000; Tedeschi et al., 1998). As was observed in the research literature, the process of recovery contains several concepts, which are also included in the definition of other concepts such as resilience and posttraumatic growth. Although the three terms (recovery, resilience and growth) are defined as distinct, their definitions and mechanisms incorporate overlapping sub-concepts such as positive adjustment, positive developmental outcomes, good coping strategies, positive perceptions about the self and good relationships with others and their context. Moreover, since most of the theories include Western concepts, several studies have emphasised the importance of a more cultural and contextual understanding of recovery (Ungar, 2008; Pals & McAdams, 2004).

In this work, the analysis of life trajectories in the aftermath of trauma has commenced with a broader understanding of recovery as a process of making meaning of one's self, others and the world (Brison, 2002; Bracken, 2002; Frank, 1995; Summerfield, 2002; Taylor, 1989). In order to proceed towards more concrete aspects of recovery, the analysis has drawn primarily on Braken's contextual approach, psychosocial and multisystemic approaches (Landau et al., 2008) as well as on conceptualisations of resilience and growth (Luthar et al., 2000; Pals & McAdam, 2004; Ungar, 2008). As some concepts overlap, the resulting conceptual framework used in this work to understand participants' journeys to recovery is described through the following main aspects: (1) constructions of the *self* (perceptions of the self, feelings, personal resources, qualities, purpose, aspirations, personal beliefs, values, etc.), (2) relationships with others (family, friends, trust, interracial relationships, forgiveness, reconciliation, etc) and (3) perceptions of the world and context (perceptions of a current social, political and economic context, community and culture).

Based on participants' narrative constructions in the three main domains mentioned above (perceptions about the self, relationships with others and perceptions of the context), the analysis revealed patterns that clustered around three main types of trajectories after trauma. They were tentatively designated in the following way: (1) "Feeling at home in the world", (2) "Still searching for significance" and (3) "Giving-up the journey". These categories do not have rigid delimitations and the decision to place participants in a certain category is tentative and artificial. However, these categories describe how people see themselves in the process of recovery, their relative positions at various times in their lives, their coping mechanisms and the factors that may have enhanced or impeded the process of recovery. In so doing, however, the purpose is not to minimise participants' individual experiences but rather to emphasise the variety of *voices* and interpretations that come together to shape various social constructs of human reality. As it will become apparent, recovery is not understood as the end of the process but rather as a continuous journey in which achievements and struggles are interwoven as an integral part of human experience.

The analysis of each narrative in the sample provided unique features regarding participants' experiences and their meaning-making process after trauma. However, what seemed to be central to all narratives was people's particular ways of repairing what trauma had destroyed in their lives, whether their trauma was related to the experience of torture and detention, a fractured identity, the loss of a dear one, losing limbs, a burned house or shattered life aspirations. This shows that the recovery process is profoundly linked with survivors' ways of interpreting their trauma and the ways in which they succeeded in *repairing* what was damaged through trauma by either redeeming or transforming it into something new. Drawing again on the metaphors used in illness narratives from Frank's (1995) *The Wounded Storyteller*, such a process would mean "repairing the wreckage" and "redrawing the map" of one's life.

The three main categories reflect participants' narrative constructions of their selves and their relationships with the world in which they currently live. Each category offers both commonalities as well as distinct meanings attributed to the process of recovery. Survivors in the first category (six participants) described their life trajectories in a positive light, emphasising the growth, fulfilment, resilience and personal effectiveness experienced in the process of recovery (Rogobete, 2013). What distinguishes people in this group from others in the sample is the fact that they have found a means to *repair* or transform the destruction produced by trauma by reconstructing new meanings for their lives and by "feeling at home in the world".

Participants in the second category (eight participants) described their journey of recovery as a mixed process containing both victories and failures experienced in various areas of their lives. Unlike the first group of participants, they are still searching for significance and for new ways to reconstruct the meaning destroyed by trauma. In some ways, it could be said that "they still haven't found what they are looking for"[1] or in Heideggerian terms, they are not yet *comfortable* with "being in the

---

[1] This is a paraphrase inspired from U2's song "I still haven't found what I'm looking for"

world". Their lives have only been partially progressing, most of them still experiencing serious challenges in the present due to poverty, dealing with loss, physical and mental illness or family difficulties. However, they remain pro-active and engaged in the process, continuing to search for meaning by investing in their own development and others around them. Unlike the participants presented in the next category, they have not given up when confronted with adversities, but remained open and committed to explore new alternatives, thus still searching.

Hence, the third category of participants (six participants) described their life trajectories after trauma as mainly negative, constructing themselves as being overwhelmed with life's difficulties. Their discourse is saturated with negative elements conveying the message (both explicitly and implicitly) that they have not recovered and would *never* be able to recover from their trauma. Listening to their stories, the reader can feel an overall sense of sadness, disillusion and pessimism. Throughout their narratives, they construct themselves as angry, embittered and disappointed about the present situation and, unlike the previous category, they have given up searching for new meanings (Rogobete, 2013).

The three categories of survivors presented above echo Gill Straker's (1992) psychological profiles of the Leandra Township youth investigated three years after the incidents of political violence they experienced in 1986. In describing them as leaders, conformists and psychological casualties, she draws attention towards the ability of youngsters to develop resilience when confronted with violence and oppression. Moreover, with regard to the meaning-making processes taking place in the aftermath of trauma, the three life trajectories of survivors presented in this study may sound closer to Frank's (1995) illness stories (restitution narratives, chaos narratives and quest narratives) mentioned in chapter three. Although this work has not focused on the impact of illness in particular, most stories of survivors of apartheid repression include micronarratives of illness and pain whether this is of a physical or psychological nature. Facing terminal or chronic illness is quite traumatic, and similar to apartheid trauma, people may feel the need to embark on a journey of making meaning of suffering and life. The remainder of this chapter will analyse the three types of life trajectories by focusing on participants' experiences as constructed in their narratives and their multiple ways of making sense of their lives after trauma.

7.1. Feeling at home in the world

The narratives of all six participants in this category are stories of achievement embedded in sophisticated ways of making meaning of life after trauma. Although most of them lived in a traumatic context characterised by multiple traumatic events due to political violence, survivors found ways to overcome adversities and even develop strengths and new coping strategies. The stories of the six participants included in this category resemble the features of progressive narratives embodied in a moral and spiritual discourse that contains predominantly positive events, characters and plots. The narrative plot develops more or less on the following line: "I was suffering… but then I worked hard to overcome difficulties… and I succeeded beyond expectations". The larger parts of the narrative text include micronarratives of success and progress that concentrate mainly on present and future situations and less on the past traumatic events. Particularly characteristic is the narrative tone of various evaluative statements and moral examples meant to construct positive perceptions of the self and an active engagement with the world in which the participants live.

The six participants in this category are currently between 44 and 73 years old (mean of 53 years) and, with one exception, they experienced trauma when they were between 14 to 25 years old. In terms of gender, three are women and three are men, out of whom four persons are Coloured, one is Black and one is White. In the present, they all have good socio-economic status, education and profession and none of them lives in township. Their health is generally good, excepting some physical difficulties related to old age and permanent disability as a result of political violence. The central themes emerging from the analysis of the six narratives highlight the ability of survivors to find new meanings in life, to build their relationships and to constructively engage with their context. These aspects, in some instances involved the possibility of redeeming the damage caused by trauma or transforming the suffering into something meaningful. This process was related in participants' narratives to constructive ways of coping with adversity, accessing available resources and support and, more importantly, developing a conceptual framework that gives meaning and purpose to the survivor's life. These themes will be analysed further by looking at the processes that come together to construct participants' understanding of their life trajectory after trauma.

The transformed self

A common theme across all six narratives included in this category is the success and achievements experienced by participants throughout their lives after trauma. Considered by various researchers as positive outcomes in the process of recovery, these constructs represent important elements in survivors' process of defining meaning of their selves and the world in which they live. There is clear evidence that participants in this category define themselves in positive terms. They display their identities emphasising their strengths, success and achievements, situating themselves in contrast with people who do not possess such qualities. They seem fully aware of the victimising connotation inferred through the victim label and prefer to call themselves survivors instead of victims. As Fowzia describes herself:

I am very strong, I'm a survivor, I can take anything! I helped many people. Other people become morbid, depressed, depending on tablets to make them sleep, tablets to wake them up. I'm not that way, I'm not that way! I find means of getting stronger because my faith is strong and I won't allow anybody to diminish my mind. Most of the time, I try my best to be the person that I am.

In similar ways Thembi refuses to be a victim, defining herself as a "*fighter*", highlighting the negative implications of the victim's status and the self's personal responsibility and agency to rise beyond this status. As she said, "*I don't want to be a victim. All my life I've been a fighter, because if you see yourself as a victim you never do anything because you always give excuses for what is happening to you. We all have been victimised but we don't have to stay there. It's not a good place to be.*" When asked what made her a fighter she replied: "*It's knowing who you are, knowing that you can do better than that. Whatever you do at that time, always trying to see what is it about me? How can I stretch myself, never be satisfied... I can walk, talk but find what is it that is about yourself.*"

Both discourses echo Frank's (1995) idea of "resisting the silence" that suffering imposes on people (p. 182). It becomes clear that through their resistance, Fowsia and Thembi found a voice, which made their suffering useful in becoming a living testimony for others. In a similar vein, Patrick is able to make connections between his involvement in the political struggle and the present benefits in terms of his ability to develop resilience:

I think this phase of being involved in the protests catapulted me into being more confident, more resilient, standing up for what I believed in. I stood up for people, I gave these moving speeches. And so this projected me into a whole new paradigm. I was confident enough, I could hold myself, people were listening to what I was saying. I spoke with authority without forcing my opinion on anyone. This has taught me invaluable skills in that the path that I am on in terms of my reconstruction was good. I had learnt such a lot out of my years in advocacy that I thought part of my healing would be catapulted further into teaching where I could be a model for the kids of how I've overcome barriers.

His reconstruction of the self is based on a coherent connection between his hero-self in the political struggle against apartheid, his confidence as a positive outcome in the present and his future ideal to become an example of resilience for the younger generation. In a similar vein, Shaheed unassumingly described his professional trajectory: *"I applied; I got the job and started my contract with them in June 2002. While teaching, I finished my teacher diploma. Afterwards I did my Masters and in the second year I got permanent employment with the university and after eight years I've got full tenureship".* His discourse displays a strong sense of mastery and self-efficacy through progressive actions and accomplishments.

One of the most important aspects regarding the ways in which participants in this category rebuilt their selves concerns the development of constructive coping skills. An important role in this process was played by an individual's ability to access internal and external resources and to pursue higher goals. Personal qualities and talent were considered by survivors an important resource in dealing with the impact of trauma and a way of creating new meanings in life. These attributes together with positive perceptions about the *self* have been considered important elements in the construction of resilience and posttraumatic growth (Tedeschi et al., 1995; Ungar, 2008).

As was observed in people's narratives, the way to developing good coping has been paved with great effort and mixed feelings. For example, Thembi expressed the struggle, loneliness and confusion she experienced in the process of finding meaning. Art became her *"escape"* and *"shelter"*:

You can be alone in the fight because you cannot express yourself, sometimes you don't know what you really want and you try to find what you really want. My art became an escape, it gave me shelter. I didn't have good schooling, good academic skills. I dropped out of school but I always felt there was nothing I could do without having good education, good family structures. I can give to other people. I felt I had that gift that I can give to other people.

Her words clearly show how the self is rebuilt and paradoxically enriched by giving to others, a fact that supports the relational dimension of the self (Ricoeur, 1992; Taylor, 1989).

Another important step for participants in developing good coping skills was to refuse passivity and victimisation. As Patrick said: *"I was not given many opportunities, but (…) I was not going to blame the legacy of apartheid or to be marginalised."* Mandy also described her attitude in the aftermath of losing her mother in the St. James Church massacre: *"I didn't have any sense of fear. I would go in the middle of the night by car in Mitchell's Plain. I would not live like a prisoner of my life. This incident will not stop me to live my life."* Such attitudes reflect a strong sense of agency and a belief in the ability to change life events and to set up personal goals. As Patrick reflected: *"I set up goals and directions for myself, things I wanted to accomplish because I didn't want to be a product of my legacy. I wanted to establish a legacy."* Thembi also remembers how she refused to listen to the voice inside that said *"You are inferior, you are nothing"* and decided to honour instead the voice saying *"you are something, you can become something".*

Pursuing and fulfilling goals (not only setting goals) was also mentioned by most participants as an important aspect of their successful life trajectories. Rhetorically, Patrick reflected*: "I was going to pursue this at whatever cost. I have already pursued other things in my life and the cost was nearly my life. So, why would I now hold back on my life in terms of shaping direction?"* In defining his coping strategies, he expressed several beliefs: (1) good decisions have to be followed by actions *("when I make up my mind about something then I go all out for it")*, (2) there are important lessons that can be learnt from mistakes *("I see failure as a growth process")*, (3) one needs to assume risks in life *("If I hadn't taken the risk, I wouldn't have accomplished what I needed to accomplish")* and (4) failure is not an end but *"another stepping stone towards getting to where I needed to go".* According to Bonano's (2004) theory of resilience, these characteristics make Patrick an ideal example of hardiness - a concept considered to be one of the "multiple and sometimes unexpected pathways to resilience" (p. 25).

Building relationships

Political violence and oppression under apartheid affected not only individuals but their relationships with others as well. Family and community relationships were shattered by job segregation, deportations, harassment, detentions and deaths. As a result, individual and communal trauma is largely represented by feelings of betrayal, loss, guilt, shame and mistrust in relationships. In order to live meaningful lives again, most survivors described their attempts to address such feelings and rebuild their relationships (Herman, 2001; Brison, 2002). This is congruent with Gergen's (2003) view that meaning is created in the context of relationships. In addition, Herman emphasised that healthy relationships and social support are essential elements in the process of recovery after trauma.

In Thembi's case, for example, managing her pain meant dealing with two significant relationships in her life: her relationship with her daughter and with her mother. On the one side she had to address her guilt for not being more present in her relationship with her daughter and on the other hand she had to deal with her sadness over the loss of her aging mother whom she never got to know very well because she had to work far from their place. Reflecting on the way she tried to make meaning of her significant relationships, she wrote a play of which she said:

> *I am a grandmother, I have reconciled with myself, I have reconciled with the situation. I have made my daughter understand the reasons for whatever she feels for me for not being with her when she was little. I wrote that play because I wanted to deal with my pain. My mother came to see my play for the first time because I have never spoken about it. My mother saw for the first time how as a young girl I was always longing to see her. She never knew my pain, I also never knew her pain...that was a way for me to reconcile with myself and forgive my parents for not being there for me, and try to put it behind.*

In order to cope and deal with her pain, Thembi wrote the play *The Woman in Waiting*. It is noteworthy how this creative engagement with past trauma empowered her to meaningfully convey childhood pain to her mother and regret to her daughter, a process that naturally involved the three women in an authentic transgenerational *rite de passage*. This process implied reconciliation with herself and the extension of forgiveness to her parents and asking forgiveness from her daughter. Whether she was forgiven or not seems less important for Thembi at this stage.

Relationships are also the context and foundation for self-construction and definition of personal identity (Ricoeur, 1992; Taylor, 1989). The participants in this category described their relationships with others in positive terms, highlighting both the importance of receiving and giving in a relationship. They invest energy and time in meaningful relationships, whether in their families or community and are influenced by their interactions with others. Participants' micronarratives include examples of various relationships in which the *self* is defined through the eyes of the *other* or in comparison with others, by highlighting personal qualities, which contribute to the development of a positive image of the self.

As can be seen in Patrick's micro-narrative, his perceptions about others are closely linked with perceptions about the self: "*I respect others because I have self respect, I respect myself. So I will respect someone else, the beggar, the vagrant, I will sit on the pavement and have a conversation with a vagrant or a beggar*". He goes on describing his encounter with the beggar and although the story's content is about the beggar, the latent meaning of the story is structured in fact to create positive images of the self. In his story, Patrick highlights some of his actions whilst trying to gain access to the beggar's world: "*That's why I sat down. I said, hold on, and I went into the shop and bought the two of us something to eat and drinks and gave it to him and I got down into his world. I was on equal level with him, I sat on the pavement and one of my students came past unbeknown to me and looked and I didn't know the student was there.*" It is noticeable that a discourse about respect for *another* becomes gradually the vehicle for a positive construction of the self as compassionate, caring, respectful, good listener, provider, showing dignity and interacting with people rejected by society. This process echoes Frank's (1995) view on storytelling being directed towards "another just as much as it is for oneself. (…) The moral genius of storytelling is that each, teller and listener, enters the space of the story for the other. Telling stories (…) attempts to change one's own life by affecting the lives of others" (p. 18).

Patrick's discourse is embedded in the political and economic realities of the South African context characterised by social and economic inequalities. Based on his experience of marginalisation, he was able to "enter" the world of the beggar and relate to him as an equal. Normalising the beggar's experience as a transitory life stage, he instils hope and trust in the beggar's ability to change ("*is only a phase of your life, it cannot be permanent unless you want it to be permanent*"). This story is also an example of an attempt to repair and transform what was destroyed by the apartheid trauma. Since Patrick's trauma was much related to marginalisation, deportation, feelings of inferiority and rejection, he finds meaning in engaging with people who feel stigmatised or have difficulties making progress in life. Moreover, his emphasis on "being equal" reveals another attempt at repairing current socio-economic inequalities in society.

This is, once again, confirming Frank's (1995) definition of listening. He considered that "one of the most difficult duties as human beings is to listen to the voices of those who suffer (…) Listening is hard, but it is also a fundamental moral act; to realize the best potential in postmodern times requires an ethics of listening. (…) Listening for the other, we listen for ourselves" (p. 25).

In addition, this micronarrative is also used by Patrick to share his identity and beliefs to teach the younger generation important values in life such as respect, dignity, social responsibility, equality and care for the marginalised. The following passage clearly reflects these constructs:

> *I said this to the kids, if we don't show dignity to people who we don't think deserve dignity, our existence is merely an existence. I don't want to be friends with people because of putting them on the same scale or level as I am. I am not going to learn anything. I need to come down, go up, come down. There needs to be an interaction between the levels, otherwise I will never know how other people feel. I think that is part of my background that somehow roots me, that keeps me where I need to be, because I am able to show an affinity toward those that are disenfranchised and marginalised because I come from there.*

Furthermore, social support was constructed in participants' narratives in terms of significant relationships with a family member or mentor and as a collective initiative coming from a group or community. Reflecting on her own life trajectory, Thembi said: "*I had good friends and my family supported me with their love*". In situations in which family support was not available, some participants mentioned the support of a mentor. In Patrick's case, in the absence of his mother, he described how his mentor was crucial in supporting him to go beyond his limits in developing his identity. As Patrick recalled, "*my mentor used to tell me, Patrick, there are certain gifts that you have that other people would love to have. (…) Who you are is not shaped by the opinions of people. Who you are is who you have decided to be and you have come through all of that.*" This quote clearly highlights the importance of healthy relationships with an adult who can nurture a wounded identity as well as modelling a pro-active attitude in dealing with hurt (Herman, 2001; Luthar et al., 2000).

Although participants in this category construct their relationships with families and friends in positive terms, they still find it difficult to trust others in new relationships. As Shaheed described it, "*for me is not easy to trust. Trust has to be won. The experiences I've been through are very tough and made me not to trust others. But on the other hand I make friends easily. I speak to anybody but to move from friends to trust is not easy. I will trust people in general. I believe most people are good but in terms of trust it takes me a while and a person would have to prove himself or herself.*" The difficulty in new relationships rests upon a sense of cautiousness when relating to new people. In a similar vein, talking about her relationships with others, Mandy said: "*to a certain extent, maybe subconsciously I'm cautious. I'm not somebody that if you meet I will give you the whole story of my life. I'm usually quiet and listen and see where are you at and where you are coming from and depending on how much you give I will reciprocate that.*"

Another aspect that was raised by participants was the issue of interracial relationships. Most participants in this category declared that they find it easy to relate to people of a different race. Some have explicitly mentioned that the skin colour or race do not play any role in the way they relate to others. In Patrick's view this is again closely related to how he constructs his own race identity. As he mentioned, "*I am comfortable in my skin. I don't have hang ups with the skin colour, because I am dealing with who you are on the inside*". In similar ways, Mandy finds it easy to relate to people of a different race, as she believes that "*if a person of a certain race will treat me strangely, I wouldn't automatically think that it is because I'm Coloured. Maybe they had a difficult upbringing, difficult experiences in their life or they just had a bad day*". However, because Thembi lived under apartheid longer than Mandy and Patrick, she sometimes finds herself automatically adopting an inferior place in her encounter with White people. As she remembered:

I was walking with my granddaughter and a White person comes across our way and I suddenly stopped. I always have been used to be the one who gives way especially to white persons. I had that in my mind and I stopped subconsciously, but she just went straight, crossing in front of that white woman. I said to her, why did you cross the way of that woman and she said: "Grandma, the other people also have eyes and they can see I'm coming. They must give me way." We have democracy now, but still I have these issues at the back of my mind.

Yet Thembi is committed to relate to people "*as equals, no matter whether they are White, Black or Red*". She enjoys living in a white area, being married to a White man and talking daily with her White neighbours. As she described it, "*I live in a very white Afrikaans suburb. When I moved there… it was strange… I come from township where you know everybody and I moved to an area where you don't know anybody. I made a mission to know my neighbours and now I know everybody. I invite them to my shows. They are Afrikaans and we stop and talk on the streets...*" There is a sense of pride and joy in her statement showing her ability to go beyond the hurt of segregation - an enormous step towards growth and transformation (Pals & McAdams, 2004; Tedeschi et al., 1998).

Issues of forgiveness and reconciliation with perpetrators did not seem to play a major role in the participants' narrative reconstructions at this stage in their lives. However, when explicitly asked for their opinions, most participants in this category emphasised several aspects. In Thembi's view, reconciliation begins within one's self, between the self and your own feelings: "*reconciliation is about yourself reconciling with the situation you are dealing with. I'm reconciling with whom? Who I am reconciling with? I'm reconciling myself with my feelings, the way I feel about things. I'm doing it for myself, through how I deal with things, through how I tried to make people not to feel inferior and try not to put people in the same situation that I have been put.*" As she perceives it, reconciliation and forgiveness is a process and is reflected in one's daily life. In a similar vein, both Mandy and Patrick extended forgiveness even if they were not even asked for it. Mentioning the perpetrators of the St. James massacre, Mandy said: "*I've forgiven them even before the TRC. (...) My faith helped me to forget these people whether they asked or not for forgiveness.* Also, Patrick: "*Hatred was not going to give me victory. I told him (a White friend) I've made peace and I forgive you, even though you didn't perform the atrocity, you still represent the race and so I forgive you. He looked at me and started crying... if I am not able to do that, I will be bitter for the rest of my life.*" Once again, a participant's constructions reflect an ability to engage and be proactive in his ways of dealing with self, others and contextual realities, these aspects being further explored in the next section.

Engaging with contextual realities

It has been argued so far that the meaning-making process after trauma is closely related to the ways in which people make sense of their selves and relationships within the social, political and cultural context (Bracken, 2002; Bruner, 1990; Gergen, 2003, Summerfield, 2002). The *self*, the *other* and the context are interrelated aspects of human experience, which are simultaneously constructed in the process of meaning making. In their efforts to define what it means to "be in the world", people in this category made reference to their values and important beliefs about life, understanding of the economic and political context, current views on past traumatic experiences and views about the future (Bracken, 2002). Their discourse is embedded in the social, economic and political realities of their communities and society as a whole. As they socially construct their worlds, both strengths and shortcomings of the various contexts become integral parts of "being in the world".

For Fr. Lapsley the context in the aftermath of trauma was defined by "*prayer, love and support*", which nurtured his process of dealing with physical pain and subsequent permanent disability. As he sustains, this context provided the way for him "*to create a good response*" during recovery. Reflecting on his journey of healing, he believes that recovery started actually when he realised he had survived the bombed attack, thus becoming a "*failed assassination*". The worldwide support received in the aftermath of the attack was an acknowledgement of his pain, which enabled Fr. Lapsley to perceive the world as a caring and friendly place. As he recalled:

> *I think there was great family support, also from the Order, strong support from the liberation movement, from the ANC, from ordinary Zimbabwean people and from all hosts that kept flooding in from across the world from different cities. I had an amazing support from children. They sent me drawings and paintings, children from Zimbabwe, from Australia, children who told their stories and also did drawings. So they also played a part in my journey.*

Besides social support, Fr. Lapsley also mentioned the importance of a "*conceptual framework that enables you to make sense of what happened*". As he explains it "*being part of the struggle, you had this conceptual framework in which risk and death was a part of reality*". An assumed risk and living with the predictability of death had a mitigating effect on the negative impact of trauma, enabling him to access higher levels of meaning thus making sense of an, otherwise, senseless situation. In his search for meaning he had a breakthrough when he understood that in his suffering there was also a gain, something he did not have before the trauma: a new voice of a new self which was his new identity as a witness of his own pain and as a responsible storyteller witnessing "from inside" to others (Frank, 1995, p. 71). In Frank's terms, his story is the rebuilding of "the shipwreck", "the finding of a voice" and the "drawing of a new map" (p.53).

Participants in this group used the support strategically that was available from their families and in the external context. They creatively found ways to mobilise relatives in the extended family to offer support in applying for scholarships in order to fulfil their dreams of having higher education and eventually transcend racial and economic boundaries.

Currently, most of them are using their work or professions to express themselves and to bear witness to other people in their community about their success. Patrick recalls the moment when he became an English teacher: *"This was a very profound moment for me because I could become a catalyst in transforming young minds from where I came from"*.

In terms of perceptions about current contextual realities, most participants emphasised the importance of continuously engaging with the context in which one lives by assuming responsibility in relating to others and defining the social context. Thembi perceived it as a daily struggle as *"dealing with people in the world, there will always be things taking you back in that situation. Each time when you wake up you have to say: Ok, I'm going out in the world today and I don't know what is gonna come. Today I don't know who I am going to meet"*. Taken in the context of her discourse, Thembi's words do not express social anxiety but rather an attitude of self-awareness within a social context that is still recovering from interracial conflicts. She also celebrates her responsibility and ability to change contextual realities. She claims that *"change doesn't come from government, the change comes from us"*, in this way showing a strong belief in her ability to change life events.

However, social change in the context of transition depends on multiple interacting factors. The intersection between identity, race and economic inequality is evident in Fowzia's perception of current contextual concerns. She emphasises the Coloured people's dilemma in constructing their identities as *"not being White enough"* during apartheid and *"not being Black enough"* in the present. She boldly asserts that *"most of the people we voted in parliament are doing the same thing as the apartheid government. I call it reverse apartheid"*. To support her arguments, she provides evidence of corruption and recent facts surfacing among the political elite.

It could be observed in most narratives, that being engaged in the social context did not mean only expressing positive views but also openly addressing issues of social concern. The slow change regarding the issue of poor housing conditions in black communities makes Shaheed affirm that *"apartheid is still there, townships are still there. If the ANC will be sincere, they will do something about townships, try to put people together..."* Being disappointed with the current economic and political situation is arguably understandable in the context of participants' personal investment and traumatic experiences in the struggle against apartheid. One the one hand, this aspect supports Crossley's (2000) idea of the self as being constructed through "historical and social structure" (p. 21). On the other hand, it highlights Taylor's (1989) concept of a "moral universe" as a context in which the self reflectively makes sense of what is "good" through responsible engagement with the world.

Furthermore, participants expressed how their values and worldviews relate to the context in which they live. For Patrick one of the greatest values is integrity which *"characterises who you are"* and *"loyalty is connected to that"*. In his view, human beings have a higher purpose and a greater destiny than the realm of animals. This means that *"our journey on earth must be in line with that purpose in order for us to get to that destiny"* otherwise *"our whole existence on earth would have been fruitless"*. Regarding his idea of a *"purposeful existence"*, Patrick believes that people *"are supposed to be making contributions, society must learn from you, you must give back to society. That distinguishes us from the animals. The animals basically have an existence, they can just exist but we have to exist more than the animals"*. In giving meaning to human existence and the world, he draws on his faith and spiritual beliefs: *"I think it has everything to do with my faith that I have. I strongly believe that we are a purpose-driven creation"*. For him, the spiritual dimension is not just another facet of the self but rather the transcendental framework in which all the other dimensions of the self (as caring, loving, capable, successful and forgiving) make sense and are able to draw their energy from. In addition, his solid conceptual framework highlights at least two meaning-making processes. First, it shows the close connection between individuals and society, stressing the importance of individuals meaningfully engaging and creating society and culture. Secondly, it gives a sense of temporal coherence in the narrative construction of the self across life, by linking past, present and future.

Views about the future were integral parts of people's understanding about the world. Participants in this category expressed both positive and ambivalent feelings about the future, placing their explanations within a context framed by direct causality between present daily work and future outcomes. As Thembi thinks, *"future is a day to day work. Is what I do today, that is going to affect my tomorrow. It is a day-to-day work. There are days when I feel optimistic about it. I feel that it must be something good that we're doing that we survived so far. I feel that we all have to do our work. We all have responsibilities as individuals"*. Although in her expression *"there are days when I feel optimistic"*, one can sense a shadow of ambivalence, still her reflection on the collective trajectory of human experience shows hope and trust in the process. This is reflected through the use of a past continuous tense that conveys continuity in the process, linking again the past (*"it must be something good that we were doing"*) with the present (*"that we've survived so far"*).

A more optimistic view about the future was expressed by Mandy who declared that she is not worried about the future. While some of her friends were thinking to move to New Zealand, she said: *"as for me and my husband this is our home. The grass is not always greener on the other side. God is in control whatever will happen. We will survive whatever will happen."* Mandy's statement (and actually her entire narrative) clearly shows a sense of hope and contentment with the world in which she lives. In this context, her values and spiritual beliefs work meaningfully together to create a purpose for her and her family. Patrick also highlighted the interplay between hope and finding solutions to problems: *"But this hope was inside of me and so part of my answer to the solution was my hope".* These findings are congruent with Bracken (2002) and Summerfield's (2002) view of recovery defined as the remaking of the practical aspects of life, which depending on people's individual experience, may involve multiple pathways as survivors continuously move across life.

Summing up, this category of life trajectories highlighted that survivors' making-meaning process included not only the development of resilience depicted through their abilities to function well in an adverse context; their narrative reconstructions showed that growth is also possible in the aftermath of long-term exposure to trauma. Using the shipwreck metaphor, it can be stated that not only were they able "to rebuild the shipwreck and redraw the map", but they built an even better ship. It can be noticed that Tedeschi et al.'s (1995) main constructs of posttraumatic growth have been confirmed in this analysis through the presence of: (1) positive self-concept, (2) good interpersonal relationships and (3) spiritual development. In addition, Pals and McAdams's (2004) narrative dimensions of posttraumatic growth have also been obvious in survivors' stories through (1) their expressed ability to integrate negative effects of trauma (*"I would not live like a prisoner of my life"* - Mandy) and (2) the positive ending of their narratives (*"I think I realised it for me that the journey was a journey of survival, to return to give my love as fully, joyfully and completely as possible. That would be my way."*– Fr. Lapsley).

Furthermore, these narratives also displayed new elements that underline growth in the process of recovery from trauma. First, not only that survivors' narratives had a positive ending but the stories as whole units contained predominantly positive language structures and a sense of hope and optimism. This becomes obvious when compared with the rest of the narratives in the sample. Second, agency and the "finding of a new voice" were also important components of people's particular pathways to growth, thus creating space for the transformation of a marginal, dehumanised self into a positive one – a self that has a new voice and is in control of his/her destiny. Finally, another contextually-specific component of growth was the ability to forgive and reconcile with oneself and with perpetrators. The narrative reconstructions pointed out that participants' ability to forgive facilitated their growth and transformation of the self. However, other narratives showed various challenges in the process of recovery as will be emphasised next.

7.2. Still searching for significance

As seen in the previous section, the stories of success and growth had a distinctive feature in terms of predominantly positive aspects, extensive descriptions of the self in everyday life and a strong sense of agency and control of life events. The eight stories included in the second category differ considerably from the previous six narratives in terms of both the form and content. First, listening to the narratives, one can sense the mix of life events depicting struggles, attempts, failures and victories that characterise the process of recovery after trauma. Participants highlight the achievements (and even growth) they have experienced in some life domains, but are still struggling to make sense of other areas in their lives. The narrative plot may sound like this: "I was suffering but after a while I got better in this area but in that area I'm still struggling... However, I keep searching...".

Second, their narratives are more concerned with disappointments with the current contextual realities rather than the reconstruction of the self and relationships with others. Third, regarding temporal framework, the stories are not chronological, nor progressive. Past and present events are interwoven together following an evaluative logic (*"I'm struggling now because in the past I suffered this..."*). Finally, an aspect more similar to previous narratives is participants' engagement and commitment in their meaning-making process. The overall message their narratives convey is that although in some areas of life they still experience suffering, it is still important to remain committed to search for the *missing pieces* that would bring clarity to the life puzzle. Similarly, in the light of the *shipwreck* metaphor, it can be asserted that these survivors, although struggling to repair the ship, they remain committed to search for new *methods* and *techniques* to rebuild the ship and redraw the map.

In terms of demographic characteristics, the eight participants included in this category are between 41 and 55 years, four women and four men: five Black, two Coloured and one White. They are all employed or are involved in self-sustained activities and one person is a pensioner. All five

Black participants still live in a township: three persons have a poor economic situation and two participants have a moderate economic situation. They experienced various traumatic events such as, arrests, beatings, police harassment, detention, torture, being shot at, loss or permanent damage of a child, family member or friend. All participants reported the experience of psychological symptoms in the aftermath of trauma such as flashbacks, nightmares, anxiety, depression, dissociation, sleep disturbance and even attempted suicide and ideation. Some participants declared the recurrence of symptoms and even currently still struggle with disability, chronic pain and illness (diabetes and high blood pressure) and depression. However, as they all emphasised, such symptoms do not impede work and they continue with their lives. They see these symptoms as part of their life: some participants have accessed medical treatment or psychological counselling but others preferred to deal with them by drawing on other types of resources such as faith and spiritual beliefs, friends, family and community. The next section will analyse the eight stories included in this category by highlighting the social processes taking place in the reconstruction of the self, relationships and the community.

The inquisitive self

Survivors in this category constructed their identity trajectory by highlighting their continuous quest and commitment to the meaning-making process. Both positive and negative aspects encountered in this journey are major constructs of their selves. The positive elements of the self were attributed to good coping mechanisms, agency, relationships and worldview, while the negative ones were related to health and economic status, as well as to injustice and societal inequalities. In order to achieve meaning in the aftermath of apartheid trauma, participants' life trajectories depict their struggles and movement between these areas of life, which work together creating meaning for the survivor's self and his/her world. A distinct identity characteristic is the inquisitive attitude in dealing with life's polarities, paradoxes and antagonisms. The contrasting aspects in people's lives at an individual level mirror in fact the macroreality of the South African society in which opposing aspects coexist and contrasts and inequalities are part of the ordinary ways of life (Kaminer & Eagle, 2010).

Mixed perceptions of the self are present in all eight narratives. For example in Sindiswa case, her narrative constructions display a strong sense of agency and good coping in spite of life adversities. This aspect is highlighted in the first sentence of her story, *"I think that the way I grew up motivated me and prepared me, giving me the strength to face the situations the way it comes to me. I grew up as a child of one parent with a single father. My mother abandoned me. I often thought what kind of mother is she? She abandoned me. What can I expect now?"* Also within the context of current difficulties, she highlights the importance of personal responsibility and pro-active attitudes as opposed to passivity, which inevitably leads to poverty:

> *I think now in general people are misinterpreting democracy and are abusing their rights. People are now sitting and relaxing beyond redemption thinking that now we have what we've been fighting for... Harasss! We are not!!! Otherwise we are being embarked in poverty. We need to say: "I have to take myself out of it. Nobody is going to take me out of it, except me!*

She presents herself as capable to take care of her family and to keep a job. However, she is unhappy about the attitudes of her children and the younger generation in general, who *"like to go out on Friday night, to parties, to the shebeen".* Also, although Sindiswa has a house in the township, she still needs money to finish it inside and buy some basic furniture. Her major concern and sadness is related to the crime, poverty and promiscuity of the context in which she has to raise her children. While we were having the interview she received a call from the local police station, announcing that her teenage daughter was threatened with a gun in their house but she managed to call the police. Also her son is currently in jail. In Sindiswa's words: *"He is 24 now and is in jail. He is usually such a good boy, nice, cute, wears nice clothes. He preached in school and was going to Germany because he plays football so well. But he messed with some bad boys".* There is clear evidence that Sindiswa's self-fulfilment is closely related to the well-being of her children. Although her past and present perceptions about herself are positive, yet future projections of *self* and family members are characterised by worries, disappointment and doubt (*"I'm in an island of doubt",* she said).

In a similar way, (and this also is a characteristic of political activists) Thulani's story shows how his heroic past, pride and agency contributed to the development of positive constructions of the self. Although he was seriously tortured and spent nine years in prison on Robben Island, he embarked while still in prison on a meaning-making process following a particular pathway to recovery. As he described the process: *"I asked myself a question when I started this process. I had two things: they would kill me or I will go to jail. They didn't kill me and they took me to jail. Luckily, I had good leaders among ourselves, people who would give us positive advice all the time. That's how I started to see the light. I started to say, no, revenge is not the best thing. That's how I was able to move forward".* From "no revenge", Thulani was able to take further steps, realising that his personal healing should begin with forgiving himself and his perpetrators - a liberating feeling that facilitated the way for him to develop healthy relationships with others and his family. He admits, *"it was not easy but what I tried to do was to heal myself, to look at me and have a different attitude towards my perpetrators and two former guards. Then I said, I must forgive me. This is how I started. That's why I'm able to work within my family, although it's still hard."*

Regarding the negative part of Thulani's story, it was interesting to notice that while recalling torture memories, Thulani did not display strong emotions. Yet when he talked about his father's permanent disability due to being shot eight times, *"just because he was the father of a 'terrorist'"*, Thulani was unable to continue the interview for a few minutes due to strong negative emotions and crying. It visibly reflects in some ways the incompleteness of his meaning-making process due to "unfinished business" and feelings of guilt and responsibility for his father's suffering. Moreover, he feels himself trapped in a type of "double-bind" situation. On the one hand, he wants to enjoy the freedom and move forward in the healing process but on the other hand, his father is a constant reminder of an unjust and cruel past that continuously creates psychological pressure and feelings of inadequacy. Describing his father's current situation, Thulani said:

> *It was very painful. He survived but he was never the same. He is in a wheelchair for the rest of his life with permanent damage. Sometimes I can't afford his medication. I try by all means to give as much as I can but sometimes I fail because medication is too expensive. One thing he doesn't like is to go to a public hospital where he has to wait in long queues. He always says "I'm in this chair because you put me in this chair." He always brings these things forward and my mother tries to give him as much support as she can. The people who did that are still OK...* (crying, not able to talk).

In a similar vein Monica describes her current struggles with permanent personal disability (she was hit with a gun and as a result developed a neurological problem) and her daughter's disability (due to teargas when she was a baby). Her unfinished journey of recovery is related to the lack of reparations after the collapse of apartheid and her mother and sister's disappearance. As she described it:

I've never seen my mother. My mother was having my sister in her arms when she was running form the police. They both disappeared. I don't even know if they killed them or what happened to them. If I can get a bone from her and my sister and bury that... this will calm me. If this will never happen, I will always have this emptiness. Even if I say that I may be able to forgive but I cannot forget this until I got the reparation, until I get the bones of my mother and my sister to bury them.

Monica's words reflect how the meaning-making process is strictly connected to the suffering produced by the disappearance of her mother and sister and the lack of reparations for her complex loss, including her permanent disability and that of her daughter. This is a serious issue within the South African context, as many disappearances have not been solved and the TRC's suggested reparations have been significantly reduced by the government (Chapman & Van der Merwe, 2008; Truth and Reconciliation Commission, 2003).

Such complex losses coupled with the lack of symbolic or financial reparations contribute to the belief that the present benefits are insignificant compared with survivors' personal investment in the political struggle against apartheid. This is obviously reflected in their inner conflicts, feelings of frustration and disappointment with their current situation. Although they have been working hard by getting several jobs in order to take care of their families and also continuing their education, they perceive their progress as being slow compared with their efforts. As Sipho described his situation: *"I still live in a shack with four kids and my wife and I fought for the freedom of this country. I'm still studying now and I am in my forties. I'm still studying because I didn't have time to study when I was young because I was fighting for this country. (…) I lost many years of my life hiding. I didn't come to Cape Town to look for jobs but I was hiding and until today I'm here. I don't feel free even today."*

However, he has positive perceptions about his self and the others, including interracial relationships: *"I'm quite fine... I'm capable of sitting with White people... but we are still suffering. I thought that I'm that sort of person... I don't hate people, I don't hate anybody but I hate the system. There are lots of people in townships who lost everything... I was one of the leaders in the liberation movement... and I'm still living in a township. There is no progress."* His current suffering is embedded in the social and political context, being profoundly related to economic inequalities and his inability to make sense of present social realities in the light of past struggle for political freedom (Summerfield, 2002).

A mixed life trajectory in the aftermath of trauma was also noticed in the stories of two survivors of the St. James Church massacre. Both Ross and Liesl have reported several positive aspects in their process of healing after trauma, yet the analysis of their narratives reveals several difficulties related to the meaning of their present situation. For example in Liesl's case, dissociation and avoidance helped her to cope in the aftermath of the massacre. As she remembered: "*I started to avoid anything that had to do with that. I didn't go to the TRC, I didn't watch TV, I didn't listen to radio... I think God is the one who judges and I didn't feel angry at them or God... I don't recall feeling angry at anybody. I just felt extremely sad but not angry.*" However, by isolating herself from the political past, ("*It was just a coping mechanism. Even today, I don't know anything about it. This is how it has been for me. I stay in my little bubble...*"). Liesl has not managed to make sense of her own self and others since the defining context is missing a temporal dimension as well as an understanding of the "unfinished business" of the past. She described her paranoid symptoms related to living and "being-in-the-world": "*But all the trauma that happened in my life made me become very paranoid. I cannot walk in my area or get out of the car by myself. I'm always conscious about what is happening around. Even with my kids, I always see the negative first instead of the positive*". However, by drawing on her spiritual beliefs she is able to remain hopeful and engaged in the process of making sense of her life: "*I see myself as a Christian and I'm thankful to God that He is in control*".

For Ross, the journey of "coming to terms as a White South African" is closely connected with White people's inability to assume responsibility for "*the evils of apartheid*". His difficulties are related both to the individual and collective dimension of his identity. Ross's narrative construction of the self is generally depicted in positive terms, emphasising attributes such as care, compassion, spiritual support and empathy for those who lost dear ones. Yet, he finds it difficult to deal with and make sense of personal and collective guilt. He finds himself in a conflicting inner space, stressed by an innate incongruence between positive values of the Christian faith and White people's denial of responsibility for apartheid. As he is trying to reflect:

> *I felt my own guilt as well. These three men* (the perpetrators) *were like this because if it weren't for the apartheid they wouldn't have had to make those decisions and I felt guilty that as a church minister I didn't speak more or have more to say. It was such an injustice that all of us in the clergy should have been in the forefront standing with the black people who have been oppressed and see, we never ever did that. Our theology was wrong which really complicates things enormously. At the end of the day, there are reasons but there are not excuses. At the end of the day we*

*have to take responsibility and until you do, there is **really no way
forward**. I think the ongoing hurt with Black people is because so many
Whites wouldn't take responsibility. Many Whites would just say "we
weren't even aware", that's … having been on the other side now with the
St. James massacre, for those who are guilty of social evil, to say "oh, we
weren't really aware", it doesn't help the situation at all. You need to be
bold enough to say "we messed it up, we messed it up. There is actually no
excuse. There are reasons, it was a very complicated thing, but we were
wrong. That has to be said, you know! I've learned those kinds of lessons
going through the TRC… In that sense, lot of goodness came out of this, I
feel, for me personally. So, that helped me come to terms as a White South
African.*

His discourse conveys a sense loneliness and alienation from his own
race due to his conflicting ways of understanding the current socio-
political context in South Africa. His political discourse is deeply rooted in
daily contextual realities, highlighting White people's individualism and
their inability to assume responsibility for the wrong doings of the past. In
his view, taking responsibility in honesty is the only *"way forward"*:
*"Instead of being defensive all the time and instead of trying to justify our
silence, if White people would say "we were part of a very wrong system,
we did benefit economically in another way from a very unjust system and
we didn't fight it nearly as much as we should have".* Such open attitudes,
in his view, would create a different type of human encounter, which
would facilitate the process of interracial reconciliation in South Africa:

*I think many Black people would be healed in the process if Whites
generally took that line. Instead of saying: 'you know, we weren't in power
at that time, we didn't know, we were just living our lives', which is just
true… but you see, there is a communal element which us Whites in South
Africa tend to downplay. And the reason why we think we can opt out of
the community responsibility is because it is typical of the West around the
world: it's this huge emphasis on individualism today and community is
not a big thing…So, it explains how psychologically, people can distance
themselves from an evil even if they benefited from it and even if they
didn't fight the evils of the apartheid. See, individualism allows you to do
that and again I feel guilty because as a Christian man, the Bible says we
should be big on community. We should have learned better.*

His narrative construction of the self highlights a sense of regret, guilt
and sadness. The *"communal element"* of his identity, which he holds
important, has been hurt by people of his race opting out of *"the
community responsibility"*. According to Ricoeur's (1992) definition of the
self, Ross's difficulty may reside in the interplay between his idem-identity

(the sense of sameness with others) and ipse-identity (the uniqueness of the self). His ipse-self is actually in conflict with the attitude of mainstream White people's in South Africa that seem to prefer to remain silent bystanders, since almost twenty years after the collapse of apartheid, there have not been many public apologies for the evils of apartheid. Although some White people from his congregation may agree with him, his attitude and behaviour remains largely unpopular, which increases his feelings of alienation both from his race and congregation. As part of his search for meaning, Ross left St. James Church and is currently a lecturer at a theological college. He finds it fulfilling to invest his time and energy in the younger generation of students from various parts of the African continent. He has been struggling with a clinical depression, which started as a fatigue syndrome, associated with flashbacks and nightmares of the massacre. However, his family's support and meaningful relationships with students and the college community seem to be significant protective factors in his recovery process. The next two sections will deal with ways in which participants in this category tried to rebuild their relationships with others and their context.

Social support and family recovery

Most survivors in the second category did not benefit from social support and a safe context in the aftermath of trauma. Even after the collapse of apartheid, the Black participants continued to live with their families in townships, being subjected to crime and poverty. The fact that survivors (even in the absence of support and a safe context) have succeeded in developing constructive coping skills and have been functional and capable of taking care of their families is a clear indication of strength and resilience amidst adversities. However, some damaged or broken relationships could never be recovered. For example, Monica was not able to recover her relationship with her husband and also she had no support apart from her older daughter. She managed to raise her children on her own and strengthen family relationships by involving her daughters in her work: *"From very early they started to be part of what I´m doing, selling second hand clothes and they also got something for them"*.

Similarly, Sindiswa has been a single mother and raised seven children on her own while continuing to fight for former victims' rights through the Khulumani Support Group. Trying to remember anybody that was helpful towards her, she said: *"Nobody… I cannot identify any… not even a family member. The people in the extended family call me when they need me to contribute for funeral costs when somebody dies in the family…nothing."*

Although she provides for her children's physical needs, she is worried about their ability to build a future: *"I always made sure they have food and clothes but they don't care now. One day I will die. What is going to happen to them?"*

In Thulani's situation, his father was shot eight times and currently *"lives in a wheelchair for the rest of his life with permanent damage"*. He feels completely responsible and guilty for his father's trauma. As he described it: *"They wanted to eliminate him. He wasn't involved in anything. He didn't even know what ANC was. He was against my involvement too. Just because he was my father...It's was so painful"*. Besides his own guilt, Thulani has to deal with his father's bitterness (*"I'm in this chair because you put me in this chair", said his father*). It is obvious from Thulani's narrative that his personal recovery is closely linked with his father's trauma. He made sense of his own suffering and decided that "revenge is not the best thing", yet his relationship with his father remains the most painful aspect of Thulani's life. What probably makes it so difficult is the perceived impossibility of redeeming what was lost in his father's life and his father's refusal to talk about his past. With great financial effort, taking his father to private hospitals is the ultimate action Thulani can perform in order to repair the evils of the past. However, Thulani has remained committed to rebuilding relationships in his community whenever he has the opportunity. As he proudly described it: *"It is surprising how in our area when people fight in the street, I'm always in the middle even if I don't know what they fight for. So, even here at work, I want there to be peace among ourselves.* His motivation is based on a belief that *"no one is born to be violent but you are trained to be violent"* (as he was in the liberation movement). Therefore he takes it as his responsibility to provide a different example in communities characterised by legacies of violence and poverty. The next section will analyse how participants in this category perceive and relate to their social context.

Searching for the missing piece of the puzzle: Economic recovery

"'Recovery' is not a discrete process: it happens in people's lives rather than in their psychologies. It is practical and unspectacular, and it is grounded in the resumption of the ordinary rhythms of everyday life - the familial, sociocultural, religious, and economic activities that make the world intelligible" (Summerfield, 2002. p. 1107).

Participants' perceptions of their context and the world in which they live was also described in mixed terms. As was discussed previously, in some areas of life, survivors are proud of their abilities to care for their families and to have a job and a house, but they are unhappy with the whole context of the economic poverty and inequality in which they live with their families. Their narrative accounts clearly underline the centrality of their beliefs about contextual realities and the inherent connection with their meaning-making processes. Survivors' recovery and ability to find new meaning are intrinsically linked with a sense of justice and economic recovery of their context. This finding supports one of Colvin's (2000) results in his study of former victims of apartheid where he considers that "healing cannot be separated from the immediate problems of survival" (p. 16).

The narrative analysis of life stories included in this category has revealed a solid sense of agency and control displayed by participants in their process of rebuilding their self and their life after trauma. Yet the process seems incomplete and similar to a jigsaw puzzle that is missing the pieces that create the scenery against which characters live their lives. According to Bracken (2002), recovery after trauma happens through survivors' practical engagement with their social and cultural context. Also, trying to understand how people rebuild their lives after trauma may involve a position of humbleness and acknowledgement of survivors' feelings, beliefs, culture and political views.

Most participants clearly described their disappointment with unemployment, poverty and crime in townships and the careless attitude of the new political elite. Their complaints are sometimes followed by practical solutions to redress the economic situation. For example, Sipho is disillusioned about his former comrades in the liberation movement who became political leaders and forgot about the masses: "*It's a very difficult struggle for those who live in poverty, because now there is money but people in power are just focusing on themselves and forgetting about the masses.(…) The leaders don't care…*". His solution is "*to go back and ask ourselves why did we fight for this country? We must deliver for the people, give them what they fought for, not just promises. I want to see things happening in this country. I need to see people having jobs in this country, people having houses in this country. I need to see people being safe.*"

In a similar vein, Sindiswa commented on unemployment and difficulties in accessing jobs, due to multiple requirements. She said: "*jobs are the most challenging in a democracy. In order to get a job, you need experience and in order to get experience, you need to be accepted to work somewhere…When you listen to all speeches at the State of the Nation address, they all talk about alleviating poverty…If those jobs require experience and qualifications, that means they are not for us."* In her view, the solution is based on a two-fold approach. On the one side people need to commit themselves to education, change their mentalities, be accountable and become empowered through training and skills' development. On the other side, the government needs to make sure their *"morality programmes"* such as Affirmative Action (AA) and the Black Economic Empowerment (BEE) *"reach the really needy people"*. As she expressed it:

> *Our government never empowered us to help ourselves. How can you wake up and help yourself? This is called 'Vuvuzenzela'… What can you do if you don't know how to do it? This is what we get from our members. We called them to meetings and they are asking when they are going to get money. Our duty is to help them get their minds off that. We had to involve them in some sorts of activities, to train them. We use artwork, body maps. It is frustrating to see them think that Khulumani is going to give them money.*

Monica brings into discussion the idea of reparations as part of the TRC's process of reconciliation and the government's legal obligation to offer a token sum to victims of gross violations of human rights during apartheid. As she stated: *"It was a bit better but not as we expected, especially the poverty. We are still struggling with poverty. There were some laws given and the TRC but they've never reached us. There was never any reparation in my situation."* As she suffered multiple losses during apartheid, she joined the Khulumani Support Group in their current struggle for justice: *"I'm insisting on the reparations. The government did nothing for us from the reparation point of view. Even the BEE, this should come back to us but it doesn't. This is supposed to help us, but it doesn't because the government is ignoring us".*

Amidst various difficulties related to the economic and political context, participants' narratives show an active engagement of the people to search for new alternatives, meanings and solutions that could bring social and material transformation. As Sean clearly described his view: *"I am a survivor, not a victim. I'm a survivor. I'll never give up and that is why we are sitting here today. I was proactive."* In addition, as part of the contextual redeeming process, Sindiswa has noticed a destructive collective pattern of attitudes towards poverty among economically disadvantaged black communities and, through her work with Khulumani, she is trying to change it:

It is such a sense of poverty and our people is nesting it as a baby,
capitalizing on poverty. Poverty is their baby. They should say no, go out,
don't stay with me, you are not my friend; I'm fighting with you. You are
the devil! So we need to implement this in our members. I'm excited about
my work. I cannot sleep if the work is not done and I'm so excited when I
get things done. I'm enjoying it. The problem is that we don't have enough
staff and support.

It is noteworthy that Sindiswa's active engagement with her social
context through her work brings her personal significance and fulfilment
in her journey to find new meaning in life. One can easily sense in her
discourse, the excitement, passion and commitment contributing to the
overall social construction of the present self.

Finally, the complexity of the meaning-making process is illustrated
also by Thelma's description of her process of recovery, thoroughly
inspired by higher moral and spiritual sources. As she said: *"Being*
Christian it's easier to forgive. We are a forgiving nation. We are! You
think of all these stories, it could have been a bloodshed country and no
South Africa by now. But because Nelson Mandela is a forgiving man we
are also forgiving people." Thelma's discourse reflects a collective or
general dimension of forgiveness, a result of people's identification with
Nelson Mandela as the prototype of forgiveness. In addition, Bishop
Tutu's identification with people's suffering through listening to their
stories and showing empathy and compassion represented a significant
acknowledgement of victims' pain, which paved the way for survivors to
respond with a forgiving attitude. However, when one particularises
human experience, one sees the ambivalence reflected both in Thelma's
feelings and in the ways she depicts contrasting events in her story:

All these things, when I talk about them, they all come back, but we are not
going to do that, because of Jesus Christ. When we were watching TRC, we
used to see Bishop Tutu crying, he used to cry and he cried. So, I can just
say that I love my church and I believe in Christ. My story is a mix. As you
could see, the policeman who arrested me was a Black man and the one
who helped me was a White man. All these things leave a mark on your life
but you just forgive, you let go, let pass because we cannot live in the past.
It's not something that we are proud of. It's a past that makes you sad. It's
a past that makes you feel sorry that you were born Black. But we don't
live on that, we need to let go. I let go.

Thelma has managed to engage with her moral and ethical dilemmas
by making appeal to what Taylor (1989) described as "strong sources" (p.
516). For her, in order to achieve the "high standards" of forgiveness, one

needs the "strong sources" of spiritual figures such as Jesus Christ and Bishop Desmond Tutu. This idea is common among the participants in the current study, as most of them have highlighted the importance of Christian faith and spiritual beliefs in the process of forgiveness and reconciliation. The next section of this chapter will analyse the life trajectories of participants who see their lives in mainly negative terms and have even stopped searching for new solutions.

7.3. Giving up the journey

The life trajectories of some survivors did not follow easy paths in their journey after trauma. A common characteristic of the stories included in this category is the overall lack of chronology and causality of life events and the absence of a narrative plot (Frank, 1995). There is also a lack of progress or even stagnation, and a sense of opaqueness regarding the search for new alternatives. The narratives' content is generally shorter than the rest of the stories and is mostly past and present oriented with no significant views about the future. Furthermore, the micronarratives predominantly convey feelings of anger, disappointment and helplessness. The language structure contains numerous negations such as *nothing, never, nobody*. Verbs are also used in the negative form (cannot, don't, didn't) and mostly in the past tense. The content of the stories contain ruminations about past and present injustices, disappointment with other people who *"do not care"*, lack of positive change and complaints about not getting any reparations for their sacrifice in the political struggle. These elements and descriptions echo Linden et al.'s (2007) concept of posttraumatic embitterment syndrome.

Regarding demographic characteristics, all participants included in this category are between 55 and 80 years old (the mean is 69 years) which means that compared to the rest of the participants in the large sample, they spent a longer time in their lives under apartheid's oppressive system. All six participants in this group are Black: four men and two women. They live in townships and have a poor economic situation. Compared to the previous two categories, these participants have experienced some of the most difficult traumatic events such as severe torture (five participants out of six) and the loss of a child. In the aftermath of trauma, they developed psychiatric pathology such as clinical depression, PTSD and suicidal ideation and attempts. Currently, most of them are under psychiatric treatment and some continue to experience flashbacks, nightmares, depression, anxiety and chronic pain. This section will deal primarily with major themes arising from the narratives included in this category, focusing particularly on participants' understanding of their lives and the world in which they live.

The embittered self

A common characteristic of survivors' narratives included in this category is the description of the self as overwhelmed by past and present injustices, anger, bitterness and disappointment. Participants in this group have negative perceptions about themselves, negative emotions and have no hopes for the future. Some of the main themes related to the construction of the self concern the following aspects: (1) a sense of unfairness in the ways they have been treated, (2) feelings of anger, sadness and regret for their involvement in the political struggle and (3) self-disgust and loss of dignity.

a) Injustices

The unfairness expressed by participants in this group is related both to the oppression they suffered under apartheid and their continued victimisation through poverty in the present. Their micronarratives include long descriptions of their suffering in the past and how such suffering has not been acknowledged or compensated in any way. For example, Alfred describes how as a result of torture during apartheid he was diagnosed with mental illness, and although he invested so much in the political struggle, he still lives in a shack with his wife and five children who are now grown up but unemployed. He complained: "*When it comes to this, it makes me over-react because I think of my commitment in the struggle and look at my kids now and where I am staying as you can see (showing his place, a single room shack). As a result of stress, I've been diagnosed with diabetes.*"

In a similar vein, Ethel describes her "*wound*" which becomes even more painful as she tries to bring back her memories: "*When I'm thinking about it, I have a wound that has not been healed. I have physical problems, heart problems because of that time. I lost my child Bishop. He was shot. I'm now a person that has lots of sicknesses. I'm still traumatised. This gives me all kind of sickness.*" Her current suffering and feelings of injustice are exacerbated by the fact that the perpetrators "*are still alive and still serving there.(…) They did not come to tell me why they tortured me or shot my son. They've never did that and I'm sure they don't care. That's why I'm saying I've got this wound inside.*"

In Cyntia's case, her whole narrative is about the killing of her son and her agony in the immediate aftermath to identify his body at the police station. A single paragraph at the end of her story describes her experience at the TRC when she offers forgiveness to the perpetrator that killed her son. However, implicitly her message also conveys sadness and disappointment over the injustice associated with the whole process:

> *But this man Mbali came to ask for forgiveness from the mothers of the seven kids. So, I said I forgive you because I can see you are almost the age of my child and is of no use holding on the revenge because my child will not come back. He is gone, he is gone… So that is the end of the TRC. Bellingham never came to ask for forgiveness himself. This was the end. Nobody was prosecuted. These are the stories that make us sad. You know being a mother… everybody was so sad.*

According to Linden et al. (2007), memories of particular events in which participants felt they had been unfairly treated represent symptoms that may suggest the presence of what he labelled as posttraumatic embitterment disorder (PTED). In addition, feelings of anger and sadness are also part of Linden et al.'s diagnostic criteria.

b) Anger, disappointment and regret

All survivors in this category acknowledged having negative feelings both in the aftermath of trauma and in the present. The experience of injustice and powerlessness to change the situation were associated in their stories with feelings of anger, frustration, regret and disappointment. As Benyi described his feelings: "*I still have anger, a never ending anger, flashbacks. Sometimes I get angry over nothing. When I'm in that mood I want to become violent and I always think that violence is the only solution to solve things*". Also Frans: "*I became very angry. I became so angry that I could not control myself…*" Alfred talks about his frustration with the government's inability to bring economic recovery for people in their situation: "*Nothing comes down to us. There is no opportunity to make a living for ourselves, as things we can do for ourselves to maintain a living. It is so chaotic that we don´t even have good roofs over our heads. We can´t see any change. We are just mingling around in mist. This is our frustration and as I´m speaking even now I get so frustrated.*" In his discourse, Alfred identifies himself with the whole group of aging victims of apartheid who have reached a dead-end in their journey after trauma. They are uneducated and overwhelmed by challenges related to aging, poverty and illness. The sense of psychological disorientation and chaos is illustrated by the words *"mingling around in mist"*. The stories in this category echo Frank's (1995) chaos narratives of illness characterised by the tellers' inability to reflect and distance themselves from life events as "the body is imprisoned by the frustrated needs of the moment" (p. 98).

In these stories, frustration also contributed to feelings of regret for getting involved in the political struggle against apartheid. As Alfred says: *"I'm regretting that I sacrificed my life... I'm ashamed to them* (his children). *I'm a laughing stock, because all that I was doing is in vain. Nothing comes in return for what I was doing in the past. There are others who did nothing and the favour is theirs."* In similar ways Benyi thinks sometimes: *"If I had stayed with my hands crossed and not do anything, it would have been better but I couldn't".* Ethel also expressed her regrets: *"I'm now rejecting all the struggle that my son was involved in, as I don't think they achieved anything. In the past I was in and out of jail, I lost my son and now I'm nothing."* When personal sacrifice for an ideal becomes worthless, the self becomes surrounded by meaninglessness and a senseless world. Human experience does not provide for alternative conclusions.

c) Self-disgust and bitterness

Constructions of the self in this situation only serve to lay the foundation for a perceived meaningless existence in a world dominated by chaos and absurdity. Survivors explicitly expressed disgust, hate and disappointment towards their own self. In their stories some even detached from their selves, adopting an external blaming voice. In Benyi's case, his encounter with the meaninglessness of life prompted him to attempt suicide. As he remembered: *"I wanted to jump head on over the hills. Again, I got scared. Then I took myself as a coward and I said to myself 'You are a coward, why don't you do it? You lost your father, you've been in prison. You've done nothing wrong but you are suffering'. So, I thought life is not worth living. I am nothing in society, I am nothing...".* Counting all her losses, Ethel also arrived at the conclusion *"I am nothing"* and *"I have a wound that has not been healed".*

As Frank (1995) noted, words do not come easily for the wounded storyteller. It was also revealing to notice the number of negative words paving the transcripts of these stories. Just on a single page of Alfred's narrative, there were over 29 negative terms and sentences such as: *"nothing comes down to us"*, *"there is no opportunity"*, *"nothing has been changed"*, *"nothing went directly to people"*, *"it never reached me"*, *"I cannot recover"*, *"nothing comes in return"*, *"others did nothing"*, *"there is no future"*, *"nothing happened to them"*, *"the poor will get nothing"*, *"there is no benefit for them"*, etc. Living in the world of *nothing* and *never* is self-alienating. Sarcasm, which sometimes may be used as a coping strategy, for Benyi becomes a tool to show more self-disgust and to portray a caricature type of *self*. In a theatrical and utterly ironic voice, he said: *"Look at the victims, all survivors of torture like myself. We are still struggling to eat meat, but we can't. Believe me, I used to walk from Langa to this office and if I need something to eat I would go to the soup kitchen. This is the man who fought for democracy!? Isn't that a joke?"* His rhetorical question could be interpreted as an attempt to break free from an absurd world. It could be also an invitation for the listener to acknowledge the ridiculous reality and disagree with the teller's negative image of the self by contributing more optimistic reflections where the wounded self fails to do that.

Arriving at the last stage of the life cycle is challenging and anxiety provoking. This is a time when people usually recount major life events including achievements and failures. For the survivors in this particular category, such an exercise is humiliating and leads to self-defeat and indignity, so that another negative construction is revealed in participants' narratives about their shattered dreams of the self, others and the world. As Benyi said:

> I'm not what I was and I'm not where I wanted to be in life. When I was at school, even before I reached matric, I wanted to become a lawyer. I'm now a mental wreck. It never happened. My ambitions, my dreams collapsed...(…). In a few days I'll be 55. It is disgusting! It is so disgusting for all who fought for the country. Until this age you have not achieved anything, but what you have done was a lot... I end up sometimes hating myself.

Unlike Frank's chaos narratives in which the storyteller dissociates herself from her illness, in the present narratives, the actual self (that is supposed to protect the narrator) dissociates from his own person, becoming an external hammering voice that joins the rest of the hostile voices in a senseless world.

Shattered relationships

Beliefs about the self as worthless have been socially constructed through the storytellers' interactions with dismissive attitudes coming from other people in their communities. As Benyi describes it: *"there are thousands of people like me that are marginalised and ignored. We are laughing stocks in our communities. I can't even ask for something from anybody. When I said people are supporting me, I talk about White people, Jewish people, Arabic people, because my own people will gossip about me, they will laugh about me, so I never go to them".* Throughout his life, he was not able to maintain a long-term relationship or job (*"it lasted for two years and we broke up, just as I lost my jobs"*) and even currently he finds it difficult to trust others (*"I don't trust other people. Even if you promise me something, I don't believe it. I don't trust"*). Experiencing failure in relationships serves to confirm personal beliefs in the worthlessness of the self.

Unlike Benyi, Frans associated himself with people willing to listen to his stories: *"I'm always with people. By talking with them about the past it gives me a comfort".* Family support is also an important resource in his life: *"My wife is very supportive. When I'm quiet she always feels and comes to me. She doesn't let me be quiet and alone in the house. Even when I'm beginning to be harsh, she has the means to calm me down."* This aspect strongly supports the importance of relationships in general and the couple relationship in particular in overcoming adversities in the aftermath of trauma (Herman, 2001; Johnson, 2002).

Nevertheless for participants in this category, their family situation remains highly problematic and often unbearable, as they currently witness not only the degradation of their lives but of their children and grandchildren as well. The next generation is also continuing the legacy of poverty, unemployment and violence. As Zitulele mentioned: *"We used to be scared of apartheid but now we are scared of our own children. Crime is just too much. They all want money from us, they want everything from us... you can't do everything."* Also in Alfred's case, none of his five adult children has a stable job and not one finished their education. He described his hopeless view using a colourful metaphor: *"When it comes to my family is like you've thrown the water on the sand, which means you cannot recover it again. And they cannot be recovered."* It becomes evident that his personal recovery is strictly linked with their family recovery. This prospect, however, remains unredeemable since the only hope for the next generation is swept away by the permanency of a destructive social context.

The dark side of the moon: Life in townships

The stories of former victims of apartheid still living in townships portray a painful image of existence. Their hopes of seeing change in their communities and a better life are collapsing in widespread and continuing patterns of antagonism. They feel doomed to live the continuous legacy of violence and poverty for which now they cannot find any justification. In addition to their difficulties in making meaning for their selves and relationships, their social context does not convey much sense either. Similarly to the apartheid times, they still perceive their world as hostile and shattered by inequalities, poverty and crime.

They are disappointed with corruption and the way the current government is dealing with issues of crime and poverty. Their despair and embitterment has not come about as a result of detrimental comparison with the new wealthy and powerful elite. In other words, their anger is not a result of relative deprivation. Rather it comes from victims' perception that people in authority are ignoring them, have become too seduced by their own power and money and, worse than anything, have stopped searching for possible solutions to problems in black communities. As Alfred stated: *"To be quite frank, there isn't much change. If you check those in the government positions, they are just making themselves rich. Nothing comes down to us"*. In a similar vein, Benyi said: *"We need reparation. This is what we need, not what we are experiencing today. We've been sacrificed for the so-called democracy. We are ignored and marginalised"*.

In addition, Frans describes the dark side of township life in the following way:

> *The crime is very bad in this area. The young ones are angry for not going to school and then not being able to further their studies because of lack of money. Then they get involved in drugs, arms and crime. We don't feel safe in our houses. These kids when they want something, they just knock at our door or kick the door and take anything they see and can sell. They are armed... You can't walk at night. Someone was killed two nights ago just around the corner, because he was running in the night. But people get killed at night all the time in this area. It is something very common. In the morning the cops just come and collect the bodies, the ones that are dead...*

People's despair is not a result of the intensity of crime only, but rather of its *banalisation* (Arendt, 1963). As Benyi noted: *"Look today... poverty, diseases among black communities, theft – it is now a usual thing... We got so used with somebody dying all the time...it's a common thing."* The dehumanising effects of poverty and illness come together to complete the chaos and to abruptly end the narrative's search for meaning.

Finally, the ultimate defeat in people's lives is the absence of any sense of future and their abdication from engaging with the world – vital aspects in the process of recovery (Bracken, 2002; Summerfield, 2002). This is clearly reflected in Alfred's statement: *"I just gave up thinking about the future. Because there is no future if you are living like this. After what I've been through there is no future for me... I just gave up."* Broken relationships and lack of support in the community have made Benyi believe that *"this is how we are, if somebody is suffering we don't go to their rescue."* People have even started questioning the idea of *Ubuntu*, thinking that the concept is just useful for ideological purposes, but that it is not practically visible in real life among people. In Ethel's view, *"Ubuntu is functioning morally not practically. When you listen to the parliamentary speeches, they are all based on the Ubuntu, but practically is not there. People are still living in that divide: I'm rich and you are poor and the rich ones do not care about the poor. That's where I see the practicality of Ubuntu. It is not there."*

Weine (2006) developed the idea of cultural trauma to describe the context in which due to trauma in society, the culture itself suffers changes in customs and behaviour. Within the South African culture, a challenge is presented not only at the peripheral cultural layers but at the core elements of the culture, represented by basic assumptions about life which are embedded in the concept of *Ubuntu*. The serious challenge to *Ubuntu* consists of the erosion of trust in relationships, extreme violence and perception of the world as an unsafe place. This creates the sensation of living in a culture in which traumatic events become individual fibres in the culture's texture. They gain a status of 'normality' in people's understanding, thus becoming an integral aspect of the way people organise their lives. People's everyday experience in townships confirm the sense of helplessness and fear related to continuous threat, violence, crime and poverty, thus contributing to the expansion of a traumatic culture or, what Straker (1987) termed as continuous traumatic stress. However, defeat is the greatest trauma in the life of nations (Kaplan, 2005) and even if some of the victims of apartheid may not live to see "the promised land", they continue to play a role in the collective meaning-making process, by bringing their own contributions to the construction of self and relationships in their communities.

7.4. Reflective review: Repairing the wreckage

Returning to the shipwreck metaphor, it can be noticed that the *wreckage* narratives in this study are somehow different from the *illness* narratives in Arthur Frank's *The Wounded Storyteller*, where (at least some of them) mention a ship that "was happily sailing on calm waters, and then the storm came". All *wreckage* narratives of trauma due to repressive political violence face storms from the outset. However, for survivors of the St. James Church massacre, for instance, the story begins directly with the destruction of the ship. Another difference is that in *illness* narratives the process of recovery from illness is usually met with care and support by the social context. On the contrary, Black victims of political violence under apartheid lived under continuous exposure to traumatic events, making it almost impossible to distinguish a clear time for beginning the recovery. This shows that the traumatic apartheid stories are profoundly shaped by the local worlds through which people move. Black and White survivors have been moving in totally different worlds. They were born and raised in different worlds, under an opposing status quo: the former as the oppressed and the latter as the beneficiaries of the repressive system. After the collapse of apartheid - a time, which at least theoretically could be considered the beginning of recovery - Blacks and Whites (with very few exceptions) continued to move in informal segregated local worlds, both in terms of their jobs and their living. Consequently, survivors' experience of trauma and recovery bear the imprints of these different local worlds. The final part of this chapter will summarise some of the main findings with regard to the three categories of life trajectories after trauma.

Sailing again

The first group of people described in this chapter, those who "feel at home in the world", have managed to rebuild their ship and are now able to sail on calmer waters. Similarly to Frank's restitution narratives, it can be said that survivors have found a new voice and have redrawn the map of their lives. The new voice tells a "good story" about the self, others and the world. The story is not only about success and achievements but also about the "wonder at all the self can be" (Frank, 1995, p. 68), including failures, which are seen as learning opportunities. The ability to redraw the map of one's life is reflected in the storyteller's capacity to be the agent of his/her life, actively involved in life decisions and making plans for the future. Their main achievement consists in their ability to repair or to transform what was destroyed by trauma.

For example, the destruction in Fowzia's life existed as her agony, knowing that her son was in detention and being severely tortured. Therefore, her only reason to live was to fight for Nazeem's liberation. Her own suffering became the vehicle for meaning-making, which was to have her son back: life started to regain meaning when her son came out of prison. Fowzia's journey of recovery was in fact Nazeem's recovery, seeing him not only free from prison, but also being able to rebuild his life by becoming a respected teacher and having a happy family. Indisputably, Nazeem's own healing in turn was heightened by his mother's progress in recovery, which in Johnson's (2002) view, signifies the importance of human connections in facing the impact of trauma, and the benefits of being together in the fight against the "dragon".

Fr. Lapsley found meaning again when he realised there is a gain beyond the loss of his limbs. He gained the ability to witness to his own pain and also bear witness to the pain of others in his encounters with trauma survivors at various institutions he founded, such as The Trauma Centre for the Survivors of Violence and The Institute for the Healing of Memories in Cape Town. Paraphrasing Frank (1995), Fr. Lapsley resisted the silence against permanent disability and through the wounds of his resistance, he gained the power "to tell and even to heal" (p. 182).

The life trajectories of people in the first category highlight the relationship between recovery as making meaning, and the ability to repair or transform the trauma. This process was related to survivors' ability to find a voice and rebuild their self as a moral, spiritual and ethical self. The self is defined in relationship with others: being both affected and affecting others with care and compassion. In addition, the rebuilt selves are constantly engaged with the world in which they live by both shaping and being shaped by their social context. In other words, they display a sense of control, agency, resilience and growth as well as a sense of consciousness and ability to reflect and continuously recreate meaning for their lives.

In trying to connect people's past, present and future, it can be noticed that most survivors in this category are younger than the rest of the participants in the large sample. This fact might indicate a possible relationship between the negative effects of trauma and a prolonged period of time spent under repression. The older survivors in this category benefited from substantial social support in the aftermath of trauma, which confirms Herman's (2001) theory regarding the importance of healthy relationships and social support as vital steps towards recovery. Finally, since none of the survivors in this category lives in a township anymore, the importance of a safe context is clearly highlighted as a crucial factor that facilitates recovery after trauma.

Rebuilding the ship

Moving now to the second category of participants analysed in this chapter (while still remaining committed to the shipwreck metaphor), their life trajectories show loyalty towards repairing the ship and redrawing the map. However, they encounter this process as challenging. Unlike previous stories, their narratives do not show "wonder at all the self can be" but rather a sense of doubt and anxiety about their ability to finally rebuild the ship. Although they lack the necessary resources and skills, they consider it is never too late to learn. However, they show a type of fixation with the absence of 'durable materials and financial means', which although they may be considered 'mere' material realities, nevertheless prove to be vital for the rebuilding of their lives. This clearly shows that making meaning of life after trauma is not merely an abstract cognitive process happening only in the mind. Recovery is "practical and unspectacular" (Summerfield, 2002, p. 1107). It is also profoundly connected, as Bracken (2002) often stressed, with "the practical ways of life", which for some survivours literally meant the rebuilding of their house or being able to feed their families. Using again Frank's analogy, it can be concluded that the redrawing of the map (signifying the mental process) becomes useless without the remaking of the ship. This is actually the main tension experienced by the majority of survivors in the second category.

For example, Sipho's trauma narrative is about his involvement in the liberation movement at a very young age, suffering severe torture, detention, exile and the loss of his youth. Hence, his story of recovery would need a minimal repair of contextual realities for which he *was ready to die*"; thus a decent material living would be an essential part of his prospective economic reality. However, Sipho has managed to draw a fairly good map of political and economic realities by accepting life's ambiguities and unfairness, including the fact that the new Black political elite *"are making themselves rich"*. Yet he cannot understand the government's careless attitude towards former victims of apartheid who *"sacrificed their lives for this country"*. His life narrative actually illustrates his wrestling with this particular incongruence, as for him, a dignifying life is strongly related to his ability to provide decent living conditions for his family. Pursuing education at this stage in his life and counselling families in his community is yet another way of repairing what was destroyed by trauma in his previous life stage.

The narratives of trauma and recovery of survivors in the second group could be said to describe an analogy between the incomplete meaning-making processes and the unfinished work on the shipwreck. The incompleteness of meaning regards not only people's dissatisfaction with economic poverty and crime, but also issues related to loss and complex grief, physical illness and depression. However, what distinguishes them from survivors in the third group is their commitment to continue the search for meaning and to rebuild the wreckage. Their narratives show an acceptance of what Herman (2001) defined as *the dialectic of trauma* in which suffering and happiness coexist in people's life as natural elements of the recovery process after trauma.

The shattered shipwreck

The third category of life narratives mainly describes challenges and failures in the process of rebuilding the meaning of life after trauma. These stories closely resemble Frank's (1995) *chaos* narratives that have no plot and no chronology. In fact, due to the abundance of negative words, these stories become non-stories. In Ethel's view, her self has been *"vandalized by the apartheid"* and as Alfred clearly declared *"there is no future... I just gave up"*. They gave up rebuilding the wreckage produced by apartheid trauma. This is also evident in Cyntia's narrative that ends abruptly by saying *"this is the end"*. There is no account of what happened with her life after the killing of her son, except her granting of forgiveness towards the perpetrator at the TRC. Her story shows in fact that there is no story to be told, as there is no storyteller. Her self has been broken by suffering and there is no recovery, just the trauma in its most overwhelming form (Brison, 2002; Herman, 2001; Janoff-Bulman, 1992).

However, the stories in this category clearly support the idea that apartheid trauma and recovery are strongly connected with issues of economic poverty, unemployment and social inequalities. The absence of a safe context in the aftermath of trauma, as well as the lack of social support and personal resources have acted as vulnerability factors in the process of recovery. Survivors' devastation and inability to heal confirm the long-term negative effects of severe torture and the loss of a child, since all participants in this category have suffered one type of these traumatic events or even both (Herman, 2001; Joseph et al., 1998; Kaminer et al., 2008; Yehuda, 1998). In addition, participants' ages (mean of 69 years) highlight once again the devastating effects of prolonged exposure to trauma, defined by Straker (1987) as continuous traumatic stress (Eagle, 2011; Kaminer & Eagle, 2010).

Finally, having analysed survivors' narratives of trauma and journeys to recovery, the discussion is now gradually approaching a concluding stage. The last chapter will provide a summary of the main ideas discussed so far interwoven with critical reflections on my personal journey of writing this book.

CHAPTER EIGHT

SUMMARY AND REFLECTION

The aim of this final chapter is to provide a summary of the main findings that have emerged from the analysis of life narratives of trauma under apartheid and journeys to reconstructing meaning. The chapter will highlight how the key elements revealed in the process of analysis relate to the existing literature and what new ideas emerged that could be considered as contributions to the field of trauma and recovery within the South African context. In addition, this chapter will include a critical reflection on the trajectory of this work, its limitations and directions for future research.

8.1. Overview of main findings

Composing an overview is in many ways similar to gazing at an Impressionist painting. One gains more of the picture by contemplating from a distance, as too close a standpoint just reveals multiple dabs of colour, which do not make much sense of the whole. An overall perspective can better be gained by achieving a certain distance from the painting, as only then can one see how the dabs of colour connect to each other to defining picture. The process of analysis can be said to mirror the painting of the dots. Hence, it is crucial at this stage to gaze at the whole picture to gain an overall perspective of the research process, its findings as well as its limitations.

An immediate feature that surfaces is the multidimensional nature of this journey that has involved many voices, which in various ways were integral part of this work. The research of numerous authors has illuminated useful ideas and concepts in the field of trauma and recovery and the current study has built on their solid foundation. In addition, participants' voices – the twenty survivors of political violence during apartheid – have brought fresh perspectives to the field from their experience of suffering and ways of rebuilding their lives after trauma. Their stories were a guiding light throughout the whole process, clarifying and giving direction to the research path. Finally, my own voice as a researcher must also be taken into consideration as an important part of the hermeneutic process. By being actively involved in listening, reading and interpreting ideas, this work carries a part of my own self, and in this way, is also becoming a part of my life journey.

From a theoretical point of view, this study has moved away from the medicalised approach to trauma and recovery, which is framed by a positivist individualist view as described by PTSD. This departure, however, does not imply that PTSD concept has been rejected, but rather acknowledged as part of the survivors' journey in the aftermath of trauma. The study also did not intend to minimise clinical and therapeutic approaches to recovery through counselling and psychotherapy, which in many cases represented an important step in people journeys to recovery. This study however did not explore the impact of a specific type of therapy but was rather more concerned with survivors' complex ways of making meaning of their suffering and their lives after more than 20 years from the traumatic events. Thus, the main concern was to find out what has been happening (after such a long time) in the lives of former victims of political violence under apartheid, what their views are on their past traumatic experiences and how they have tried to make sense of their lives again. In so doing, the purpose was to understand the impact of trauma on their lives and what aspects contributed or impeded their process of recovery from the aftermath of trauma up to the present.

In working with trauma narratives, one is always tempted to be distracted by the modernist emphasis on "fixing" and often becomes committed to projects attending to "what is fixable". This is due to the fact that, as Frank (1995) noted, "society prefers medical diagnoses that admit treatment, not social diagnoses that require massive change in the premises of what that social body includes as parts of itself" (p. 113). In trying to avoid this pressure, I have attempted in the conceptual framework of this study to draw upon contextual and relational approaches to trauma that highlight the importance of the historical, social, political, economic and cultural contexts in shaping survivors' experience of trauma and their journey to recovery (Bracken, 2002; Brison, 2002; Herman, 2001; Straker, 1992; Summerfield, 1998, 2002). In the meaning-making process, people continuously reinterpret their experiences and social realities in order to make sense of themselves and the world in which they live. Thus, the trauma narratives of the twenty survivors reflect the wider impact of oppression and political violence inflicted on individuals, families and communities during apartheid. Within this context, recovery is understood as a multidimensional process, which is profoundly embedded in the social, political and economic context of South African society.

The analysis process has been continuously moving between general and specific aspects of the narratives, trying to include both the specific within the wholeness of each narrative and the common elements, by observing various patterns across the sample. The study did not find any single profile that could describe the experience of trauma under apartheid but rather multiple ways of experiencing and understanding suffering and healing. From an early stage in the narrative analysis, a first cluster of experiences was observed taking place between narratives of trauma due to political violence coming from state repression and those caused by anti-apartheid movements. Consequently, the results presented in the following paragraphs, bear the imprints of race identity, ideology and the politics of segregation during apartheid in South Africa as well as the characteristics of the social, political and cultural context after the collapse of apartheid.

Trauma, race and political violence

The experience of trauma under apartheid was profoundly shaped by the ideology of racial segregation and the politics of repression, which determined different types of experience within different contextual realities across racial divides. One cannot discuss trauma under apartheid generally without highlighting the contextual differences with regard to the nature of traumatic events experienced by black communities compared to those of the White victims. This is not to compare different types of traumatic events experienced across the racial divide but rather to emphasise that in the case of black communities shattered by continuous oppression, trauma can be better understood within the framework of a *traumatic context* and not as a result of one or more *traumatic events.*

For victims of state repressive structures under apartheid, particularly Black and Coloured participants, trauma was experienced as an *engulfing process* characterised by *loss of meaning* described through the shattering of the self and relationships within families and communities, due to ongoing oppressive processes such as police harassment, beatings, humiliation, deportation, detention and torture. At an individual level, trauma was reconstructed in terms of helplessness, anger and despair due to injustice and marginalisation during apartheid. However, some Black survivors described their current suffering as a continuation of past trauma that is more related currently to the present economic poverty and living under ongoing threat rather than to past traumatic experiences during apartheid.

In addition, although the study did not include a clinical evaluation of participants' mental status by using DSM IV, all Black participants involved in the present study reported the experience of psychological symptoms (flashbacks, nightmares, anxiety, depression, etc.) both during repressive times and for several years after. The survivors still claiming such symptoms (in the present) had experienced torture or the loss of a child in the political struggle. Three survivors of torture are still under psychiatric treatment. The rest of the Black and Coloured participants (including the other torture survivors) in the sample, although they continue to experience some of these symptoms, they however consider them as a natural part of life and do not seem to be largely affected by them; they are able to carry on their regular daily activities and maintain healthy relationships with others.

As revealed through the narrative analysis, political violence perpetrated by means of the repressive structures of apartheid on the Black population had a traumatic impact not only on individuals but on families and communities as well, carrying its vicious legacy even up to the present time (Colvin, 2000; Gobodo-Madikizela, 2009; Kaminer & Eagle, 2010). Trauma within families during apartheid was related to the overwhelming effect of multiple traumatic events experienced by family members, such as the loss of a child or parent, detention and torture of a family member, permanent disability, illness and separation. The multiple forms of repressive violence had a destructive impact on family dynamic, generating more instability, chaos and broken relationships. The results highlighted that women (mothers in particular) often had to deal both with the effects of repression and the family responsibilities of raising the children and protecting them from violence. The majority of women's narratives reflect the struggles and complex loss experienced by Black South African women due to separation, divorce or the killing of a child, thus highlighting the intricate interplay between gender, race and ideology during apartheid (Shefer, 2010). Their stories also show an active involvement in the liberation movement against apartheid, portraying themselves at the heart of the battleground (Sideris, 2003).

An important component of trauma highlighted in this study was the communal dimension of suffering during apartheid repression. Narratives of participants living in black communities portrayed their communities as a "theatre of violence", shattered by police harassments, continuous terror and control, abuses, violence, burning of houses, removals, shootings, arrests and killings (Foster et al., 2005). In addition, black communities were affected by what Foster et al. (2005) labelled as lateral violence, depicting the aggression and violence happening among members of black communities due to suspicion of collaboration with the apartheid structures. Furthermore, witnessing pain and atrocities became a transmission mechanism that contributed to the expansion of the communal effects of trauma in black communities shattered by apartheid repression.

On a rather different note, the analysis of survivors' narratives involved in the St. James Church massacre showed a closer similitude to Western conceptualisations of trauma. Their narratives commenced directly with the experience of the massacre and the description of its devastating effects in the aftermath. However, overall, the narrative reconstruction did not focus exclusively on individual symptoms. On the contrary, these became secondary in comparison with the communal experience of the massacre mediated by participants' religious beliefs as related to the political, spiritual and social context. Within this framework, trauma was perceived as a consequence of living in a "fallen world" and humanity was seen as perverted/corrupt - a view that nevertheless implies serious political consequences as well as moral and ethical responsibilities for both sides of the conflict. For example, as was discussed previously, Rev. Ross Anderson who was leading the church service on the night of the massacre remains with an ongoing dilemma, consisting of the fact that neither White nor Black people in South Africa have been able to assume responsibility for their wrongdoings. These findings highlight once again the complex experience of trauma under apartheid and the ongoing social processes and personal beliefs that shape it. Such results confirm postmodern ideas that trauma is not universal and there is no direct causality between traumatic events and the experience of trauma. Although in the aftermath of trauma survivors may experience pathological symptoms as described by earlier works and DSM IV, their experience of trauma is more complex than this as it is mediated by people's sophisticated interactions with the social world, through language, beliefs and cultural values. This is even more evident in survivors' journeys in the wake of trauma, particularly after the collapse of apartheid.

Recovery as finding meaning

Recovery from trauma is not a straightforward phenomenon but rather a multidimensional process that takes place in several domains of life - a journey full of contradictions and ambiguities. There is clear evidence in this work that psychological recovery is strictly connected with relational recovery and economic recovery. In other words, results showed that participants have been able to make progress in their journey to recovery by rebuilding their selves, relationships with others and their living context. Such findings strongly support Bracken's (2002) contextual understanding of recovery as the remaking of the "practical ways of life," involving a search for meaning within the social, politic and cultural context. In this work, if trauma was understood as *loss of meaning* and *shattering of the self*, recovery was thus defined as *making meaning* of life and *rebuilding the self*. This is to say, survivors make meaning of their lives after trauma as they reconstruct their self in relation to others and their social context through reflexivity and language as explained below.

An important vehicle in the meaning making process was the narrative reconstruction of the self by the rebuilding of the "narrative function" of the self through language and interpretation of the self in relation to the world (Crossley, 2000). There is sufficient evidence in participants' narratives confirming that there is a strong connection between survivors' recovery and the language structures that they use to construct their stories. An important finding discovered at an earlier stage of the narrative analysis highlighted the clear relationship between the length of the narrative and the progress made in the journey to recovery. There are several aspects that need to be emphasised at this point with regard to the language, form, sequence and content of the narratives.

First, the stories of survivors who achieved recovery are longer in length than those still struggling in this process, or those who gave up searching for meaning. Second, successful recovery narratives deal more with journeys after trauma, while non-recovery stories deal more with past trauma and disappointment with life in the present. Third, recovery stories are present and future oriented, while non-recovery stories are mostly past-oriented with inserts about current disillusionment. Finally, recovery stories contain ample positive descriptions of the self, of others and various life events. Such stories have a plot, events are usually chronological and the self is presented (through the use of active voice, verbs and the "I" pronoun) as active and engaged with the world. On the contrary, in the rest of the narratives, the shorter the distance covered on the road to recovery, the more negative language structures are used throughout the narrative in the form of negations (*never, nobody, nothing*), passive voice, and the use of the "he" or "they" pronoun (e.g., *they took me, I was sent*).

One of the most important findings of the present study lies in regard to the three types of life trajectories that describe survivors' ways of making meaning after trauma in three main areas of life: (1) the reconstruction of the self, (2) relationships with others and (3) the world as represented through their views in the social, political and cultural context.

Depending on their progress and relative location in the recovery process, participants' experiences clustered around the following main categories: (1) "Feeling at home in the world" (depicting those who made the most progress in recovery), (2) "Still searching for significance" (describing those who find the process of recovery challenging but are committed to continue) and (3) "Giving-up the journey" (illustrating those who have not made much progress and have given up the search for meaning). The three categories were relatively heterogeneous in terms of race, gender, age, education and social status in the first and second category but became more homogeneous in the third category as all participants in this group were Black, economically poor and older that the rest of participants. An interesting result was that the number of narratives included in each category followed a perfect Gauss curve with six narratives in the first group, eight in the second, and six in the third group.

Apparently there is no clear or straightforward answer as to why some survivors managed to recover and others did not, as the same factors that had a protective role in the life of some survivors, did not function in similar ways for other participants in the study. For example, there was clear evidence that for some survivors, a safe context and social support in the aftermath of trauma contributed significantly to their process of recovery. Yet not all participants who benefited from a safe context and healthy relationships made the same progress. There were additional processes taking place in other areas of life where the reconstruction of meaning had not so far been achieved. For example, in Ross's case (survivor of the St. James church massacre), although he has been benefiting from family and social support and a safe context (including psychological counselling), it seems that he is still struggling in the process of rebuilding his self (a sense of alienation from his own race, as discussed previously) and finding meaning in an unjust world.

Some findings showed that survivors' lack of progress in the process of recovery is related to the experience of torture, economic poverty and lack of education. However, while this is valid for some participants in the sample, there are other survivors of torture in the sample who made significant progress towards recovery. A possible explanation or a key to dealing with this dilemma may be found in Ungar's (2008) indicated tension between individuals' needs and the ability of their context to meaningfully provide the necessary resources for the healing process. As the author exemplified, in other words, good fishing abilities are pointless if there are no fish in the pond. Therefore, another major finding for the understanding of recovery lies in the match between peoples' psychological capabilities (in terms of their agency, pursuing education, aspirations, goals, etc.) and the ability of their social, political and cultural context to facilitate the fulfilment and development of these specific capabilities.

While the study could not find a unique or universal way to present such complexities, it was, however, illuminating to examine the above-mentioned aspects within the context of participants' life narratives. It was helpful to see how meaning was achieved and what aspects facilitated or hindered this process across the narratives' spectrum. A crucial element in all narratives and also a reliable indicator of progress in the recovery process was the survivors' ability to *repair* or *transform* what was destroyed by trauma in their lives. Thus, the first category of stories are described as successful recovery narratives as they emphasise the self's ability to reconstruct meaning, repair damages related to past trauma and enjoy life again. These stories could be considered also narratives of resilience, as they highlighted positive adjustment within the context of adversity through participants' effectiveness, success and agency in dealing with life events (Garmezy, 1991). Furthermore, the stories in this category explicitly conveyed the idea of positive transformation and spiritual growth as a result of trauma (Pals & McAdams, 2004; Tedeschi, 1999). An important characteristic of such narratives is people's success in *repairing* or *transforming* the destructions produced by trauma in their lives through an active process of meaning reconstruction. Within the boundaries of this category, analysis highlighted several aspects that facilitated the process of recovery. It is thus safe to assert that a sense of agency and purpose, positive perceptions of the self, self-efficacy, spiritual beliefs, supportive relationships, forgiveness, community involvement and education acted as facilitating factors in participants' journeys to recovery.

The second category designated by those who are "still searching" for meaning included stories that highlight both achievements and failures throughout the life trajectories, as survivors struggle to overcome current challenges. In many ways, these stories could more probably be considered narratives of resilience than the stories in the previous category, as they describe the commitment of the self to continue the search for meaning in spite of life's adversities (Luthar et al., 2000; Ong et al., 2006). Participants in this category have not managed to achieve meaning in some areas of life and they have not yet repaired the damage produced by trauma in their lives. In the analysis, vulnerability factors impeding the process of recovery seemed to be related to: loss and complex grief, economic poverty, social inequalities, lack of education and physical or mental illness. However, positive factors such as agency, community involvement and commitment to search for new meanings were also highlighted as facilitating the recovery process.

Finally, the narratives in the third category mostly described a lack of recovery and an abandonment of the search for meaning. Such stories resemble in many ways Straker's (1992) category of psychological casualties and Frank's (1995) *chaos narratives* of illness. The narrative analysis has revealed predominantly negative constructs of the self and relationships with others as well as an image of the world as a hostile place. The self was constructed as angered, helpless, embittered, disappointed, marginalised, traumatised and defeated by difficulties. Such elements can be found in Linden et al.'s (2007) symptoms of posttraumatic embitterment syndrome and Straker's (1987) concept of continuous traumatic stress. As major vulnerability factors, findings highlighted the experience of living under continuous threat (due to poverty and crime in black townships), torture and the loss of a child. It must be stressed, however, that although the stories convey a sense of hopelessness, they have a positive message for the next generation of youngsters to encourage them in pursuing education as the most important aspect in life (Weine et al., 2004).

Resilience, growth and forgiveness

In the unfolding of recovery narratives, predominantly the first and second category of life trajectories highlighted a complex relationship between the understanding of recovery and patterns of *resilience, growth and forgiveness*. A major finding in this context is that throughout the process of making meaning, patterns of resilience and growth have coexisted and have been interwoven, rather than strictly separated. This finding contradicts Bonano's (2004) understanding of the three concepts (*recovery, resilience and growth*) as being distinct. He considers that recovery is defined by the return of normal functioning to "pre-event levels", while resilience reflects the capacity "to maintain a stable equilibrium" when confronted with adversities (ibidem, p. 20). Especially within the context of recovery after apartheid trauma, Bonano's firm demarcation between resilience and recovery, measuring the present outcomes against "pre-event" levels, is problematic and therefore, not useful within this particular framework for the following reasons.

First, not only in this study but also more broadly, the "pre-event" characteristics are impossible to assess with precision. Once a certain event is part of the past, the only elements available for researchers to include in their studies are perceptions about that particular past event, which cannot be equated with the event itself as it is always shaped by interpretations (Antze & Lambeck, 1996). Second, even if a pre-event level is taken into consideration, within the context of prolonged trauma or multiple traumatic events, it becomes highly complicated to decide which one among the many events should be considered as a "pre-event". Consequently, the idea of measuring current perceptions against pre-event levels would not bear much relevance within the context of the present study, as the characteristics of the pre-event situation are hard to pin down.

Another finding of this study highlighted that a majority of life narratives within the whole sample contained patterns of resilient behaviour identified by positive functioning even within the context of adversity. Results, however, did not point towards a common pathway leading directly to the achievement of resilience. The multiple ways in which survivors have developed resilience in their journey to recovery (discussed in Chapter 7) were related to various aspects such as good coping skills, agency and control, positive self-concepts, healthy relationships with others, spiritual development and active engagement in communities. This situation confirms Bonano's (2005) statement that resilience is more common than is often believed and that it can be achieved through multiple pathways.

It was also observed that when survivors' resilience encountered a social context that could provide access to resources and personal development, participants experienced significant progress on their journey to recovery. This finding highlights Ungar's (2008) understanding of *resilience* as defined not only in terms of individuals' efforts "to navigate their way to health-sustaining resources" but also as a characteristic of their environment as being able to provide the necessary resources in "culturally meaningful ways" (p. 225). Such an environment could also facilitate *growth* and *transformation of the self* in the process of making meaning after trauma. In this work, survivors who "feel at home in the world" (first category of life trajectories) have experienced *growth* in the majority of life domains, defined by Tedeschi's conceptual framework as related to: (1) positive self-concepts, (2) constructive relationships and (3) spiritual development.

This analysis identified specific elements reflecting a positive self-concept pertaining to *growth* defined as "feeling comfortable in one's skin" which, for most of the Black survivors, meant overcoming feelings of inferiority and marginalisation and being proud of one's achievements in the face of adversities. Regarding the second domain of healthy relationships, results revealed survivors' ability to construct themselves as being capable of reconciling and developing interracial relationships.

Finally, spiritual development was strongly connected with a construction of the self as inherently spiritual, possessing religious beliefs and the ability to forgive.

Further findings of this study have shown that while elements of *resilience* and *growth* were part of most narratives in the first and second categories, only a minority of participants made spontaneous reference to the concept of *forgiveness* in their stories. However, throughout the whole narrative sample, there seems to be a relationship between survivors' progress to recovery and their ability to forgive and reconcile with perpetrators (whether they are perceived as distinct identifiable persons or just as the apartheid repressive system in general). Although this particular relationship has not been the main focus of the present study (and therefore has not been directly explored), there is however both explicit and implicit evidence pointing to such a relationship.

Explicit evidence in support of this relationship has come from participants' own experiences linking directly their making-meaning process with the ability to forgive. Forgiveness as well as the process of healing were placed within a spiritual framework in which both healing and forgiveness can take place. This is obvious in Thelma's conclusion: *"but we are not going to do that* (to take revenge) *because of Jesus Christ (...) So, I can just say that I love my church and I believe in Christ"*. Her Christian faith, as a transcendental foundation, allows her to make meaning of life, to heal and to forgive (Ogden et al., 2000). This argument strongly supports Taylor's (1989) concept of the moral self (discussed in Chapter 2) as being profoundly spiritual and rooted in supreme sacrificial love, since forgiveness is embedded in self-sacrifice (Griswold, 2007; Tutu, 1999).

Other evidence supporting a possible relationship between *recovery* and *forgiveness* was drawn from the meaning of *growth* and *self-transformation*. According to Tedeschi's (1999) conceptualisation, the first category of narratives ("Feeling at home in the world") analysed in chapter seven, could be defined as growth narratives, as they all emphasise the three main dimensions of posttraumatic growth mentioned above. The analysis showed that the ability to forgive is a critical component of spiritual development and wisdom (the third dimension of growth) and therefore it implicitly underlines the connection between survivors' recovery from trauma, growth and their ability to forgive their perpetrator. *Forgiveness* is probably one element that, in general terms, could distinguish *growth* from *resilience* and *recovery*. Such an argument is, however, speculative. In order to clearly differentiate between these three constructs, one needs to take into consideration the multiple dimensions of forgiveness and its intricate mechanisms within the context of relationships shattered by trauma. Therefore, given the conceptual boundaries of the current study, such complex issues must await further exploration.

8.2. Implications and contributions

Within the context of what has been mentioned above, it is important to look now at the implications of the current findings with regard to the theoretical and methodological framework for the understanding of apartheid trauma and the process of recovery, within the South African context. Perhaps most importantly, the present work has revealed a lack of attention given to the study of trauma and recovery of former victims of apartheid in South Africa. I have encountered only a few empirical narrative studies dealing specifically with this topic (Ogden et al., 2000; Skinner, 1998 – conducted during 1994 – 1995). Although this may not be the place to embark on an adventure to find an explanation for such a complex phenomenon, I will, however, take the risk of just pointing to some possible explanations, which future research studies may be able to confirm or invalidate. One explanation could be that there is no clear or straightforward answer to issues raised by such topic. From a political point of view, it may be argued that the TRC's work became such a prominent process after the collapse of apartheid, that the research focus shifted from victims to perpetrators and then to issues of forgiveness and national reconciliation (Chapman & Van der Merwe, 2008; Hamber, 1995). Thus researchers worldwide have become more interested in finding out the premises, mechanisms and results of such issues in particular. In addition, one could think that at the TRC's hearings, victims had the opportunity to deal with their trauma and therefore have rapidly embarked on a process to recovery (Summerfield, 2002). Yet another explanation for the *silence* surrounding the issue of trauma and recovery could be just the natural need of individuals and society in general, to close a painful chapter in their history and move on, especially within the context in which other types of trauma (such as rape, murders, women and child abuse, HIV, drug abuse, etc.) seem to have greater prevalence (Kaminer & Eagle, 2010; Shefer, 2010).

However, perhaps the most plausible explanation for the lack of research in this field could be allied with Frank's (1995) argument describing societies' preference for medical diagnoses as opposed to social ones. A medical condition can be treated through medication, while a social one may need changes that society is not able or willing to adopt. As controversial as it may sound, it may prove, in fact, more opportune to entirely give up the term *trauma* when referring to contexts of oppression and political violence. In society in general, trauma is automatically associated with mental dysfunction, and recovery is perceived as the responsibility of psychiatric institutions. Hence, reframing the victims' reality by removing them from the medical paradigm may have a beneficial effect both for the victims and for society. It may increase the moral and ethical responsibility of individuals, communities and societies to attend to conditions that should be considered as relating to and affecting their own existence.

In order to facilitate the expression of complex and diverse experiences related to survivors' perceptions of past trauma and recovery, this work adopted a multidimensional contextual framework by taking into consideration the historical, social, political and cultural context in which perceptions were shaped. Such an approach has two major implications: first, it emphasises the fact that PTSD is not a sufficient framework for the exploration of current challenges facing survivors of apartheid trauma and second, it highlights once again the dynamic, elusive and multifaceted nature of trauma as being continuously shaped by people's social worlds. With regard to the first implication, within the context of black communities, a psychiatric diagnosis does not necessarily generate compassion, care and recognition, as Herman (2001) argued, but rather it leads to further stigmatisation and social alienation (Colvin, 2000; Skinner, 1998). In addition, victims' struggle with economic poverty further undermines their dignity and increases their sense of helplessness and isolation. Moreover, such a situation impedes listening to victims' stories of apartheid since their discourses are interpreted as being the effect of mental illness and therefore inaccurate. As a result, former victims of apartheid repression become victims again, this time victims of the current socio-political context, thus perpetuating the ongoing cycle of victimhood.

Consequently, this study joins previous works on trauma and recovery in challenging the concept of PTSD as a universal conceptual framework for the understanding of trauma (Bracken, 2002; Summerfield, 1998; Young, 1995). In so doing, PTSD has not been rejected, but acknowledged as part of survivors' journeys to recovery at a certain moment in time; this journey is not a static process but is continuously being shaped by people's beliefs, cultural values and social realities. This study has therefore shown that trauma and recovery are not two separate processes but are interconnected and overlap in the process of making meaning of life after trauma. Consequently, since trauma during apartheid seriously affected individuals and had a devastating impact on family relationships and communities, the recovery process cannot be conceived in individual terms only but rather as profoundly linked with the rebuilding of relationships and the contexts in which people currently live. Although the conceptual framework of this work has not aligned itself entirely with Bracken's (2002) framework, his argument regarding the importance of the social, political and cultural context for the understanding of trauma and recovery has been thoroughly confirmed throughout the whole analysis.

As a mark of the ever-changing aspect of trauma, this study has highlighted both continuities and differences with regard to survivors' perceptions of trauma. Continuity was conveyed through survivors' current constructions of the self in relation to their *heroic* past experiences and their future aspirations and goals. Differences were related to the retrospective construction of trauma, which in the past was embedded in the ideology of racial segregation and political violence, while in the present is rooted in the current contextual realities of economic and social inequalities. Systemically framing the process of recovery in terms of survivors' openness and commitment to the meaning-making process, this study was able to avoid the dead-end type of positivist conceptualisations in which recovery is defined through the mere absence of pathological symptoms, thus ignoring other meaningful realities that participants mention in their narratives.

Consequently, Bracken's definition of recovery as a search for meaning and the remaking of the practical ways of life have opened new avenues in the current study for the exploration of a particular understanding of such concepts within the South African context. Therefore, this study was able to show that survivors' progress on their journey to recovery is related to their abilities and multiple ways of repairing or transforming what trauma had destroyed in their lives. For most Black survivors it explicitly meant having a house and a job or to be able to care for their families. Similar findings were also provided by other studies in non-Western cultures such as those of Summerfield and Toser (1991) in Nicaragua, Bracken (2002) and Giller (1998) in Uganda, Sideris (2003) with Mozambican women refugees in South Africa, and Weine et al. (2004) with Bosnian refugee families in Chicago. These aspects point towards another major theoretical implication - the fact that recovery is an ongoing process of making meaning, happening not only at the intra-psychic level of individuals' lives but mostly in their interactions with their social worlds (Summerfield, 2002).

Probably the most important contribution of this work concerns the process of recovery within the South African context and the three main types of life trajectories of survivors after apartheid trauma. Through the three main categories of meaning-making journeys, this work has illuminated a notion of the self as diverse, multifaceted, contradictory and continuously changing. The notion of the narrative self highlighted the importance of language and culture in the reconstruction of the self through stories shaped in their turn by the self's own belief system, spiritual values and contextual realities (Crossley, 2000; Ricoeur, 1984). Thus this study highlighted the victory of recovery in the narratives of growth and resilience as a triumph in the battle against trauma; it also emphasised the image of suffering as the dissolution of the self in the absence of language or a story to be told. Furthermore, drawing on Taylor's (1989) moral universe, this study was also able to emphasise the underlying mechanisms contributing to recovery through faith, social support and a self as inherently spiritual. Most participants that made progress in the process of recovery have placed spiritual values at the core of their being as elements that enabled both recovery and growth in their lives. On the contrary, the narratives describing disappointment and lack of recovery do not display these values as part of their reconstruction of events, perceptions or interpretations. A possible explanation for this fact may be that within the overall spiritual discourse on forgiveness and reconciliation within the South African society, some former victims find it difficult to reconcile the largely negative view of their lives with the immaculate image of religion.

By taking into consideration the family context, the current study was able to show that the process of individual recovery is strongly connected with the family dynamic. On the one hand, the family is the context in which healing can take place and the family's resources are important protective factors in one's journey to recovery. On the other hand, the recovery of an individual member is closely related with the recovery of the family as a whole, and the analysis clearly emphasised such specific situations in the lives of participants in this study. These aspects strongly confirm the importance of a safe context and healthy relationships for recovery (Herman, 2001; Johnson, 2002; Weingarten, 2000, 2004).

Regarding the various pathways to recovery, this study both agreed and disagreed with Bonano's (2004) definition of resilience as being completely different from recovery and growth. Findings showed agreement with regard to the multiple ways in which people develop resilience but it disagreed with his strict delimitation between recovery, resilience and growth. In this work, these three processes were complementary and overlapping rather than completely separate. In fact, Bonano's argument is in some ways contradictory, as on the one hand, he states that recovery is different from resilience and posttraumatic growth, yet, on the other hand, he admits that there are "multiple pathways to resilience", out of which some of them overlap. In order to exemplify these, he lists among others the term *hardiness*, described as commitment to finding purpose in life, agency and control, and ability to learn from negative experiences (p. 25). Since such attributes constitute in fact positive beliefs about the self, they are essential characteristics of both recovery and posttraumatic growth experienced by survivors in their process of making meaning of life after trauma. Furthermore, in the case of trauma, Ungar (2008) considers that resilience is an indicator of recovery after trauma. Therefore, in this study, while exploring survivors' own meanings of recovery through their "practical engagement with their social and cultural environment" (Bracken, 2002, p. 211), both resilience and growth were identified at various stages of life trajectory.

Crucial in the process of recovery is the remaking of the context. Within the South African context, what some survivors would need in order to make more progress in their healing process, is a more resourceful environment able to respond in meaningful ways to victims' efforts to rebuild their lives after suffering (Ungar, 2008). By providing the necessary resources for their economic recovery, this gesture would convey dignity and appreciation for survivors' past and would honour their stories of suffering, such a crucial aspect for the rebuilding of a shattered self (Brison, 2002; Etherington, 2003; Frank, 1995). In many ways, participants' stories mirror the contradictions and polarities reflected both within the cultural diversity as well as in the social and economic inequalities in South Africa. As a new construct of economic imbalance, besides interracial inequalities, a new intra-racial component has emerged between the black political elite and former victims of apartheid.

From a methodological point of view, by including both victims of repressive violence and victims of liberation movements, this study highlighted on the one side, the difference between trauma caused by single traumatic events and prolonged trauma, and on the other side it emphasised the role of ideologies and interracial conflict in relation to the widespread impact of political violence on individuals, families and communities. Also, by having a diverse sample in terms of race, the study was able to illuminate how the experience of trauma and the process of recovery were different across race, and how these aspects were highly influenced by survivors' ability to experience a safe context and social support in the aftermath of trauma. In addition, by allowing participants to decide whether or not they wanted their real name to be used, the narrative method of this study created the opportunity for survivors to find their voice and rebuild their narrative self. The fact that 18 participants out of 20 opted to have their real name used, highlighted survivors' need to tell their stories in their own voice in the presence of an empathic listener with the hope of being heard by others and in this way helping themselves to become responsible witnesses of their own stories (Frank, 1995).

Finally, it must be also mentioned that although this research was not oriented towards finding a model or a specific interventions for working with trauma survivors, the findings of this study lead however to some important implications for the field of clinical psychology and psychotherapy. Thus, in the light of what was mentioned above, strategies of support and interventions with trauma survivors can adopt a more holistic, multi-disciplinary and collaborative approach. In order to explore survivors own meanings of suffering and healing, clinicians should look beyond individual treatment and lists of symptoms by trying to explore survivors experiences in a more collaborative manner. Also, instead of "talk therapy" and strategic interventions, "non-interventive support" may prove to be even more beneficial (Bracken, 2002; Kaminer & Eagle, 2010; Summerfield, 2002). In addition, connecting with other governmental institutions and non-governmental organisations (in communities, education, legal, security and social system) in order to assist survivors to rebuild their "practical ways of life" can indicate that professionals are actively listening to their clients' needs. An attitude of authentic care, empathy and preoccupation for the most vulnerable may contribute to survivors' recovery more than many hours of cognitive processing.

8.3. Limitations of the study and directions for future research

The work has several limitations related to its methodological and conceptual framework. First, since the study employed narrative methods, the findings cannot be generalised outside the limits of the sample and therefore some conclusions may not reflect the current reality on a larger scale. Survivors of political violence during apartheid are currently living in various parts of South Africa and the world. Their stories might be very different from those included in the current sample. In addition, since participants in this sample were selected through institutions such as the Institute of Justice and Reconciliation and Khulumani Support Group, other former victims not registered with these organisations could not be reached. The inclusion of such participants in the study might have changed some findings with regard to the process of recovery. Also the inclusion of family members, second-generation survivors and groups from various communities might be an important direction for further research. Such studies could provide a more comprehensive picture of the impact of repression on families and communities by exploring the family and group dynamic, life experiences of survivors' children, the impact of witnessing trauma in families and communities and what socially and culturally meaningful factors have been related to the process of making meaning of life in contemporary South African society.

Second, the research sample was heterogeneous with regard to type of traumatic events, race, gender and age. Perhaps a more homogeneous sample could have allowed the process of analysis to establish more connections between various constructs that define the understanding of trauma and the process of meaning-making within current social and cultural realities. However, a diverse sample contributes to a richer interpretation of life experiences (this actually being an important aim of this work) through the multiple voices that come together to represent pieces of a much wider and more complex reality. In addition, gender identity did not seem to highlight major differences in participants' reconstructions of trauma and recovery. However, this does not mean that such differences do not exist. Although the study did not focus directly on this aspect, some gender-specific constructions were mentioned at various points in the analysis. Gender differences related to the experience of trauma and recovery could be better explored in further research based on a comparative study using larger samples of men and women survivors of apartheid trauma (Shefer, 2010).

Furthermore, it can be considered that the research topic itself induced some limitations, since people's narratives have been framed by the overarching topic of suffering under apartheid. A different question might have generated different stories imbedded in different language structures and meanings. Also, suffering may have meaning in itself, an aspect that has been only briefly mentioned (Frank, 1995; Morris, 2003).

Third, this study attempted to develop a conceptual framework that is broad enough to explore the complexities of survivors' experiences within the South African multicultural context, in which Western and non-Western cultural values coexist. Such an attempt had both advantages (mentioned in the previous two sections) and possible shortcomings. Thus, it may be possible that the study has been caught within tensions and polarities inherent in a theoretical framework that has been influenced by philosophical and anthropological ideas (even without claiming a thorough understanding of their complexities); at the same time there was an attempt to divert from clinical approaches to trauma and recovery without perhaps entirely succeeding. This dialectic may in fact mirror the journey of apartheid trauma in contemporary society. It is therefore the task of future research in this field to fine-tune the approach in order to find the right balance both within the South African context and other non-Western cultures.

Finally, it has been often said that a life narrative is not the life *per se*, and an analysis of a narrative is not the narrative itself. By comparing the presentation of findings with the actual life narratives, the former seem an oversimplification of an exceedingly complex reality. Since each narrative could have been a study in and of itself, the richness and particularities of individual narratives have not been made sufficiently visible. However, I hope that the multiple quotations interwoven with interpretive statements were able to bring to life participants' voices and show the uniqueness and particularities of each story, in the context of the whole study. Future research should continue to explore the life narratives of former victims of political violence during apartheid while they are still alive. As Desmond Tutu often said, it is never too much to talk and reflect about what happened during apartheid. Many researchers have pointed to various legacies of apartheid; thus these efforts could be seen as an ongoing dialogue meant to assist individuals and communities to negotiate their subjective locations in the process of transformation in contemporary South Africa.

8.4. Reflection on my journey

"Reflection on one's own narrative preferences and discomforts is a moral problem, since in both listening to others and telling our own stories, we become who we are"
(Frank, 1995, p. 77)

Whilst I was finalising the work and tidying up the threads at the end of the writing process, the image of Fisher's labyrinth became vivid again. In some ways, I feel as if I have arrived at the end of the labyrinth and looking back now, not only that I cannot see the labyrinth anymore but I realise how much this journey has become my own story. On the one hand this is a story of development in terms of my own thinking while making sense of theory and concepts I used throughout the research process. On the other hand, this work has become an important context that has shaped my *self* in relation to the world at this particular stage in my life.

Reflecting on this journey, I remember the insecurities and anxiety surrounding the beginning stage of the process and the alternating phases of either an overwhelming flow of ideas or just a blank wordless mind. However, as I started the interviewing process, I gradually gained more confidence in my abilities as an empathic listener and responsible witness of survivors' stories. The experience of interviewing some of the participants in their homes in townships has opened a new world for me. Not only that it made me gain a more profound view of their everyday realities but it helped me grasp the extent of social and economic inequalities that characterise the polarised South African society, a crucial aspect in the process of analysis.

The period of interviews was both fascinating and difficult at the same time. From the beginning of this phase I was faced with a dilemma regarding the drawing of flexible boundaries between my immersion into peoples' narratives and the ability to maintain relative neutrality (Johnson, 2002). While I managed to go fairly well through this stage, after several weeks of continuously and repeatedly listening to the trauma stories while transcribing each interview, I vicariously experienced the anxiety infused in the stories through nightmares and panic attacks carrying a fear over faceless images of people moving through unfamiliar places and undefined times. The supervision sessions helped me regain balance and make sense of my cognitive and emotional saturation in relation to participants' trauma, to other stories of trauma and even to my own anxieties related to the unknown ahead of me waiting to be made known. Although painful, I valued this experience as it allowed me to gain access into victims' lives and become a witness of both their suffering and of my own fears. Although the interviews were not framed by a therapeutic context, this profound experience and my interaction with the participants during the interview allowed me to enter their lives and be "changed by this encounter", since "we are, all of us, in this together" (Yalom, 1989, p. 14).

This experience, however, became an opportunity for new insights, and similar to the "wounded storytellers" in this study, I could gradually distinguish a new voice of my *self* breaking out of psychic and hermeneutic wrestles with new ideas and concepts while trying to make sense of painful realities (Frank, 1995). Retrospectively, I see my new voice not as a recipient of new knowledge but rather as one voice among many voices who contribute to the co-creation of meaning and the understanding of human suffering and healing. As a psychologist, I have been trained through a positivist framework and although my training in systemic thinking has opened wider perspectives, I have still sensed an attitude shift in myself towards becoming more comfortable with ambiguities, and with the fact that some aspects of human existence and suffering are not totally comprehensible. This fact echoes the Corinthian verse "for now we see only a reflection as in a mirror" (1Cor. 13:12, New International Version), which highlights the human impossibility to grasp or reflect reality in a "perfect" manner (Freeman, 1993). Consequently, in order to capture the complexities of survivors' experiences, Taylor's (1989) notion of a moral universe and Bracken's (2002) ethical contextual approach to suffering seemed an appropriate alternative.

This journey has also been a journey of making meaning of my own self at this particular stage in my life in relation to my family and my relationships with others, which have been also shaped by history and culture. For example, listening to Thelma's story, I understood how the experience of repression makes people deny or minimise their pain in the same way their identity was minimised and denied during repression. Reflecting on my own experience of living under totalitarian communism for twenty two years, I understood why so often I felt that my opinion or my story was less important than other people's experiences. The constant pressure to "be equal" imposed by communist repression had a quite similar effect to that of the inferiority feelings experienced by Black people under apartheid. It made us believe that our ideas were not worth telling or that there is no interesting story to be told. By losing their voices, victims have joined the repressive state in facilitating the conspiracy of silence (Danieli, 1998). This work has taught me that victims of political violence during apartheid have "something to teach" if they will find listeners willing to hear their stories.

Finally, towards the end of the process I experienced another paradox: the writing of the last pages was essentially solitary, yet I have never felt more in touch with others. The journey towards myself has become a journey towards others, an experience perhaps best described by Paul Ricoeur's (1992) *Oneself-as-Another*.

8.5. Concluding remarks

The desire to forget the painful past, to move on and engage with more optimistic issues is understandable, to some extent, in any post-conflict society. However, while at a macro-level such a tendency may be a natural phenomenon, at a micro-level, some individuals and groups may still struggle to adopt the new rhythm while others have even decided to give up the *run*. It is therefore to be expected that, in a still highly unequal society such as South Africa, people's trajectories of recovery would be quite diverse. Hence, this work started from a concern about the current situation of former victims of political violence during apartheid with a real interest to find out what their subjective location is on their journey to recovery.

The study had a two-fold focus. First it explored the complex reconstructions of apartheid trauma and its impact on individuals, families and communities through the life narratives of survivors of political violence during apartheid in South Africa. Second and related to the above, this study analysed participants' life trajectories after trauma up until the present time with the aim of revealing survivors' pathways on their journey to recovery. In so doing, the theoretical framework has departed from individual positivist approaches to trauma and adopted a broader contextual framework in an attempt to integrate a view of suffering and healing as dynamic, relational and continuously shaped by social, political and cultural contexts. Therefore trauma was considered as a loss of meaning and shattering of the self, and recovery as a journey of making meaning of the self and life through commitment and engagement with the social world.

By using a narrative methodology, this study has shown how individuals reconstruct their life trajectories after trauma by making sense of who they are in relation to others and their context within a temporal framework that links their past, present and future. This process has revealed that survivors' memories of apartheid trauma are still alive and very vivid. For the victims of repressive violence, the reconstruction of trauma was closely related to past racial discrimination, injustice, humiliation and multiple losses, which, as they said, "will never be forgotten". Yet, the more they were able to rebuild their lives, the less they were preoccupied with their past suffering and the more they became able to invest their lives in the present and future. Achievements and success were related to the spiritual dimension of the self which is reflected in a moral engagement with the world, a "purposeful life" and the wisdom to cope, transform and grow in spite of adversities. Psychological recovery, in their view, is closely linked with economic recovery, family recovery and the recovery of significant relationships in their lives. This meant the remaking of the "practical ways of life" and the redeeming of what trauma had destroyed in their lives, which in concrete terms referred to having higher education, a higher status in society, a good job, a house and/or a healthy family. The inability of some survivors to make progress in their journey to recovery is a reflection of the painful reality of former victims of torture who, besides multiple illness and loss, have to deal also with aging and economic poverty. This work has been an attempt, in Frank's (1995) words, to honour their stories and create a context for them to be heard, in the hope that they may find meaning in suffering as "suffering comes to understand itself by hearing its own testimony" (p. 169) or even that they may engage "to wrestle with God" (p. 182).

Finally, by paraphrasing Bar-On (1999), this work has been, in many ways, an attempt to describe the "indescribable" and to discuss the "undiscussable" - yet, another paradox. I feel there is still much more to say about survivors' lives and their complex ways of "rebuilding the wreckage and redrawing of a map". This endeavour then, can be seen as another voice trying to break the silence of suffering, as another attempt to wrestle with the chaos, confusion and disillusionment produced by repressive regimes in people's lives, with the hope of becoming a responsible witness in the listening and honouring of these stories. Ultimately, besides trauma and suffering, these narratives have also been stories of recovery and healing. Without this important part, this study would have shown just "the dark side of the moon". The majority of survivors in the study, through their commitment and creative ways of making sense of life again, confirm that recovery is possible even in an unjust world. The *rainbow* nation has multiple resources and the existing South Africa is a testimony to this fact. This work is, therefore, a tribute to survivors' ability to repair the "shipwreck" and a celebration of their intricate ways of reconstructing meaning after trauma.

APPENDIX A:
CORE NARRATIVES

1. Alfred[a]: "We cannot be recovered... we are just mingling around in mist"

Alfred (72 years old, Black) is a Khulumani member and a pensioner. He lives with his wife and five children in a shack. During apartheid he was beaten and severely tortured. As a result he ended up in a psychiatric hospital, being considered mentally disturbed. Because of stress, he was also diagnosed with diabetes. He feels frustrated and angry because "nothing has changed for the people in need" and those in government positions just "make themselves rich". When talking about his family he believes that "they cannot be recovered". His children have no stable jobs and none of them finished education because they did not have money to continue their school. He gave up thinking about the future because he believes "there is no future if you are living like this". Regarding the TRC, Alfred thinks that the TRC favoured perpetrators and believes there is no reconciliation. Even Ubuntu, in his view, is "just a vehicle for people in power to collect things from other countries" and "there is no evidence of its practical existence". He wants to tell the young generation that "their anger is not getting them anywhere" and they should pursue education.

2. Benyi[*]: "This is the man who fought for democracy... Isn't that a joke?"

Benyi (55 years old, Black) is single and rents one room in a shack in a township. He was introduced to Steve Biko and joined the liberation movement in March 1973 at the age of 19 years. He remembers that during that time black communities were destroyed by fire and they were forced to carry pass cards. In 1980 he was arrested for political reasons

---

[a] Core narratives are listed in alphabetical order according to participants' names
[*] Names marked by an asterisk (*) are fictitious and any resemblance to real persons is entirely unintended.

and put in solitary confinement. For six days he was brutally tortured by being repeatedly beaten (his teeth were kicked out), electrocuted, blindfolded and forced to stay naked. After he was released from prison he was under continuous surveillance by the security branch. He submitted a statement at the TRC and was invited to speak in a public hearing but he refused being afraid that he would lose his job with some "White people". Since then he has struggled with the effects of trauma, being under psychiatric treatment and counselling at the Trauma Centre. He was diagnosed with amnesia and made two suicide attempts. Benyi could not keep a steady job or a relationship. He is disappointed with the present situation as he lives on a disability grant and feels that former victims are marginalised and ignored by the new government. He feels that all his dreams and ambitions in life have been shattered by the effects of trauma and is angry that he received no reparations for sacrificing his life in the struggle against apartheid. He is embittered, hates himself, cannot trust others and regrets his involvement in the political struggle.

3. Cyntia: "These are the stories that make us sad"

Cyntia (68 years old, Black) is one of the mothers whose son was shot dead by the police in the "Gugulethu 7" attack on 3 March 1986. She told her story at the TRC and granted forgiveness to her son's killer. However, the person who gave the orders did not ask for amnesty or forgiveness and he was never prosecuted. Cyntia is a widow as her husband died 12 years ago. She has been struggling to recover, while still living in poverty and in a very unsafe context. Although there have been over 25 years since the loss of her son, she is still in pain and suffering. She is also disappointed with the current economic situation as she still lives in a township with one of her sons' family and grandchildren. All these memories bring to her feelings of sadness and unfairness.

4. Ethel: "I'm a vandalized person by the apartheid"

Ethel (64 years old, Black) lives by herself in a shack. She was born in Eastern Cape and moved to Cape Town in 1971 to be with her husband and to look for a job. At the beginning, she left her children with her mother in Eastern Cape but because her mother was struggling with poverty, Ethel had to bring her children to Cape Town. While in Cape Town she experienced repeated harassment from the police, detention and even torture. Her eldest son was heavily involved in the struggle as an ANC leader in the youth sector in Crossroads. He was shot when he was

19 years old and became paralysed on the right side and mentally disturbed. He needed permanent assistance during the whole time he was awake. As this was not possible sometimes, in 2005 he died hit by a car close to his home. For Ethel this is "a wound that has not been healed". She still feels traumatised and physically sick, having heart problems and lots of pain in her body. She still considers herself as having been "vandalised" by the apartheid regime. She could never find out why she was tortured and why her son was shot. She considers that *Ubuntu* is functioning just morally not practically, as "the rich ones do not care about the poor". Ethel believes that education is the key and encourages the youngsters to get educated.

5. Fowzia Lowe: "I had to be there, fighting for my son"

Mrs. Lowe (73 years old, Coloured) got involved in the anti-apartheid movement in 1985 because her son was arrested, badly tortured and condemned to 10 years imprisonment for 'terrorism'. She connected with the other mothers of the youngsters that were arrested and organised various forms of protests asking for the liberation of their sons and daughters who "were not terrorists but freedom fighters". She was many times put in prison and threatened with death. However, the goal of saving her son's life was above her own life. She had a special relationship with her son. The whole time while her son was detained and tortured she could not sleep, could not eat, but was always thinking what she could do to get him out. She organised protests together with other mothers who had their sons in prison. She instructed them about what to expect in prison, and the necessary things they needed to have with them in case they were arrested. With no support from her husband and struggling with epilepsy and a hysterectomy, her life was often in danger. In spite of various traumatic events that she experienced, she considers that the thought of losing her son was the most traumatic. She was very happy when her son was liberated together with other youngsters in 1991 and although since then she has experienced flashbacks and nightmares, she has had the ability "to let go and move on". She is very disappointed with political corruption saying that if she were young again she would start protesting against it. Currently, she defines herself as a happy elderly person who has many friends and family support.

6. Frans: "The only thing left for me now is to get this pension from the government"

Frans (74 years old, Black) is currently a pensioner. He has eight children in total from two wives and seven grandchildren. His family is made up of thirteen people living in two rooms of a shack. During apartheid, he was arrested and harassed many times and in 1986 his house was completely burnt by the police during the forced removal. He remembers his frustration at having to work for a small amount of money and several times being fired from the job and not paid anything. However, what affected him the most was the death of his six months old son due to teargas inhalation. He became very angry with White people, aggressive and not able to control himself. What he finds helpful for his healing is talking with other people about the past. His wife is also very supportive and helps him calm down when he is angry. His only hope for the future is to get his pension and to see his children having jobs and grandchildren being educated. Currently, he thinks that compared with the apartheid time, the situation has changed only in terms of political freedom but that they still live with fear of crime and poverty.

7. Fr. Lapsley: "Prayer, love and support of people from around the world"

Fr. Lapsley (61 years old, White) was born in New Zealand. He went to Australia to become a priest of the Anglican Church. He was transferred to South Africa to study Mission and Psychology in Durban. He became Chaplin of the campus and of other two black campuses. In 1976 (during the Soweto uprisings), he became the national Chaplin and started to minister to students who were detained. During that time, he began to speak out against injustices, torture and detention in South Africa. As a result, he was expelled from the country and went to Lesotho to join the ANC. He spent 16 years there as a member of the ANC and the ANC's Chaplin. On the 28th of April 1990, he was sent a letter bomb, which exploded in his arms, making him lose both his hands and the sight of one eye. He received medical treatment in Zimbabwe and Australia for seven months. Fr. Lapsley considers that the journey to healing started when he realised that he had survived what he calls "a failed assassination". The prayer, love and support of people from around the world helped him recover both emotionally and physically. What contributed also to his recovery was his "conceptual framework" in which the possibility of death was part of everyday reality. However, what he was not prepared for was living with "permanent major physical disability". This was his greatest challenge. Founding and getting involved in the Trauma Centre for the Victims of Violence and Torture in Cape Town gave him a sense that there was not just loss but also gain from his trauma, as he was now more qualified to do certain things that he was not qualified to do before. Another important aspect in his recovery was to develop a "healthy interdependence: not to be totally dependent and not to be totally independent". Fr. Lapsley founded the Institute for the Healing of Memories whose major activity is the facilitation of workshops with victims of various traumas, who are encouraged to tell their stories of suffering and embark on a journey of healing. In Fr. Lapsley's words, this is a "journey to survival, to return, to give my love as fully, joyfully and completely as possible".

8. Liesl: "I stay in my little bubble"

Liesl (36 years old, Coloured) was involved in the St. James massacre in 1993. She was 17 years old at that time and her best friend and the mother of her boyfriend (her current husband) were killed next to her. As did all participants involved in this massacre, Liesl also initially believed that what was happening was a show put on by the youth of the church. She could make sense of the reality only after the shooting stopped and the perpetrators ran away. She felt devastated seeing the people around bleeding or dying. She went in the ambulance with her boyfriend and his injured mother who died on the way to hospital. Witnessing her boyfriend's loss and suffering was overwhelming. Soon after the event, she started to experience nightmares, sleeplessness and high anxiety. Any noise would almost make her have a panic attack. However, in contrast with these feelings, she remembered going back to church and feeling very peaceful, trusting God that "He is in control of everything". She admitted that she dissociated and tried to avoid anything that had to do with the massacre. She did not watch TV, did not listen to radio and did not go to the TRC. She does not remember being angry with the perpetrators or God and considers that avoidance was her major coping mechanism that helped her at that time. These painful experiences triggered for Liesl previous memories of traumatic experiences and vulnerabilities. She is still struggling to work through various types of trauma and dealing with fear when she is alone with her two children. She finds it difficult to relate to others and often becomes angry with herself and isolates herself in her "little bubble". What kept her going were her supportive husband and her belief in God.

9. Mandy: "God is in control whatever will happen"

Mandy (30 years old, Coloured) was 14 years old when her mother and a good friend of hers were killed in the massacre at St. James Church in Kenilworth, Cape Town. She was sitting in the same pew as her large family when "two black men came through the front door" and started shooting and threw grenades down the aisle. Her mother was killed by a chip from a nail grenade and died on the way to hospital. Her friend (a young man) was killed by a bullet in his head, while he was trying to shield two girls sitting next to him with his own body. The two girls were saved but he died instantly. Mandy recalls a sense of unreality and although everything happened quite quickly, all the actions seemed like watching a movie in slow motion. She felt a strange sense of peace at that time and could not feel any anger towards those who killed her mother and friend. Later on, while growing up and going through different stages in her development as a young adult she found it difficult to deal with her anger towards God, and raised the question "where was God when all that happened?" She became rebellious, could not trust people and started to experience broken and destructive types of relationships. Various stages of individual and family life cycle involving stressful changes (such as her father's remarriage and her brother's marriage) would bring back to her feelings of loss, abandonment and anger. She went to the TRC hearings hoping to understand "why those men did that", but came out disappointed for not finding the answer. She perceived that the two men were avoiding most of the questions, providing irrelevant information, which did not make sense to her. However, she felt the healing power of her handshake with the two men after they apologized and asked for forgiveness. Nevertheless, she forgave them even before they asked for forgiveness. She had a significant experience at the St. James Church during the "Wholeness in Christ" workshop when for the first time she realised how angry she was. She was angry with God for not being there when the massacre happened, with her mother for leaving her, with her father who remarried after two years, with her brother (her best friend) for getting married and with herself for making such bad decisions in her life. She felt abandoned by all the important people in her life and realised the need to forgive and reconcile first with herself and then with her past. She considers that God enabled her to put an end to her anger, bring closure to her painful past and move on. Mandy is now married and is eight months pregnant with her first baby. Becoming a mother is yet another important stage in her life, which brings back traumatic memories of her own mother who is not there to assist her to become a mother herself.

10. Monica: "If I can get a bone of my mother and sister to bury"

Monica (53 years old, Black) remembers growing up without her mother whom she never knew. She was raised by her father who was struggling himself with the loss of his wife. Monica's mother and her baby sister disappeared when Monica was just a child and up to the present, they have no explanation for their disappearing. She was told that her mother was harassed by the police, as she was against the government. Monica also remembers that her father had to hide from the police and so could not keep a job. In 1976, Monica went to Cape Town to look for work. She got involved in the uprisings taking place at that time and was arrested several times by the police and badly beaten. She later joined the UDF. In 1986, when the police started to burn houses in black settlements, Monica was hit by a policeman with a gun on her right ear. She has a blood block and cannot hear with the right ear. Her baby daughter was damaged by the teargas and was left with a permanent disability. Because of continuous harassment, Monica recalls not being able to spend time with her husband. As a result, he left her for another woman and in the end they divorced. She has been struggling to raise her two daughters by selling second hand clothes. Currently, she lives with her two daughters (28 and 21 years old) in a small house in a township. Monica learned to manage the little money she had, so that a part is used to buy groceries and the rest to reinvest in second hand clothes. Her daughters have been helping with the second hand clothes and, in this way, they are able to support their family. Monica is still disappointed and cannot rest until she finds out what happened with her mother and sister.

11. Patrick: "Whatever I put my mind to, I can accomplish"

Patrick (44 years old, Coloured) was only twelve years old when he came from school one day and found his mother carrying furniture into trucks and being very reluctant to give him explanations. They were living in District 6 at that time and were forcedly moved to Mitchell's Plain. He remembers this time as being very difficult for him and his mother who was a single parent trying to raise eight children on her own. He recalls all the confusion and helplessness regarding his inability to change anything in that particular situation. These feelings were magnified by the fact that everyone in the neighbourhood was submissively doing the same thing. These events, together with other stories in which he was discriminated against contributed to his image of the injustices of apartheid. Later on while a student at UWC, he became heavily involved in the political struggle against apartheid being part of many protests, having to hide, being tear-gassed and detained by the police. Being the youngest among his siblings he always had a special relationship with his mother as his father left her six months before he was even born. She has always encouraged him to study, pursue higher education and get a good job in the future. This became the legacy of Patrick's life and his way of coming out of the inferiority status prescribed by the repressive apartheid regime. His mother transmitted her Christian values to him and he integrated them as core values into his life. He had meaningful guidance from other spiritual friends who supported him emotionally and spiritually. He was able to achieve important things in his life: higher education, a good job, family and travelling on three continents. He was able to forgive those who made him and his family suffer not because they apologised or showed remorse but because he decided to step beyond hate and revenge. He decided to situate himself on a higher plane, that of offering forgiveness and finding new meaning for his life. His dream of becoming an English teacher has come true and he is now able to invest in the new generation. Reconciliation for him requires the telling of the truth, but just the truth is not enough. It is a matter of decision for the victim to give up the old ways of stereotype thinking and move on to cooperation. Patrick is much appreciated by other teachers in his school, by his students and by parents as well.

12. Ross: "We were part of a very wrong system…"

Ross (54 years old, White) was one of the ministers of St. James Church in Cape Town who was leading the family service when the massacre took place on the 25 July 1993. He remembers the feeling of disbelief and the delay in realising what was happening when the shooting started. It was inconceivable for him that anyone would attack "defenceless people" in a church. During the attack he remembers telling people to stay flat on the ground. After the last grenade went off and the perpetrators ran, he went to the pulpit to give directions, asked for doctors and nurses to come forward and asked somebody to call the police and ambulance. The days following the attack, Ross was very busy visiting those who were hurt, planning the funerals and giving lots of interviews. He found this particular time helpful in processing the trauma, especially that he had to answer some difficult questions from family members who lost their dear ones. He considers the TRC even more traumatic than the massacre. The fact that the perpetrators kept blaming their commanders and did not want to assume responsibility made him imagine how Black people may feel when they hear Whites blaming the national government instead of assuming responsibility for the racial oppression. In his view reconciliation depends on assuming responsibility for the wrong doings on both sides of the racial divide. He realised at the TRC that as a White South African, he should be the first one to apologise and assume responsibility for the evils of apartheid so that the Black perpetrators would be able to assume responsibility for killing people in the massacre. In his view, real forgiveness depends on a deep human encounter between victims and perpetrators. In the absence of such an encounter, the forgiveness is superficial and cheap, which is worse than no forgiveness at all. Real reconciliation can happen only in the context of Christian love. Ross has been struggling lately with symptoms of PTSD and depression (nightmares of the massacre), which he connects with being tired and involved in too many activities at the church. He finally resigned from being the minister of St. James Church and is now a lecturer in theology. He is pessimistic when thinking of the state of social welfare but is optimistic that God is in control.

13. Sean: "Betrayal is my biggest fear"

Sean (43 years old, Coloured) was involved in the anti-apartheid movement from when he was in high school and continued as a student at UWC. He was in prison, tortured and lost one tooth when he was beaten. He was in terrible pain and was given medical care only after two days. However, his most traumatic event was when his best friend died as a result of betrayal by one of their team members. It was very difficult for him to recover after that. He could not trust people anymore and all his following relationships were destroyed. Reflecting on the aftermath of those events he remembers his efforts of trying to forget, hide his feelings and not talk about it. He did not have much support after these events since all his family, excepting his mother, were against him. Moreover, different words and attitudes of the people around him triggered his feelings of betrayal, making him suspicious and frustrated. As his frustration increased he would become excessively angry and react with violence towards others around him. His previous relationships were mainly with White women towards whom he was aggressive and eventually the relationships broke up. He had a very short relationship with a Coloured woman who betrayed him by not being honest about her intention to become pregnant. As a result he has now an 11 years old son with whom he is in regular contact. He worked as a sports journalist but lost his job because of his aggressiveness. He has been unemployed since 2008. He started lately to experience flashbacks and nightmares about his traumatic experiences during apartheid. He has no place to live and temporarily is living in his mother's one room apartment. Although his present situation is difficult, he defines himself as a survivor and fighter, who "will never give up" searching for solutions to problems. He is actively involved in applying for jobs and writing project proposals. Sean is disappointed with the current economic and political situation in general but is hopeful about his future.

14. Shaheed: "They could imprison the body, but not the mind"

Shaheed (47 years old, Coloured, Indian) became aware of the injustices of apartheid from a very early age in his life when he was only in primary school and recalls writing a play about White people who oppress the Blacks. In 1976, when he was only 13 years old, he got involved in the students' uprising in Cape Town. In 1980 he became a leading activist, organising school boycotts. He was arrested over 15 times, put in solitary confinement and tortured. The torture was more psychological, by locking him in a cell with a criminal, making threats about his mother and sister and not allowing him to sleep for a long time. In solitary confinement, he developed coping mechanisms to survive either by use of his imagination, writing on the walls, or exercising to keep fit. He has never thought of giving up fighting. He joined the Unemployed Workers Movement (UWM), which got in conflict with the Communist Party. His mother's death in 1990 was very traumatic for him. He also recalls the difficulties of keeping in touch with friends and family, as he did not want to put them in danger because of his political involvement. After the collapse of apartheid he remained part of UWM and was unemployed for seven years, until 2001 when he received a teaching job. While unemployed, in order to survive he used to write complaint letters on behalf of employees to their employer and for radio stations. Currently, he prefers to keep his past away from others and does not trust people easily. Even his family does not know much about his past. He is currently a lecturer, is married and has a four-year-old son.

15. Sindiswa: "Nobody is going to take me out of it, except me!"

Sindiswa (52 years old, Black) is single now (had two relationships in the past) and has seven children. She had a difficult upbringing as a child of one parent – a single father – who took good care of her. Sindiswa still finds it difficult to understand why her mother abandoned her. She got involved in the struggle in the 70s when there were no forms of liberation movements yet. Taking part in numerous protests, she was shot in her leg and lived with the bullet in her body until freedom came. One of the most traumatic events she experienced was when her first baby boy was ten months old and they were in the hiding, as the police were looking for Sindiswa to arrest her. While she was boiling water, the baby pulled the pot and the boiling water went all over his body. Since Sindiswa could not go out, she asked a woman to take the child to hospital and she stayed behind crying and not knowing if her baby would live. The baby was left with serious marks on his head and arms and is now in jail, as he got involved with "some bad boys". After the collapse of apartheid, Sindiswa became a member and an employee of the Khulumani Support Group. She is upset about the attitude of the young generation who like to party and are not disciplined enough to finish their studies. They "misinterpret democracy and are abusing their rights". She had no support and everything she achieved was through her own effort. People in her extended family call her only when they need her to contribute for funeral costs. Sindiswa is pessimistic about the future and does not trust other people and institutions. Through her work at Khulumani she wants to help other former victims become more active and stop "capitalising on poverty".

16. Sipho*: "I'm still studying now and I'm in my forties"

Sipho (42 years old, Black) is married with four children and has a stable job. He grew up in Eastern Cape and has had clear memories since he was about seven years old, about his parents being harassed by the police and his uncle being in jail for political reasons. In 1983, being only 15 years old, he got involved in the struggle against apartheid. He was detained that year and put in prison until 1984. During the first fifteen days of detention he was badly beaten and tortured with the wet plastic bag, needles under his nails and hit on his feet and genitals. Five of his friends were killed in detention during that time. The security police told his parents that he had killed himself, as they were planning to kill him too.

After being released, he went into hiding for two years in some places in the Cape Town area and has remained in Cape Town until now. He is deeply affected by all these traumatic events and regrets the time lost in hiding when he could have studied. He decided to continue his education and is determined to complete his undergraduate studies. Sipho is disappointed with the current political situation, corruption, poverty and crime. Although he is proud of having been a leader in the liberation movement, he currently believes that Black people are still suffering, Whites are still controlling the finances and the Black elite is focusing only on themselves to become rich. He is happy to make a difference in other people's lives through his job and believes that education is the only way to succeed in life and the only future for the country.

17. Thelma: "Because Nelson Mandela is a forgiving man, we are also forgiving people"

Thelma (75 years old, Black) was an assistant nurse before she retired. Her husband died and she lives now with her daughter and her two kids. She suffered multiple traumas during apartheid. One trauma was the experience of forced displacement, when they were taken away without any notice and removed from Retreat to Nyanga. Their belongings were taken on a big truck and dumped on an empty field. Another traumatic experience was when her 12-year-old son was nearly shot by a policeman because he did not stop when the police asked him to stop. Since it was during the children's revolt, her son was scared of the policeman and ran to his mother. Thelma was terrified seeing the policeman with a gun pointing at her son's head. Her husband's arrest was also traumatic for her. It happened in the sixties during the time of Robert Sobukwe. He was arrested together with many other men, badly beaten and all kept in inhumane conditions, in very small confinement, one bleeding on top of the other as there was no place to move away. A two-year-old child of her relative was shot because the parents did not stop as they were hurrying to take the sick child to the hospital. Something that left an impact on Thelma was her own arrest one morning while she was trying to buy milk for her kids left asleep in the house. She was arrested by a Black policeman, but was set free by a White policeman who felt sorry for her seeing her crying desperately because her kids were left alone and the house unlocked. In the present, she is disappointed with the fact that even now she still has to walk a long way to the toilet where she lives in Gugulethu. However, she is able to forgive and move on as in her view "we cannot live in the past".

What gives her strength to forgive are her Christian values and the example of Nelson Mandela and Desmond Tutu.

18. Thembi: "All my life I've been a fighter"

Thembi (62 years old, Black) is an actress, singer, playwright and composer. Her life story is illustrated in "A woman in waiting", a play she co-wrote and starred in. Her traumatic experiences during apartheid are described through her pain as a little girl who had to live without her parents. She had to live with her grandmother in Eastern Cape because her parents worked in Western Cape and were able to come home only for Christmas. She recalls her mother's humiliation by her White boss and her acute desire to be White as, for her, "anything white was better". Similar to her mother, she also became a domestic worker playing with the White kids while her child "was playing in the dusty streets in townships". As her parents separated when she was a teenager, and also being the oldest among siblings, she soon became a kind of mother in the family. She was arrested several times because she did not have a pass. The most traumatic experience for the whole family was when her sister was almost necklaced. Through her friends in the UDF, Thembi managed to save her sister. This experience had a devastating impact on Thembi's sister; although she is currently in her forties, she still lives with her mother and cannot keep a job or a relationship. In Thembi's view both reconciliation and forgiveness is a process and a "continuous struggle with yourself". She uses the stage to express herself and to be a "voice for the voiceless". She is proud to have good relationships with her family and other people in her neighbourhood - a predominantly white suburb.

19. Thulani: "I'm trying to give as much as I can to our community"

Thulani (50 years old, Black) is married and has four children. He was just fifteen when he got involved in the struggle. He was part of a group of young people who were trained to use hand grenades and guns. He was given a unit and the mission to put a bomb in a building in Johannesburg. At a short time after the explosion of the building, he was arrested while he had a grenade and was intending to blow himself up. For six months he was brutally tortured with various forms of cruelty: wet bag, electrocuted, pushed faeces into his mouth, stayed naked, burnt testicles with a cigar, etc. Afterwards it was announced that he was sentenced to death. By pleading guilty, although he did not agree with this at the beginning,

Thulani was sentenced to 18 years in prison on Robben Island. He stayed in prison from 1982 to 1991. Compared with his treatment in solitary confinement, when he went to this prison, he felt like "a president going to the palace". Although life in prison was difficult, he came to appreciate the important lessons and skills he learned from older detainees such as Mr. Kathrada and Tokyo Sexwale. They would read the Bible every day, wash their clothes and read foreign books smuggled into the prison in mysterious ways. They learned life skills in prison and befriended the guards. His former guard is still his friend in the present. In prison they were busy planning the future and thinking about what kind of South Africa they wanted when apartheid would be over. Thulani's major suffering is related to his father's shooting by the security police, while he was coming to visit Thulani in prison. Without any involvement in the struggle, just because he was Thulani's father, he was shot eight times and is now in a wheelchair, having a permanent disability. He constantly reminds Thulani that he is responsible for his condition and expects him to pay for his treatment even if sometimes Thulani cannot afford the medication. Thulani lives with his family in a township and wants to provide support and change some of the people's attitudes in the community. He believes that revenge is not the best thing. He started first to forgive himself and then his attitude towards his perpetrators and former guards changed as well. He "was able to move forward" and wants to bring peace wherever he is as "no one is born to be violent but you are trained to be violent".

20. Zitulele: "We are scared now of our own children"

Zitulele (80 years old, Black) was born in Eastern Cape and moved to Cape Town in 1950. Since he did not have a pass, he was many times arrested and beaten by the police. In 1966 he brought his wife, who also was arrested by the police as they knew she did not have a pass. The police used to come in the middle of the night, kick the door open and enter by force to search for her. They did not care if she was undressed or even if she had the baby in her arms. Zitulele had to keep paying to get her back. He is very disappointed with the current situation, the poverty and crime. He admitted living in constant fear of his own children. Before he retired, he was a driver. He lives now with his wife, but his children and grandchildren are still asking money from him. They have no stable jobs and have not completed their education. He feels that "crime is just too much" and he cannot cope with all the requests from their children who force him to give them his own money.

APPENDIX B:
GLOSSARY AND ACRONYMS

AA	Affirmative Action
Afrikaans	Language, evolved mainly from Dutch; spoken by Afrikaners and majority of Coloured people
ANC	African National Congress
APA	American Psychiatric Association
APLA	Azanian People's Liberation Army
AZAPO	Azanian People's Organisation
Bantu Education	Legally imposed inferior education for Africans in 1953
BBE	Black Economic Empowerment
COSATU	Congress of South African Trade Union
CSVR	Centre for the Study of Violence and Reconciliation
DSM	Diagnostic Statistic Manual
FAMSA	Family and Marriage Association of South Africa
ICD	International Classification of Diseases
IDASA	Institute for Democracy in South Africa
IJR	Institute of Justice and Reconciliation

LHS	Linking Human Systems: a systemic therapeutic program of working with families and communities affected by mass trauma
Matric	Short for matriculation; final examination taken at the end of high school
Necklacing	The method of execution carried out by forcing a rubber tyre, filled with petrol, around a victims chest and setting it on fire
PAC	Pan Africanist Congress: broke away from ANC in 1959
Pass/ passbook	Identity document required for Africans over sixteen to restrict their movement; abolished in 1986 and replaced by other means of control
PTSD	Posttraumatic Stress Disorder
PTG	Posttraumatic Growth
RDP	Reconstruction and Development Programme
SACP	South African Communist Party
SEP	Stanford Encyclopaedia of Philosophy
Shebeen	An illegal drinking place with live music
Standard	Grade in school: standard six is the equivalent of the eight grade
Township	Black residential ghettoes located near cities
TRC	Truth and Reconciliation Commission
TRC	Act Promotion of National Unity and Reconciliation Act

Ubuntu   A classical African concept emphasising the
                         importance of relationships: "I am what I am because
                         of who we all are"

UDF   United Democratic Front

UWM   Unemployed Workers Movement

BIBLIOGRAPHY

Abell, J., Stokoe, E. H. & Billing, M. (2000). Narrative and discursive (re)construction of events. In M. Andrews, S. D. Sclater, C. Squire & A. Trecher (Eds.). *Lines of narrative: Psychosocial perspectives* (pp. 180-192). London: Routledge.

Abbott, P. (2008). *The Cambridge introduction to narrative* (2nd edition). Cambridge University Press.

Adhikari, M. (Ed.). (2009). *Burden by race: Coloured identities in southern Africa*. University of Cape Town Press.

Alasuutari, P. (1995). *Researching culture: Qualitative method and cultural studies*. Thousand Oaks, CA: Sage.

Allwood, C. (1986). Violence: The psychological toll. *Race Relations News*, July, 5.

American Psychological Association. (2010). *Publication manual of the American Psychological Association* (6th edition). Washington, DC: American Psychological Association.

Andreasen, N. C. (1985). Posttraumatic stress disorder. In H. I. Kaplan & B. J. Sadock (Eds.). *Comprehensive textbook of psychiatry* (pp. 918-924). Baltimore: Williams and Wilkins.

Andrews, M., Sclater, S., Squire, C. & Treacher, A. (2000). *Lines of narrative: Psychosocial perspectives*. London: Routledge.

Antze, P. (1996). Telling stories, making selves. In P. Antze & M. Lambeck (Eds). *Tense past: Cultural essays in trauma and memory* (pp. 3-25). New York: Routledge.

Antze, P. & Lambeck, M. (Eds.). (1996). *Tense past: Cultural essays in trauma and memory*. New York: Routledge.

APA (1952). *Diagnostic and statistical manual of mental disorders* (1st edition). Washington, DC: American Psychiatric Association.

APA (1968). *Diagnostic and statistical manual of mental disorders* (2st edition). Washington, DC: American Psychiatric Association.

APA (1980). *Diagnostic and statistical manual of mental disorders* (3st edition). Washington, DC: American Psychiatric Association.

APA (1987). *Diagnostic and statistical manual of mental disorders* (3st edition, revised). Washington, DC: American Psychiatric Association.

APA (1994). *Diagnostic and statistical manual of mental disorders* (4st edition). Washington, DC: American Psychiatric Association.

Arendt, H. (1963). *Eichman in Jerusalem: A report on the banality of evil.* New York: Viking.

Arrington, E. G., & Wilson, M. N. (2000). A re-examination of risk and resilience during adolescence: Incorporating culture and diversity. *Journal of Child and Family Studies, 9*(2), 221-230.

Asmal, K., Roberts, R. S. & Asmal, L. (1998). *Reconciliation through truth: A reckoning of apartheid's criminal governance.* New York: Palgrave Macmillan.

Auerhahn, N. C. & Laub, D. (1998). Intergenerational Memory of the Holocaust. In Y. Danieli (Ed.). *Intergenerational handbook of multigenerational legacies of trauma* (pp. 21-42) New York: Plenum Press.

Baker, D. (2010). Watching a bargain unravel? A panel study of victim's attitudes about transitional justice in Cape Town, South Africa. *The International Journal of Transitional Justice, 4*, 443 – 456.

Baldwin, A. L., Baldwin, C. P., Kasser, T., Zax, M., Sameroff, A. & Seifer, R. (1993). Contextual risk and resiliency during late adolescence. *Development and Psychopathology, 5,* 741-761.

Bar-On, D. (1999). *The indescribable and the undiscussable.* Budapest: Central European University Press.

—. (2000). From intractable conflict through conflict resolution to reconciliation: Psychological analysis. *Political Psychology, 21*(2), 351-365.

Bateson, G. (1972). *Steps to an ecology of mind.* San Francisco, CA: Chandler.

Bateson, G., Jackson, D. D., Haley, J. & Weakland, J. (1956). Towards a theory of schizophrenia. *Behavioral Science, 1*, 251-264.

Berger, P. L. & Luckman, T. (1967). *The social construction of reality.* Garden City, NY: Doubleday.

Bertando, P. (2000). Text and context: Narrative, postmodernism and cybernetics. *Journal of Family Therapy, 22,* 83-103.

Bhavnani, K. K. (1990). What's power got to do with it? Empowerment and social research. In I. Parker & J. Shotter (Eds.). *Deconstructing social psychology* (pp. 141-152). London: Routhledge.

Blake, D. D., Albano, A. M. & Keane, T. M. (1992). Twenty years of trauma: Psychological abstracts 1970 through 1989. *Journal of Traumatic Stress, 5,* 477-484.

Bogdan, R. C. & Biklen, S. K. (1992). *Qualitative research for education: An introduction to theory and methods* (2nd edition). Boston: Allyn and Bacon.

Bonanno, G. A. (2004). Loss, trauma, and human resilience: Have we underestimated the human capacity to thrive after extremely aversive events? *American Psychologist, 59,* 20-28.

—. (2005). Clarifying and extending the construct of adult resilience. *American Psychologist, 60,* 265-267.

Boraine, A., Levy, J. & Scheffer, R. (Eds) (1994). *Dealing with the past: Truth and reconciliation in South Africa.* Cape Town: Institute for Democracy in South Africa (IDASA).

Bracken P. (2002). *Trauma: Culture, meaning and philosophy.* London: Whurr.

—. (2007). Beyond models, beyond paradigms: The radical interpretation of recovery. In P. Stastny and P. Lehmann (Eds.). *Alternatives beyond psychiatry* (pp. 400-401). Berlin: Peter Lehmann.

Bracken P., Giller J.E. & Summerfield. D. (1995). Psychological responses to war and atrocity: the limitations of current concepts. *Social Science and Medicine, 40,* 1073-1082.

Bracken, P. & Petty, C. (Eds.). (1998). *Rethinking the trauma of war.* London: Free Association Press.

Bracken P. & Thomas P. (2001). Postpsychiatry: A new direction for mental health. *British Medical Journal, 322,* 724-727.

Bracken P. & Thomas, P. (2005). *Postpsychiatry: Mental health in a postmodern world.* Oxford: Oxford University Press.

Braun, V. & Clarke, V. (2006). Using thematic analysis in psychology. *Qualitative Research in Psychology, 3,* 77-101.

Breslau, N. (1998). Epidemiology of trauma and posttraumatic stress disorder. In R. Yehuda (Ed.). *Psychological trauma* (pp. 1-30). Washington, DC: American Psychiatric Press.

Brewin, C. R., Andrews, B. & Valentine, J. D. (2000). Meta-analysis of risk factors for posttraumatic stress disorder in trauma-exposed adults. *Journal of Consulting and Clinical Psychology, 68,* 748-766.

Brison, S. (2002). *Aftermath: Violence and the remaking of a self.* Princeton University Press.

Bruner, J. (1990). *Acts of meaning.* Harvard University Press.

—. (1991). The narrative construction of reality. *Critical Inquiry, 18,* 1-21.

Burr, V. (1998). Overview: Realism, relativism, social constructionism and discourse. In I. Parker (Ed.). *Social constructionism, discourse and realism* (pp. 13-27). London: Sage.

Business Report. (2011). *South Africa most unequal society in the world.* Retrieved May 20, 2011, from http://www.iol.co.za/business/business-news/sa-most-unequal-society-in-the-world-1.1064335

Cairns, E. & Lewis, C. A. (1999). Collective memories, political violence and mental health in Northern Ireland. *British Journal of Psychology, 90*, 25-33.

Cassey, E. (1987). *Remembering: A phenomenological study.* Bloomington: Indiana University Press.

Carey, P. D., Stein, D. J., Zungu-Dirwayi, N. & Seedat, S. (2003). Trauma and posttraumatic stress disorder in an urban Xhosa primary care population: Prevalence, comorbidity, and service use patterns. *Journal of Nervous and Mental Disease, 19*(4), 230-236.

Carr, A. (2006). *Family therapy: Concepts, process and practice (2nd edition).* Chichester: John Wiley and Sons.

Carrigan, C. J. (1996). *Jacques Derrida, deconstructionism and postmodernism.* Retrieved September 25, 2010 from http://www.ontruth.com/derrida.html

Cerny, J. A., Barlow, D. H., Craske, M. G. & Himadi, W. G. (1987). Couples treatment of agoraphobia: A two year follow-up. *Behaviour Therapy, 18,* 401-415.

Chapman, A. (2008). Perspectives on the role of forgiveness in the human rights violations hearings. In A. Chapman & H. van der Merwe . *Truth and reconciliation in South Africa: Did the TRC deliver?* (pp. 66-89). Philadelphia: University of Pennsylvania Press.

Chapman, A. & Van der Merwe, H. (2008). *Truth and reconciliation in South Africa: Did the TRC deliver?* Philadelphia: University of Pennsylvania Press.

Cichetti, D., & Garmezy, N. (Eds.). (1993). Milestones in the development of resilience [Special issue]. *Development and Psychopatology, 5*(4). 497-774.

Cichetti, D., & Schneider-Rosen, K. (1986). An organisational approach to childhood depression. In M. Rutter, C. Izard, & P. Read (Eds.). *Depression in young people, clinical and developmental perspectives* (pp. 71-134). New York: Guilford.

Chikane, F. (1986). Children in turmoil: The effects of unrest on township children. In S. Burman & P. Reynolds (Eds.). *Growing up in a divided society* (pp. 333-345). Johannesburg: Ravan Press.

Colvin, C. (2000). *We are still struggling: Story telling, reparations and reconciliation after the TRC.* Retrieved February 12, 2010, from http://www.csvr.org.za/docs/trc/wearestillstruggling.pdf

—. (2006). Shifting geographies of suffering and recovery: Traumatic storytelling after apartheid. In T. Luedke & H. West (Eds.). *Borders and healers: Brokering therapeutic resources* (pp. 166-183). Bloomington: Indiana University Press.

Creswell, J. (2003). *Research design: Qualitative, quantitative and mixed methods approaches.* CA: Sage.

Creswell, J. W., & Miller, D. L. (2000). Determining validity in qualitative inquiry. *Theory into Practice, 39(3),* 124-130.

Cronen, V. & Pearce, W. (1985). Toward an explanation of how the Milan method works: An invitation to a systemic epistemology and the evolution of family systems. In D. Campbell & R. Draper (Eds.). *Applications of systemic family therapy: The Milan approach (pp. 69-84).* London: Grune and Stratton.

Crossley, M. (2000). *Introducing narrative psychology: Self, trauma and the construction of meaning.* Buckingham: Open University Press.

Crotty, M. (1998). *The foundation of social research: Meaning and perspective in the research process.* London: Sage.

Cushman, P. (1990). Why the self is empty: Toward a historically situated psychology. *American Psychologist, 45,* 599-611.

—. (1995). *Constructing the self, constructing America.* New York: Addison-Wesley.

Daly, E. & Sarkin, J. (2007). *Reconciliation in divided societies: Finding common ground.* Philadelphia: University of Pennsylvania Press.

Danieli, Y. (Ed.). (1998). *Intergenerational handbook of multigenerational legacies of trauma.* New York: Plenum Press.

Davies, B. (1998). Psychology's subject: A commentary on the relativism/realism debate. In I. Parker (Ed.). *Social constructionism, discourse and realism* (pp. 13-27). London: Sage.

De la Rey, C. (1999). *Career narratives of women professors in South Africa.* Unpublished doctoral dissertation. University of Cape Town, South Africa.

De la Rey, C., Duncan, N., Shefer, T. & Niekerk, A. (Eds.). (1997). *Contemporary issues in human development: A South African focus.* Durban: International Thomson.

Dawes, A. & Tredoux, C. (1989). Emotional status of children exposed to political violence in the Crossroads squatter area during 1986-1987. *Psychology in Society, 12,* 33-47.

Doxtader, E. & Salazar P. (2007). *Truth and reconciliation in South Africa. The fundamental documents.* Cape Town: Institute of Justice and Reconciliation.

Duncan, N. & Rock, B. (1997). The impact of political violence on the lives of South African children. In C. de la Rey, N. Duncan, T. Shefer, & A. Niekerk (Eds.). *Contemporary issues in human development: A South African focus* (pp. 133-155). Durban: International Thomson.

Du Plessis, C. (2010, August 6). *Corruption is killing us.* The Cape Times, p. A1.

Du Toit, A. (1990). Disc ourses on political violence. In N. C. Manganyi & A. du Toit (Eds.). *Political violence and the struggle in South Africa* (pp. 87-130). Hampshire: MacMillan.

Eagle, G. (2011, June). *Comparing complex and continuous traumatic stress: Diagnostic and treatment implications.* Paper presented at the second national symposium on continuous traumatic stress in South Africa, Cape Town, South Africa.

Edwards, D. (2009). The lasting legacy of trauma. In P. Gobodo-Madikizela & C. Van der Merwe (Eds.). *Memory, narrative and forgiveness* (pp. 47-75). Newcastle: Cambridge Scholars.

Eliot, S. & Whitlock, K. (Eds.). (1992). *The enlightenment: Texts II.* Milton Keynes: The Open University.

Ercikan, K. & Roth, W. (2009). *Generalizing from educational research: Beyond qualitative and quantitative polarization.* New York: Routledge.

Etherington, K. (2003). *Trauma, the body and transformation.* London: Jessica Kingsley.

Everatt, D. & Sisulu, E. (Eds.) (1992). *Black youth in crisis.* Braamfontein: Ravan Press.

Falicov, C. (2007). Working with transnational immigrants: Expanding meanings of family, community and culture. *Family Process, 46*(2). 157-171.

Felsen, I. (1998). Transgenerational transmission of the effects of the Holocaust: The North American research perspective. In Y. Danieli (Ed.). *Intergenerational handbook of multigenerational legacies of trauma* (pp. 43-68) New York: Plenum Press.

Foa, E. & Meadows, E. (1998). Psychosocial treatments for posttraumatic stress disorder. In R. Yehuda (Ed.). *Psychological trauma* (pp. 179-204). Washington, DC: American Psychiatric Press.

Foster, D. (1991). Social influence 1: Ideology. In D. Foster & J. Low-Potgieter (Eds.). *Social psychology in South Africa* (pp. 345-391). Johannesburg: Lexicon.

—. (1993). On racism: Virulent mythologies and fragile threads. In L. Nicholas (Ed.). *Psychology and oppression* (pp. 55-80). Johannesburg: Skotaville.

—. (1995). *Advanced studies in racism and the psychology of intergroup relations.* Unpublished report. University of Cape Town.

Foster, D., Davis, D. & Sandler, D. (1987). *Detention and torture in South Africa.* Cape Town: David Philip.

Foster, D., Haupt, P. & de Beer, M. (2005). *The theatre of violence.* Cape Town: HSRC Press.

Foster, D. & Sandler, D. (1985). *A study of detention and torture in South Africa.* Preliminary report. Institute of Criminology: University of Cape Town.

Foster, D. & Skinner, D. (1990). Detention and violence: Beyond victimology. In N. C. Manganyi & A. du Toit (Eds.). *Political violence and the struggle in South Africa* (pp. 205-234). Hampshire: Macmillan.

Foucault, M. (1972). *The archaeology of knowledge and the discourse on language.* London: Tavistock.

—. (1979). *Discipline and punish: The birth of the prison.* New York: Vintage.

—. (1980). *The history of sexuality* (Vol I). New York: Vintage.

Frank, A. (1995). *The wounded storyteller.* Chicago: The University of Chicago Press.

Freeman, M. (1993). *Rewriting the self: History, memory, narrative.* London: Routledge.

Freud, S. (1894). On the grounds for detaching a particular syndrome from neurasthenia under the description 'anxiety neurosis'. *The standard edition of the complete psychological works of Sigmund Freud* (Vol. 3). London: Hogarth Press.

—. (1919). *Introduction to the psychology of the war neurosis* (Standard Edition, Vol. 18). London: Hogarth Press.

Garmezy, N. (1985). The NIMH-Israeli high-risk study: Commendation, comments, and cautions. *Schizophrenia Bulletin, 11*, 349-353.

—. (1991). Resilience in children's adaptation to negative life events and stressed environments. *Paediatrics, 20*, 459-466.

Gavreliuc, A. (Coord.), Bozian, M., Gavreliuc, D., Rogobete, I. & Vochin-Bartl (2006). *Psihologia interculturala: Impactul determinarilor culturale asupra fenomenelor psihosociale.* West University of Timisoara, Romania.

Gergen, K. (1973). Social psychology as history. *Journal of Personality and Social Psychology, 26*, 309-320.

—. (1991). *The saturated self: Dilemmas of identity in contemporary life.* New York: Basic Books.

—. (2003). Knowledge as socially constructed. In M. Gergen and K. Gergen (Eds.). *Social construction: A reader* (pp. 15-22). London: Sage.

Gergen, M. & Gergen, K. (1993). Narratives of the gendered body in popular autobiography. In R. Josselson & A. Lieblich (Eds.). *The narrative study of lives* (Vol. 1) (pp. 191-218). Newbury Park, CA: Sage.

Gergen, M. & Gergen, K. (Eds.). (2003). *Social construction: A reader.* London: Sage.

Gibson, J. (2004). *Overcoming apartheid: Can truth reconcile a divided nation?* New York: Russell Sage Foundation.

Gibson, K. (1989). Children in political violence. *Social Science Medical Journal, 28*(7), 659-667.

Giddens, A. (1979). *Central problems in social theory: Action, structure and contradiction in social analysis.* London: Macmillan.

Giller, J. E. (1998). Caring for 'victims of torture' in Uganda: Some personal reflections. In P. Bracken & C. Petty (Eds.). *Rethinking the trauma of war* (pp. 128-145). London: Free Association Press.

Gobodo-Madikizela, P. (2003). *A human being died that night.* New York: First Mariner Books.

—. (2009). Working through the past: Some thoughts on forgiveness in cultural context. In P. Gobodo-Madikizela & C. Van der Merwe (Eds.). *Memory, narrative and forgiveness* (pp. 148-170). Newcastle: Cambridge Scholars.

Gobodo-Madikizela, P. & Van der Merwe, C. (Eds.) (2009). *Memory, narrative and forgiveness.* Newcastle: Cambridge Scholars.

Goldenberg, H. and Goldenberg, I. (2008). *Family therapy: An overview.* Belmont: Thomson Brooks/Cole.

Griswold, C. (2007). *Forgiveness: A philosophical exploration.* New York: Cambridge University Press.

—. (2009). Forgiveness and narrative. In P. Gobodo-Madikizela and C. van der Merwe (Eds.). *Memory, narrative and forgiveness* (pp. 98-112). Newcastle: Cambridge Scholars.

Guthrey, H. (2015). *Victim healing and truth commissions.* New York: Springer. DOI: 10.1007/998-3-319-12487-2

Haley, J. (1967). Toward a theory of pathological systems. In G. Zuk, & I. Boszormenyi-Nagy (Eds.). *Family therapy and disturbed families* (pp. 11-27). Palo Alto, CA: Science and Behavior Books.

Hamber, B. (1995). *Do sleeping dogs lie? The psychological implications of the TRC in South Africa.* Retrieved September, 17, 2008, from www.csvr.org.za/papers/papbh&rw.htm

—. (1998). Conclusion: A truth commission for Northern Ireland? In B. Hamber (Ed.). *Past imperfect: Dealing with the past in Northern*

Ireland and societies in transition. Derry, Londonderry: University of Ulster. Retrieved November 7, 2010, from http://www.brandonhamber.com/publications/Chap%207%20-%20SA%20&%20NI%20Brandon%20Hamber.pdf

—. (2000). Repairing the irreparable: Dealing with double-binds of making reparations for crimes of the past. *Ethnicity and Health, 5(3-4),* 215-226. Retrieved October 2, 2009, from http://www.csvr.org.za/docs/trc/repairingtheirreparable.pdf

—. (2004). *The impact of trauma: A psychosocial approach.* Retrieved September 17, 2008, from www.csvr.org.za/papers/papbh&rw.htm

—. (2009). *Transforming societies after political violence.* Springer.

Hamber, B. & Wilson, R. (1999). *Symbolic closure through memory, reparation and revenge in post-conflict societies.* Retrieved September 17, 2008, from http://www.csvr.org.za/index.php?option=com_content&view=article&id=1716%3Asymbolic-closure-through-memory-reparation-and-revenge-in-post-conflict-societies&Itemid=2

Hammersley, M. (1992). *What's wrong with ethnography? – Methodological explorations.* London: Routledge.

Hardtmann, G. (1998). Children of Nazis: A psychodynamic perspective. In Y. Danieli (Ed.). *Intergenerational handbook of multigenerational legacies of trauma* (pp. 85-96). New York: Plenum Press.

Hare-Mustin, R., (1986). The problem of gender in family therapy theory. *Family Process, 26,* 15-27.

Harvey, D. (1993). *The condition of postmodernity.* Oxford: Blackwell.

Harvey, M., Mondesir, A. & Aldrich, H. (2007). Fostering resilience in traumatized communities: A community empowerment model of intervention. In M. R. Harvey & P. Tummala-Narra (Eds.). Sources of expressions of resilience in trauma survivors: Ecological theory, multicultural practice. *Journal of Aggression, Maltreatment and Trauma, 14,* Retrieved September 8, 2009, from http://www.challiance.org/vov/publications/Fostering%20resilience%20in%20traumatized%20communities.pdf

Hassan, I. (1996). Postmodernism: A paracritical bibliography. In L. Cahoon, (Ed.). *From modernism to postmodernism: An anthology* (pp. 325-335). Oxford: Blackwell.

Herman, J. (2001). *Trauma and recovery* (4th edition). London: Pandora.

Hirschowitz, R., Milner, S. & Everatt, D. (1992). *Growing up in a divided society.* Braamfontain: CASE.

Hirschowitz, R. & Orkin, M. (1997). Trauma and mental health in South Africa. *Social Indicators Research, 41,* 169-182.

Hoffman, L. (1985). Beyond power and control: Toward a "second order" family systems therapy. *Family Systems Medicine, 2,* 381-396.

Hook, D. & Harris, B. (2000). Discourses of order and their disruption: The texts of the South African Truth and Reconciliation Commission. *South African Journal of Psychology, 30*(1), 14-22.

Horowitz, M. J. (1975). Intrusive and repetitive thoughts after stress. *Archives of General Psychiatry, 32,* 1457-1463.

Human Science Research Council. (2004, July 26). Fact sheet: Poverty in South Africa. In *South African Regional Poverty Report.* Retrieved March 3, 2011, from http://www.sarpn.org.za/documents/d0000990/

Hutnik N. (2005). Toward holistic, compassionate, professional care: Using a cultural lens to examine the practice of contemporary psychotherapy in the West. *Contemporary Family Therapy, 10,* 383-402.

Ide, N & Paez, A. (2000). Complex PTSD: A review of current issues. *International Journal of Emergency Mental Health, 2,* 43-49.

Ivey, A.E., D'Andrea, M., Ivey, M.B., Simek-Morgan, L. (Eds.). (2002). *Theories of counselling and psychotherapy: A multicultural perspective* (5th edition). Boston: Allyn and Bacon.

Janoff-Bulman, R. (1989). Assumptive worlds and the stress of traumatic events: Applications of the schema construct. *Social Cognition, 7,* 113-136.

—. (1992). *Shattered assumptions: Towards a new psychology of trauma.* New York: The Free Press.

Jenkins, H. (1986). A family and other systems: Treatment within a structural-strategic framework. *Maladjustment and Therapeutic Education, 4(2),* 33-41.

Johnson, H., Thompson, A. & Downs, M. (2009). Non-western interpreters' experiences of trauma: The protective role of culture following exposure to oppression. *Ethnicity and Health, 14*(4), 407-418.

Johnson, S. (2002). *Emotionally focused couple therapy with trauma survivors.* New York: The Guilford Press.

Joseph, S., Williams, R. and Yule, W. (1998). *Understanding post-traumatic stress.* New York: John Wiley and Sons.

Kaminer, D. (2006). Healing processes in trauma narratives: A review. *South African Journal of Psychology, 36*(3), 481-499.

—. (2011, June). *Introduction and overview of symposium aims.* Paper presented at the second national symposium on continuous traumatic stress in South Africa, Cape Town, South Africa.

Kaminer, D. & Eagle, G. (2010). *Traumatic stress in South Africa.* Johannesburg: Wits University Press.

Kaminer, D., Grimsrud, A., Myer, L., Stein, D. & Williams (2008). Risk for post-traumatic stress disorder associated with different forms of interpersonal violence in South Africa. *Social Science and Medicine, 67,* 1589-1595.

Kaminer, D., Stein, D., Mbanga, I. & Zungu-Dirwayi, N. (2001). The Truth and Reconciliation Commission in South Africa: Relation to psychiatric status and forgiveness among survivors of human rights abuses. *The British Journal of Psychiatry, 178,* 373-377.

Kardiner, A. (1941). *The traumatic neurosis of war. Psychosomatic medicine monograph II-III.* New York: Paul B. Hoeber.

Kaplan, E.A. (2005). *Trauma culture: Politics of terror and loss in media and literature.* New Jersey: Rutgers University Press.

Kgalema, L. (2002). *Making amends: The psychological impact of South Africa's Truth and Reconciliation Commission on victims of gross human rights violations.* Unpublished master's thesis. University of Cape Town. South Africa.

Khulumani Support Group (2011, May 11). *Khulumani comments on government gazette general notice 282.* Retrieved June 3, 2011, from http://www.khulumani.net/reparations/government/2011-regulations/item/481-i-introduction-comments-on-the-draft-regulations-published-by-the-department-of-justice-dealing-with-reparations-for-apartheid-era-victims.html

Khulumani Support Group (2015). Retrieved May 30, 2015, from http://www.khulumani.net/khulumani/about-us.html

Kirk, J. & Miller, M. L. (1986). *Reliability and validity in qualitative research.* Beverly Hills, CA: Sage.

Kraeplin, E. (1886). *Psychiatrie* (Vol. 5). Leipzig: Barth.

Kuhn, T. (2003). On scientific paradigms. In M. Gergen & K. Gergen (Eds.). *Social construction: A reader* (pp. 7-10). London: Sage.

Kvale, S. (Ed.). (1992). *Psychology and postmodernism.* London: Sage.

Landau, J. (2007). Enhancing resilience: Families and communities as agents for change. *Family Process, 46,* 351-365.

Landau, J & Garrett, J. (2006). *Invitational intervention: A step-by step guide for clinicians helping families engage resistant substance abusers in treatment.* BookSurge.com: BookSurge.

Landau, J. & Saul, J. (2004). Facilitating family and community resilience in response to major disaster. In F. Walsh & M. McGoldrick (Eds.). *Living beyond loss* (pp. 285-309). New York: Norton.

Landau, J., Mittal, M. & Wieling, E. (2008). Linking human systems: Strengthening individuals, families and communities in the wake of mass trauma. *Journal of Marital and Family Therapy, 34*(2), 193-209.

Lifton, R. J. (1993). *The Protean self: Human resilience in an age of fragmentation.* New York: Basic Books.

Lincoln, Y. S. & Guba, E. G. (1985). *Naturalistic inquiry.* Beverly Hills, CA: Sage.

Linden, M., Rotter, M., Baumann, K. & Lieberei, B. (2007). *Posttraumatic embitterment disorder: Definition, evidence, diagnosis, treatment.* Cambridge, MA: Hogrefe and Huber.

Lum, W. (2002). The use of the self of the therapist. *Contemporary Family Therapy, 24*(1). 181-197.

Luthar, S., Cichetti, D. & Becker, B. (2000). The construct of resilience: A critical evaluation and guidelines for future work. *Child Development, 71*(3), 543-562.

Lutz, C. (2003). Emotion: The universal as local. In M. Gergen & K. Gergen (Eds.). *Social construction: A reader* (pp. 39-43). London: Sage.

Mamdani, M. (1996). Reconciliation without justice. *Southern African Review of Books*, November/December, 3-5.

Mannheim, K. (1936). *Ideology and utopia: An introduction to the sociology of knowledge.* New York: Harcourt Brace and World.

Manganyi, N. C. & du Toit, A. (Eds.). (1990). *Political violence and the struggle in South Africa.* Hampshire: Macmillan.

Marks, M. (2001). *Young warriors: Youth, politics, identity and violence in South Africa.* Johannesburg: University of Witwatersrand.

Marks S. & Andersson N. (1990). The epidemiology and culture of violence. In N. C. Manganyi & A. du Toit (Eds.). *Political violence and the struggle in South Africa* (pp. 29-69). Hampshire: Macmillan.

McGoldrick, M. & Carter, E. (1982). The family life cycle. In F. Walsh. (Ed.). *Normal family process* (pp. 167-195). New York: Guilford Press.

Mengel, E., Bnorzaga, M. & Orantes, K. (Eds.). (2010). *Trauma, memory, and narrative in South Africa.* Amsterdam: Rodopi.

Miles, R. (1989). *Racism.* London: Routledge.

Minuchin, S. (1974). *Families and family therapy.* London: Tavistock.

Moon, C. (2008). *Narrating political reconciliation: South Africa's Truth and Reconciliation Commission.* Maryland: Lexington Books.

Moon, C. (2009). Healing past violence: Traumatic assumptions and therapeutic interventions in war and reconciliation. *Journal of Human Rights, 8*, 71-91.

Morris, D. (2003). The meaning of pain. In M. Gergen & K. Gergen (Eds.). *Social construction: A reader* (pp. 43-47). London: Sage.

Mott, F. W. (1919). *War neuroses and shell shock.* London: Oxford University Press.

Nabbaro-Rubinstein, N. (1992, November). *Systemic insight: A concept in interactional context.* Workshop presented at the European Family Therapy Association International Congress: Feelings and Systems, Sorrento, Italy.

Nichols, M. (2009). *Family therapy: Concepts and methods (9th edition).* Upper Saddle River, NJ: Prentice Hall.

Ogden, C. J., Kaminer, D., Van Kradenburg, J., Seedat, S. & Stein, D. J. (2000). Narrative themes in response to trauma in a religious community. *Central African Journal of Medicine, 46*(7), 178-184.

Ong, A. D., Bergeman, C. S., Bisconti, T. L. & Wallace, K. A. (2006). Psychological resilience, positive emotions and successful adaptation to stress in later life. *Journal of Personality and Social Psychology, 91*(4), 730-749.

Pals, J. L. & McAdams, D. P. (2004). The transformed self: A narrative understanding of posttraumatic growth. *Psychological Inquiry, 15*(1), 65-69.

Pare, D.A. (1996). Culture and meaning: Expanding the metaphorical repertoire of family therapy. *Family Process, 35,* 21-42.

Parker, I. (1998). *Social constructionism, discourse and realism.* London: Sage.

Parkes, J. and Unterhalter, E. (2009). Violence and the struggle for coherence in South African transformation. In P. Gobodo-Madikizela and C. van der Merwe (pp. 400-427). *Memory, narrative and forgiveness.* Newcastle: Cambridge Scholars.

Pillay, B. (2000). Providing mental health services to survivors: A KwaZulu-Natal perspective. *Ethnicity and Health, 5*(3-4), 369-272.

Polkinghorne, D. P. (1988). *Narrative knowing and the human science.* New York: Sunny Press.

Posel, D. (1990). Symbolizing violence: State and the media discourse in television coverage of township protest, 1985-7. In N. C. Manganyi & A. du Toit (Eds.). *Political violence and the struggle in South Africa* (pp. 154-171). Hampshire: Macmillan.

Price, L. (2002). *Making sense of political activism: Life narratives of activists from the South African liberation movement.* Unpublished doctoral dissertation. University of Cape Town, South Africa.

Rachman, S. (1980). Emotional processing. *Behaviour Research and Therapy, 18,* 51-60.

Rampage, C. (1994). Power, gender and marital intimacy. *Journal of Family Therapy, 16*, 125-137.

Ramphele, M. (1996). Political widowhood in South Africa: The embodiment of ambiguity. *Daedalus, 125*(1), 99-117.

Raport final (2006). *Comisia prezidentiala pentru analiza dictaturii comuniste in Romania*. Bucuresti. Retrieved on 2 March, 2015 from http://www.presidency.ro/static/ordine/RAPORT_FINAL_CPADCR.p df

Ricoeur, P. (1984). *Time and narrative*. University of Chicago Press.

—. (1992). *Oneself as another*. University of Chicago Press.

Riessman, C. K. (1993). *Narrative analysis*. Newbury Park, CA: Sage.

—. (2008). *Narrative methods for the human sciences*. Los Angeles: Sage.

Ritchie, J. & Lewis, J. (2003). *Qualitative research practice*. London: Sage.

Rogobete, I. (2011). *Reconstructing trauma and recovery: Life narratives of survivors of political violence during apartheid in South Africa*. Unpublished doctoral dissertation. University of Cape Town.

—. (2013). Legacies of repressive regimes: Life trajectories in the aftermath of political trauma. In P. Runcan, M. Rata & A. Gavreliuc (Eds.). *Applied social sciences: Psychology, physical education and social medicine* (pp. 83-90). Newcastle: Cambridge Scholars Publishing.

Rogobete, I. & Rogobete, S. (2014). Narrative constructs of resilience in post-apartheid South Africa. In S. Ionescu (Ed.). *From Person to Society: The Second International Congres on Resilience* (pp. 761-766). Bologna: Medimond.

Rogobete, S. (2011). The interplay of ethnic and religious identities in Europe: A possible mapping of a complex territory. In E. Eynikel & A. Ziaka (Eds.). *Religion and conflict: Essays on the origins of religious conflicts and resolution approaches* (pp. 259-277). London: Harptree.

Rosenthal G. & Volter B. (1998). Three generations within Jewish and non-Jewish German families after the unification of Germany. In Y. Danieli (Ed.). *Intergenerational handbook of multigenerational legacies of trauma* (pp. 297-314). New York: Plenum Press.

Sampson, E. (1989). The deconstruction of the self. In J. Shotter & K. Gergen (Eds.). *Texts of identity* (pp. 1-19). London: Sage.

Sarbin, T & Kitsuse, J. (1994). *Constructing the social*. London: Sage.

Satir, V. & Baldwin, M. (1983). *Satir step by step: A guide to creating change in families*. Palo Alto, CA: Science and Behaviour Books.

Saussure, F. de (2006). *Writings in general linguistics* (English translation). Oxford University Press.

Scarry, E. (1985). *The body in pain: The making and unmaking of the world.* New York: Oxford University Press.

Seligman, M. E. & Maier, S. F. (1967). Failure to escape traumatic shock. *Journal of Experiential Psychology, 74*, 1-9.

Shalev, A. & Yehuda, R. (1998). Longitudinal development of traumatic stress disorder. In R. Yehuda (Ed.). *Psychological trauma* (pp. 31-66). Washington, DC: American Psychiatric Press.

Shefer, T. (2010). Narrating gender and sex in and through apartheid divides. *South African Journal of Psychology, 40*(4), 382-396.

Shotter, J. and Gergen, K. (Eds.) (1989). *Texts of identity.* London: Sage.

Sideris, T. (2003). War, gender and culture: Mozambican women refugees. *Social Science and Medicine, 56*, 713-724.

Silverman, D. (2000). *Doing qualitative research: A practical handbook* (1st edition). London: Sage.

Silverman, D. (Ed.). (2010). *Doing qualitative research: A practical handbook* (3rd edition). London: Sage.

Simpson, M. A. (1998). The second bullet: Transgenerational impacts of the trauma of conflict within a South African and world context. In Y. Danieli (Ed.). *International handbook of multigenerational legacies of trauma* (pp. 487-512). New York: Plenum Press.

Simpson, G. & Van Zyl, P. (1995). South Africa's Truth and Reconciliation Commission. *Temps Modernes, 585*, 394-407. Retrieved April 15, 2009, from http://www.csvr.org.za/wits/papers/papgspv.htm

Skaar, E. (2009, January 18). Review of the book *Truth and reconciliation in South Africa: Did the TRC deliver?* by A. R. Chapman and H. van der Merwe. *The International Journal of Transitional Justice, 3*(1), 150-152.

Skinner, D. (1998). *Apartheid's violent legacy: A report on trauma in the Western Cape.* Cape Town: The Trauma Centre for Victims of Violence and Torture.

Solomon, Z. (1990). Does the war end when the shooting stops? The psychological toll of war. *Journal of Applied Social Psychology, 20*, 1733.

—. (1998). Transgenerational effects of the holocaust: The Israeli research perspective. In Y. Danieli (Ed.). *Intergenerational handbook of multigenerational legacies of trauma* (pp. 69-84). New York: Plenum Press.

Southward, E. E. (1919). *Shell shock and neuropsychiatric problems.* Boston: Leonard.

Sprenkle, D. H. & Piercy, F. P. (Eds.). (2005). *Research methods in family therapy*. New York: The Guilford Press.

Stanford Encyclopedia of Philosophy (2002). *Paul Ricoeur*. Retrieved October 19, 2010, from http://plato.stanford.edu/entries/ricoeur/

Statman, J. M. (2000). Performing the truth: The social-psychological context of the TRC narratives. *South African Journal of Psychology, 30*(1), 23-32.

Staub, E. (2006). Reconciliation after genocide, mass killing, or intractable conflict: Understanding the roots of violence, psychological recovery, and steps toward a general theory. *Political Psychology, 27*(6), 867-893.

Stein, D., Seedat, S., Herman, A., Moomal, H., Heeringa, S. & Kessler, R. (2008). Lifetime prevalence of psychiatric disorders in South Africa. *British Journal of Psychiatry, 192*(2), 112-117.

Stein, M., Walker, J., Hazen, A. & Forde, D. (1997). Full and partial post-traumatic stress disorder: Findings form a community survey. *American Journal of Psychiatry, 154*, 1114 – 1119.

Straker, G. (1992). *Faces in the revolution: The psychological effects of violence on township youth in South Africa*. Cape Town: David Philip.

Straker, G., Mendelsohn, M., Moosa, F. & Tudin, P. (1996). Violent political contexts and the emotional concerns of township youth. *Child Development, 67*, 46-54.

Straker, G. & The Sanctuaries Counselling Team. (1987). The continuous traumatic stress syndrome: The single therapeutic interview. *Psychology in Society, 8,* 48-78.

Summerfield, D. (1991). The rise of post-traumatic stress disorders. *British Medical Journal, 303*, 1271.

—. (1997). South Africa: Does a truth commission promote social reconciliation? *British Medical Journal, 315*, 1393.

—. (1998). The social experience of war and some issues for the humanitarian field. In P. Bracken & C. Petty (Eds.). *Rethinking the trauma of war* (pp. 9-35). London: Free Association Press.

—. (1999). A critique of seven assumptions behind psychological trauma programmes in war-affected areas. *Social Science and Medicine, 48*(10), 1449-1462.

—. (2002). Effects of war: Moral knowledge, revenge, reconciliation, and medicalised concepts of recovery. *British Medical Journal. 325*, 1105-1107.

Summerfield, D. & Toser, L. (1991). 'Low intensity' war and mental trauma in Nicaragua: A study in a rural community. *Medicine and War, 7*, 84-99.

Swartz, L., Gibson, K. & Swartz, S. (1990). State violence in South Africa and the development of a progressive psychology. In N. C. Manganyi & A. du Toit (Eds.). *Political violence and the struggle in South Africa* (pp. 234-265). Hampshire: MacMillan.

Swartz, L. & Levett, A. (1990). Political oppression and children in South Africa: The social construction of damaging effects. In N. C. Manganyi & A. du Toit (Eds.). *Political violence and the struggle in South Africa* (pp. 265-287). Hampshire: Macmillan.

Taylor, C. (1989). *Sources of the self: The Making of the modern self.* Cambridge University Press.

Tedeschi, R. G. (1999). Violence transformed: Posttraumatic growth in survivors and their societies. *Aggression and Violent Behaviour, 4(3),* 319-341.

Tedeschi, R. G. & Calhoun, L. G. (1995). *Trauma and transformation: Growing in the aftermath of suffering.* Thousand Oaks, CA: Sage.

Tedeschi, R. G. & Calhoun, L. G. (1996). The posttraumatic growth inventory: Measuring the positive legacy of trauma. *Journal of Traumatic Stress, 9,* 455-471.

Tedeschi, R. G., Park, & Calhoun, L. G. (1998). *Posttraumatic growth: Positive changes in the aftermath of crisis.* Mahwah: Laurence Erlbaum.

Therborn, G. (1980). *The ideology of power and the power of ideology.* London: Verso.

Thomas, P. & Bracken, P. (2008). Power, freedom and mental health: A postpsychiatry perspective. In: C. Cohen & S. Timimi (Eds.). *Liberatory psychiatry: Philosophy, politics, and mental health* (pp. 35-53). Cambridge University Press.

Thompson, J. B. (1984). *Studies in the theory of ideology.* Cambridge: Polity Press.

Tismaneanu, V. (2008). Democracy and memory: Romania confronts its communist past. *The Annals of the American Academy of Political and Social Science, 617(1):* 166-180.

Truth and Reconciliation Commission. (1998). *Truth and Reconciliation Commission of South Africa Report* (Vol. 1-5). Cape Town: CTP.

Truth and Reconciliation Commission. (2003). *Truth and Reconciliation Commission of South Africa Report* (Vol. 6-7). Cape Town: Juta.

Tutu, D. (1999). *No future without forgiveness.* New York: Doubleday.

Ungar, M. (2008). Resilience across cultures. *British Journal of Social Work, 38,* 218-235.

Van der Berg, S. (2014). South Africa will remain a hugely unequal society for a long time. *The Conversation.* Retrieved May 4, 2015, from http://theconversation.com/south-africa-will-remain-a-hugely-unequal-society-for-a-long-time-25949

Van der Kolk, B. (1996). *Traumatic stress: The effects of overwhelming experience on mind, body and society.* New York: Guilford Press.

Van der Kolk, B., Roth, S., Pelcovitz, D., Sunday, S., & Spinazzola, J. (2005). Disorders of extreme stress: The empirical foundation of a complex adaptation to trauma. *Journal of Traumatic Stress, 18*, 389-39.

Van der Merwe, C. & Gobodo-Madikizela, P. (Eds.). (2007). *Narrating our healing: Perspectives on working through trauma.* Newcastle: Cambridge Scholars.

Van der Merwe, H. (1999). *Community reconciliation in South Africa: Lessons from the TRC's intervention in two communities.* Paper presented at Sociology Department seminar, University of Witwatersrand, Johannesburg, South Africa.

Van der Merwe, H. (2001). Reconciliation in South Africa: Lessons from the TRC's community interventions. In M. A. Nimer (Ed.). *Reconciliation, justice and coexistence* (pp. 187-208). Lanham: Lexington Books.

Van der Merwe, H. & Chapman, A. (2008). Did the TRC deliver? In A. Chapman & H. van der Merwe. *Truth and reconciliation in South Africa: Did the TRC deliver?* (pp. 241-279). Philadelphia: University of Pennsylvania Press.

Van Zyl, S. (1990). *Explaining violence in South Africa: Some psychoanalytic considerations.* Retrieved September 17, 2008, from http://www.csvr.org.za/wits/papers/papsvanz.htm

Venturi, R. (1996). Complexity and contradiction in architecture. In Cahoon, L. (Ed.). *From modernism to postmodernism: An anthology* (pp. 325-335). Oxford: Blackwell.

Villa-Vicencio, C. & Du Toit, F. (2006). *Truth and Reconciliation in South Africa: Ten years on.* Cape Town: Institute for Justice and Reconciliation.

Villa-Vicencio, C. & Verwoerd, W. (Eds.) (2000). *Looking back reaching forward: Reflections on the Truth and Reconciliation Commission of South Africa.* University of Cape Town Press.

Vogelman, L. & Simpson, G. (1990). *Apartheid's violent legacy.* Retrieved September, 17, 2008, from http://www.csvr.org.za/wits/articles/artapart.htm

Volkan, V (2009). The next chapter: Consequences of societal trauma. In P. Gobodo-Madikizela & C. Van der Merwe (Eds.). *Memory, narrative and forgiveness* (pp. 1-23). Newcastle: Cambridge Scholars.

Watzlawick, P. (1978). *The language of change*. New York: WW Norton.
Watzlawick, P., Weakland, J. & Fish, R. (1974). *Change: Principles of problem formation and resolution*. New York: WW Norton.
Weine, S. (2006). *Testimony after catastrophe: Narrating the traumas of political violence*. Evanston: Northwestern University Press.
Weine, S., Muzurovic, N., Kulauzovic, Y., Besic, S., Lezic, A., Mujagic, A., ... Pavkovic, I. (2004). Family consequences of refugee trauma. *Family Process, 43*(2), 147-160.
Weingarten, K. (2000). Witnessing, wonder and hope. *Family Process, 39*, 389-402.
—. (2004). Witnessing the effects of political violence in families: Mechanisms of intergenerational transmission of trauma and clinical interventions. *Journal of Marital Family Therapy, 30*(1), 45-59.
Weiss, T. & Berger, R. (Eds.) (2010). *Posttraumatic growth and culturally competent practice: Lessons learned from around the globe*. New Jersey: John Wiley & Sons.
Werner, E. & Smith, R. (1992). *Vulnerable but invincible: A study of resilient children*. New York: McGaw-Hill.
Wilson, J. P. (1994). The historical evolution of PTSD diagnostic criteria from Freud to DSM IV. *Journal of Traumatic Stress, 7*(3), 681-698.
World Bank. Gini index (World Bank estimates). Retrieved May 15, 2015, from http://data.worldbank.org/indicator/SI.POV.GINI
Yalom, I. (1989). *Love's executioner and other tales of psychotherapy*. New York: Basic Books.
Yehuda, R. (Ed.). (1998). *Psychological trauma* (pp. 31-66). Washington, DC: American Psychiatric Press.
Young, A. (1995). *The harmony of illusions: Inventing post-traumatic stress disorder*. Princeton University Press.

INDEX